The
UNLIKELY FARMER

The
UNLIKELY FARMER

Biography of a Vermont Hill Farmer

GEORGE KEMPTON

MILL CITY PRESS

Mill City Press, Inc.
2301 Lucien Way #415
Maitland, FL 32751
407.339.4217
www.millcitypress.net

Printed in the United States of America.

ISBN-13: 978-1-54563-239-0

TIMELINE

1887	George's mother Annie Shears born London, England
1906	George's father Leonard Kempton born Springfield, Vermont
1924	Annie Shears marries Albert Blodgett
1927	Half sister Shirley Blodgett born
1929	Half sister Corinne Blodgett born
1929	Annie and Albert Blodgett divorce
1930	Annie marries Leonard Kempton
1931	George Kempton born Springfield, Vermont
1931	Patricia (Patty) Gulick born Summit, New Jersey
1943	George enters Newton School, Windham, Vermont
1945	First farm job, Dutton farm, Windham
1946	Stanley Clay farm, Reading
1947	Gerald Holland farm, Reading
1948	Graduates Newton School
1948	Farm at children's school, Newington, Connecticut
1949	Work on Alaska Railroad
1950	David Claghorn farm, Perkinsville
1950	Enters University of Connecticut School of Agriculture
1951	George Farnham farm, Connecticut
1952	Graduates UConn in May
1952	David Claghorn farm
1952	Drafted into Army December 2, serves in Austria
1954	Discharged from Army in November
1955	Herdsman and teacher, UConn School of Agriculture
1955	David Claghorn farm
1955	Meets Patricia Gulick at Newton School, deer season
1956	Marries Patty in Summit, New Jersey

1956   Sam Kempton born
1957   Fred Knapp farm, Dummerston
1957   Jennifer Kempton born
1958   David Kempton born
1959   George's mother Annie dies
1960   Annie Kempton born
1961   Matthew Kempton born
1962   Purchase Craig Farm, Peacham, Vermont
1975   Purchase Miller Farm, Peacham
1985   Farm partnership formed: George & Patty, Matthew & Dawn
1999   George's father Leonard dies
2012   Patricia Kempton dies

INTRODUCTION

T HIS BOOK, LIKE THE "BIG-HOUSE, LITTLE-HOUSE, back-house, barn" arrangement that characterizes old Vermont farmsteads, is a comfortable assembly of parts – histories, diary, and commentary – that George Kempton fitted together to describe his bountiful life.

It's the narrative of a man whose intelligence and charm-filled personality were born into unpromising circumstances but were recognized time and again by people who saw promise and were moved to present opportunities for that promise to ripen. It's a description of farming in the mid-1900s in Vermont. It's a farm wife's daily journal, providing an uncensored view into the raising of a big family in the 1960s and the struggle to grow a farm when farms in Vermont were going out of business. One of the "outbuildings," or chapters, is the result of George's desire finally to discover the mystery of his mother's background.

The main story, the big house, to which all the other tales are appended, is a story of love, the love of two people for their living, their family, their farm, each other.

George grew up in southern Vermont, the son of hardworking parents who struggled to make a life for themselves and their family. His English mother was a domestic worker in wealthy homes. His father, a native Vermonter beset with illness and bad luck, moved from job to job. George early learned that he had to fend for himself, and worked as a farm laborer. He had the great fortune to attend a private boarding school near home in Windham, Vermont, having attracted the attention of the headmaster, who waived his tuition. Through the Newton School George was introduced not only to a new life, but to his wife, Patricia (Patty) Gulick.

Patty was born the same year as George, 1931. The similarities of their early years end about there. Patty grew up in a stable, church-going, middle-class home in Summit, New Jersey. Her dad worked for New Jersey Public Service for 51 years. Her mother was a homemaker. While George was sweating out farm chores and taking his tired baths in the brook, Patty was playing tennis at the club, having dancing lessons, travelling, sailing, and socializing with her friends – she was popular with the girls as well as the boys. The likely sequel was that she would marry one of her suitors and settle in a New Jersey suburb.

Patty and George met when a mutual friend invited her to Vermont and the annual hunting season reunion at the Newton School. Hunting season at Newton amounted to a religious calling for George. If it was humanly possible, he was there. The mutual friend who brought Patty that November holiday asked George to be her escort. Strolling through the woods pretending to hunt but actually falling in love, George told Patty his unlikely dream of owning his own farm, of being a farmer. It struck an immediate and joyful chord with the 24-year-old Patty. Somewhere among those dancing and sailing lessons and the urban scenes of her nursing school days, a seed must have lodged, the concept of a life of nurture in the country. Of course, being there that deer-hunting weekend at the Newton School – itself an old farmhouse on a dead-end country road – with a crowd of ruddy deer hunters, square dances, Mom Newton baking bread – probably worked on her. "I was able to hook on to that charm," George would say.

The couple pretty much settled their future that weekend. Less than four months later they married.

That was 1956, and a pivotal moment in George's journey from "unlikely" to "here I am, here we are." The whole journey is recorded in these pages.

Lynne Lawson
Peacham, Vermont
April 2018

1887-1930

"Dad would have been swept off his feet
with this beautiful, mature English woman."

M Y MOTHER, ANNIE SHEARS, WAS BORN IN THE
district of Poplar in the East End of London between 1887-
1889. Poplar, recently popularized by the BBC television series "Call
the Midwife," was a place of docks and ports and industries related
to shipping: warehousing, ship building, rope making. Its residents
were laborers, and poor. Mother was the second youngest of seven
children, with Charlotte, Louisa, Caroline, Henry, and Elizabeth
(Bess) older, and Joseph younger. Their parents were Henry Shears
and Caroline Eliza Godden.[1] All of their birth dates are approxi-
mate due to different dates being listed on official documents – censuses, institutional forms, ships' manifests.

Caroline, my grandmother, died when she was around 40 years
old, leaving six young children (young Henry had only lived one
year). Apparently my grandfather couldn't cope with the situation,
because at various times he sent four of his children – Mother, Aunt
Caroline, Aunt Bess, and Uncle Joseph – to the Forest Gate District
School, essentially a local orphanage. I remember Mother talking
about the orphanage, telling that they saw an orange once a year at
Christmas, and they never had a toothbrush. Bess's granddaught⟋
Diane Krupsky Coughlin told me that the children worked for t¹
keep in the orphanage; Aunt Bess worked in the kitchen, v

---

[1] Birth dates: Charlotte ca.1872. Louisa ca.1879. Caroline ca.1⸁
ca.1880. Elizabeth ca.1885. Joseph ca.1886. Henry Sr. ca.1852. ⸀
ca.1856.

1

would have been the start of a lifelong career as a cook in restaurants and wealthy homes.

There is an article written in 1897 about life in the Forest Gate School. The unnamed author spoke glowingly about the facilities, their cleanliness, and the kindness of the staff. In a description of the Christmas Day dinner, I was amazed to read that at the end of the meal every child was given a present, a paper bag containing two oranges and crack-nuts, confirming my mother's story about getting an orange at Christmas. There was also a "swimming bath" or pool, which explains what Mother said about her life after the orphanage, how she did a lot of swimming and diving.

During the First World War Mother said she worked in a factory sewing wings for war planes. Uncle Joseph, she said, joined the Army and was killed in the war. Aunt Louisa married John Wheeler in 1910, and in the 1911 England census, both Bess and Mother were listed as domestic workers in the Wheeler's home: Aunt Bess was a cook and Mother was a housemaid. I have another document showing that Mother was a domestic in at least one other home, of Mrs. Thomas in Kensington, London.

Around 1916 Aunt Bess fell in love with a World War I soldier, Raymond Bigelow, who was born in 1895 in Newbury, Vermont, but joined the Canadian army and went to England in April 1916. Bess and Raymond married in London in the summer of 1917. Through Raymond, both Bess and eventually my mother emigrated to the United States and Canada.

I'm not sure why Raymond went from Danville, Vermont – his residence at the time – to Canada and joined the army there. The U.S. wasn't in the war yet, but the Canadian army was actively recruiting. Raymond joined the 244th Battalion, nicknamed "Kitchener's Own" after the British war minister Lord Kitchener. For unknown reasons he returned to the U.S. before the war was over. His young wife Bess wasn't able to go with him immediately and had to wait for word. I guess it took a while for him to send for her, because when Aunt Bess arrived in New York in September 1918 on the ship Olympic, their daughter Josephine, born in England April 20, was already five months old.

On the Olympic's manifest, Bess listed Danville, Vermont as her intended destination in the U.S., and in the 1920 U.S. census, Bess, Raymond, and Josephine are living on Eastern Avenue in nearby St. Johnsbury. Three years later the family was in Springfield, Vermont, Bess was working as a cook for the Hartness family. Aunt Bess was very homesick, and wrote to her sister Annie – my mother – to encourage her to come over from England. Bess's granddaughter Diane told me that my mother was not able to get a visa to the United States, so she came to Canada. She arrived in Quebec on October 12, 1923 on the ship Montrose sailing from Liverpool. A form that Mother filled out on arrival in Canada is interesting. She reported that she had "no living relatives," but she had friends in England, Mr. and Mrs. Farres in Kensington. She said she had $10 in her possession. A Mr. and Mrs. J. Hamilton Roberts from Kingston, Ontario, Mother reported, had paid her passage, and the Roberts' home was her destination in Canada, she was going to work there as a domestic. (It was common at that time for Canadian households to import domestic help from other countries, particularly England.)

Major-General J. Hamilton Roberts was a decorated and acclaimed officer with a long and distinguished career in the Canadian military, serving in both World Wars. In the 1921 Canadian census, just after the First World War and two years before my mother arrived in Canada, Roberts was living with his wife and children and two domestic workers in Kingston, Ontario. One would assume that Mother went to Kingston to work for the Roberts as she had declared on her immigration form.

This, however, is unlikely, because by August 1924, less than a year after arriving in Canada, Mother was married and living in Springfield, Vermont. Did she say she was employed by the Roberts in order to get permission to immigrate, without ever intending to work for them? How did she know of the Roberts at all? Were they in on a scheme (not likely given Roberts' upstanding reputation)? Had Mother's brother-in-law Raymond Bigelow heard of Roberts, or met him, during the war? Perhaps Mother actually did go to Ontario for a few months, and then left her employer to come join her sister Bess and Bess's husband Raymond in America.

Bess's granddaughter Diane told me that her grandfather Raymond was able to persuade the Springfield police chief to go up to the Canadian border and bring my mother into Vermont. This seems farfetched, but it was the beginning of Prohibition, and Raymond (and the police chief?) may have been familiar with crossing the border. However and whenever Mother came to this country, she seems to have come illegally. There is no record of legal immigration, and on her marriage certificate she lists Stratford, Connecticut as her birthplace, apparently not wanting to raise any red flags. Once in the U.S., Mother joined Bess, at that time a live-in cook for the Hartness family in Springfield, Vermont. She would have been 35-37 years old.

I think I should tell a little about James Hartness and Springfield's machine tool industry, since they played such a large role, not only in Aunt Bess's, but also in both my parents' working lives. In 1888 Adna Brown (I remember a hotel with that name in downtown Springfield) bought the Jones and Lamson machine shop, which was located in Windsor, Vermont. Brown moved the shop to Springfield and hired James Hartness to manage it. Hartness discontinued the many things the shop had made and concentrated on making a lathe of his own design. His lathe sold very well, and he was paid a royalty in addition to his salary for each sale. In subsequent years Hartness set his most promising young engineers up in their own companies: Fellows Gear Shaper and Bryant Chuck and Grinder, for example. These precision-tool companies were an economic engine for Springfield and were going full-time day and night during the Second World War, making Springfield a boomtown.

In addition to being an engineer and businessman, Hartness had a brief political career as Governor of Vermont for one term, 1921-23, and I think Aunt Bess would have been working for the Hartnesses then – Hartness and his wife Lena Pond. The Hartness's two daughters – Anna (Hartness) Beardsley and Helen (Hartness) Flanders – both married engineers. Both husbands worked for their father-in-law in the shops. Helen's husband Ralph Flanders – who interestingly was born in Barnet, Vermont – went on to be a U. S. Senator. During the Cold War in the 1950s, Flanders got national recognition for getting the Senate to censure Senator Joseph

4

McCarthy for accusing people in this country of being Communists without adequate evidence, thus causing them undue hardship. When Mother moved in with Bess at the Hartness home in Springfield in 1924 there began a relationship of working for and living with the Hartness family of successful businessmen and politicians that would last more than 20 years. (Years later, after I was born, I remember playing in the Hartness's home; on the third floor there were the most amazing toys, I could play for hours, and the cellar had an underground hallway that led to a telescope – what a place for a little boy to fantasize! I loved it when I got to stay there with Mother.)

Bess's husband Raymond had a friend named Albert Blodgett, born in Rockingham, Vermont in 1899. Blodgett enlisted in the U.S. Army in September 1918, but I never heard of his having gone to war. By 1920 he was in Springfield working in an iron foundry. Mother married him on August 18, 1924 in Springfield. They had two daughters–Shirley, born April 2, 1927, and Corinne, born January 30, 1929. It would turn out that Albert didn't fill the normal father-husband role, but his parents Ed and May Blodgett lived in downtown Springfield and were very supportive. Ed and May lived in a tenement on the upper end of Main Street; I think they were quite poor. (Even after Mother had divorced Albert, remarried, and had me, I visited Ed and May. I remember having lunch with them and eating salt pork and gravy–it was a white and salty dish, a Depression dish, that I had difficulty eating–but I found my Blodgett grandparents to be very nice people.)

Mother's life at that period, with two small children and what seems to have been a bum of a husband, was a disaster; the two redeeming features were the Hartness family and her in-laws Ed and May. Aunt Bess's marriage was also a failure, I can only imagine how she and Mother handled these years. Later I remember them getting together and having fun; but before that happened, in 1930 Aunt Bess, Raymond, and their daughter had moved to Hartford, Connecticut, then Bess left Raymond and took her daughter Josephine to New Britain, Connecticut, where she had gotten a job cooking for another wealthy family.

Mother stayed in Springfield, divorced Albert on February 12, 1929 – two weeks after their daughter Corinne was born – and married my father Leonard Kempton a year later, April 19, 1930. In the 1930 U.S. census, before marrying Mother, my father was living with his parents, and his occupation was listed as "Chauffeur." Could he have met my mother chauffering for Anna Hartness Beardsley, who had taken over the Hartness home where Mother was working?

I have wondered how my mother, a woman in 1929, was able to get a divorce from Albert, even though he was a no-good. The reason given on the divorce papers is "refusal to support," but my cousin Diane Coughlin says that Albert gave my mother syphilis. Either reason would have given Mother legitimate grounds for divorce. So there you have it, a wronged, 41-year-old woman in need of a good man, and Dad, the 24-year-old chauffeur, a good, honest, big-hearted, hard-working man in need of love and direction: a perfect fit.

When Mother and Dad married in April 1930, the only people at the wedding were Dad's uncle Frank Fletcher and his wife Clara, who "stood up" for them. Neither Dad's parents nor his sister Francis (Fran) attended, nor did any of the Hartness family. Aunt Bess was working in Connecticut. The absence of Dad's parents at the wedding and various innuendoes I recall lead me to believe that Dad's father never approved of Mother or the marriage. Mother was older than Dad (older even than the marriage certificate claims, which is that she was 34; according to the more reliable English censuses she would actually have been 41; a friend of mine recently called Mother "resourceful"), and she had two very young children.

Father

My father Leonard Kempton was born in Springfield, Vermont in August 1906. His father George Leonard Kempton, my namesake, and his mother Ethel Fletcher Kempton, moved from Claremont, New Hampshire to Springfield in the early 1900s because of the machine tool industry – Grandpa worked at Jones and Lamson machine shop his whole working life. In contrast with my mother's unsettled and at times homeless childhood, Dad was raised in a stable environment with both parents and lived in the same house all his life until he married. In 1924, when Dad was on a high school senior class trip, he caught undulant fever, which reoccurred for several years afterwards. Undulant fever is commonly caused by drinking unpasteurized milk from cows with brucellosis. Dad would have suffered remittent fever, weakness, weight loss, and headache.

I'm not sure what his plans would have been after graduating from high school, but the fever would have changed them. It would have been natural for him to follow his father into Jones and Lamson or another of Hartness's companies, but I believe he worked instead in a milk plant. I also think that Dad and his father didn't get along well, perhaps my grandfather was domineering, though very little was said that I remember. Or maybe Dad just didn't want to work in a shop. For whatever reason, Dad hadn't started on a career when he met Mother, and with the start of the Depression it would get more difficult.

Mother must have thought her life had finally turned around when she met Dad, a young, handsome, honest man that loved her, and Dad would have been swept off his feet with this beautiful, mature English woman that loved and needed him.

1931-1937

"It must have been very difficult, and I don't know
how or where we all lived during this time."

I WAS BORN IN GRANDPA KEMPTON'S HOUSE ON 9
High Street on May 31, 1931. I assume we were living there when
I was born, perhaps my half-sisters Shirley and Corinne as well, but
I don't know for how long. I spent a lot of time in that house, I
remember it well. It was a two-story house with attached woodshed,
garage and barn. I suppose when my grandparents moved there the
garage would have housed a buggy and/or wagon, and the barn a
horse or two, perhaps a cow and some chickens. There was a well
out back that was shared by several homes in the neighborhood.
Grandmother had a pump at the kitchen sink; later the neighborhood built a water tower, and it ran water into each home by gravity.
After that, Grandma had a copper-lined cistern with a faucet by the
sink where the pump had been; I think she was very pleased with it.

I remember the iceman coming with his horse and cart.
Grandma had a square card with numbers on each edge–25, 50, 75,
100–that she put in the window; in the icebox the iceman would
put a chunk of ice, the weight matching the number on top of the
card. He would often give me pieces of ice to chew on. There was
a large lawn, reaching to the neighboring house, and a big garden.
Grandpa had a push mower that he kept sharp and well oiled, and I
would sometimes mow the lawn. Often, before I mowed, Grandpa
would remind me that the eaves on the neighbor's house dripped
onto his land, and to be sure to mow right up to the house. (Many
years later, Jim Craig, who sold me the Village Farm in Peacham,

8

told me the same thing about the Peacham Historical building–that its eaves dripped on land that came with the Village Farm I was buying. With today's zoning laws this wouldn't happen.) Both my grandparents loved me, "Little Georgie."

I have pictures that help me remember things from my childhood. There are photos of our camping on Mt. Ascutney when I was very young – Mother and Dad, Aunt Bess and her friend Jane Goodrich and their boyfriends. Jane worked with Bess in New Britain, Connecticut, and they would come up to visit us in Vermont. The two of them were a lot of fun on these camping trips, squealing and carrying on about the threat of wild animals.

I know that during this period of my early childhood, living with my Kempton grandparents, Dad had an accident. He was splitting wood with an axe and it slipped, cutting off his thumb. This accident would have been not only shocking and painful, but it would have made it even more difficult for Dad to find work. The first job I'm aware of his having was called the "Bug Job." It was a Government program designed to eliminate Tent Caterpillars that were defoliating trees. Dad worked on Stratton Mountain for a dollar a day. It must have been very difficult, and I don't know how or where we all lived during these early years. I wish I had started this story when my half-sister Corinne was alive, she would have remembered more of everything. I know we lived in several houses or apartments, but I don't remember when or how many of us, Corinne would.

1938-1942

"Living in the cellar might not have been too bad
if the deck hadn't leaked."

WHEN I WAS SIX OR SEVEN, DAD WAS WORKING for the Modern Oil Burner Co. in Springfield. I remember a picture of a pickup truck piled high with crated stoves. I would sometimes ride with Dad when he went to Gardner, Massachusetts to get these stoves. This was a time when people were switching from wood to oil. Dad not only installed new stoves but converted many wood stoves to oil. I remember a story of Dad being nearly trapped in a cellar during the hurricane-flood of 1938. He was pulling an oil burner out of a furnace when the water smashed through the windows, flooding the cellar. I remember the giant trees that were blown over; their 12- to 15-foot-high roots towered over me.

It would have been about this time, 1938 or '39, that Dad and Mother bought a house lot on the Pleasant Valley Road midway between Springfield and Chester, off Route 11. This was a big step, an effort to get the family together. Dad tried to build the house himself. I think he had the skills to do it, and he certainly worked hard enough, but he always lacked self-confidence and may not have thought things through well enough. We eventually hired the house built, but not before digging a cellar, covering the deck or floor with tar paper, and trying to live in it. Living in the cellar might not have been too bad if the deck hadn't leaked. I don't think Mother was there at the cellar phase – she was living and working for Anna Hartness Beardsley – but Corinne and Shirley were. We would catch the school bus; I would get off at a one-room schoolhouse

10

called the Slab-Hollow School on the road to Springfield. The thing I remember about that school was I didn't like the hot lunch.

The family was still making camping trips to Mt. Ascutney: I have pictures of my parents, me, Shirley and Corinne, and Bess's daughter Josephine. Josephine was around 20 then, and in the pictures is with Steve Krupsky, her future husband. They were living in Springfield, they probably met in high school. They soon married and had two daughters, Diane and Stephanie.

Corinne, Shirley, Dad, and I left our cellar home sometime in the winter and moved, probably back to Springfield, but I know that at some point that year Corinne and I ended up living with Dad in Concord, New Hampshire. I don't remember what job Dad was doing in Concord, but I do remember it was the fourth school I had been in that year. I was in the fourth grade, and I remember Corinne using flash cards to help me learn the multiplication tables. It must have been a crazy time for Dad and Mother, but by 1941 I think this chaotic lifestyle ended with the whole family living together back in the newly-finished house on Pleasant Valley Road.

I went with Dad one Sunday morning, December 7, 1941, to help a neighbor with an oil burner. While there, we learned about Pearl Harbor. Dad was soon working at Fellows Gear Shaper in Springfield, and life settled down for us. Corinne, Shirley, and I caught the bus to school, Dad worked in the shop, Mother was home, sounds like the American dream. However, for reasons known only to Dad and perhaps Mother, we left this stable situation and bought a farm in Windham, Vermont. We moved there in May 1943.

Windham is located on a road that runs southerly from Route 11 near Londonderry over the shoulder of Glebe Mountain (Magic Mountain ski area) and down to West Townsend on Route 30. The farm was on a cutoff road between Windham and South Windham that went by Burbee Pond. It consisted of a rambling house, a barn, and a two-car garage across and down the road a bit. The garage didn't seem to fit with the rest of the buildings. The farm had been owned for a number of years by summer people, and it is my guess that they built the garage. I'm sure they remodeled the house for their convenience, which apparently didn't include heating the place in winter or keeping the water from freezing. If Mother's health had been better, or Dad hadn't been working 12 hours a day, 7 days a week in the Gear Shaper, and if he hadn't had a 30-mile drive to work, we might have been able to cope. As it was, we gave up during the second winter. Our farming venture, however, wasn't a complete loss. In fact, my life changed completely and for the better because of this move to Windham.

1943-1944

"Dave Newton asked if I would like to go to his prep school."

THE FIRST SUMMER WE WERE ON THE WINDHAM farm, a neighbor Dave Newton stopped and asked if he could cut our hay. He would put hay enough in our barn for our cow and two horses, and he would have the rest. This worked well for us, since we couldn't cut the hay anyway, but more importantly, the Newtons also introduced us to a new social life. They ran a boys prep school and farm about four miles away; they also had a summer program for young people. As part of the young people's entertainment, they would go to local square dances once or twice a week. On their way to a dance, the Newtons would stop and pick us up – Shirley, Corinne, and me. We loved it, and it was a natural way to get to know the four Newton kids. Margaret Newton, the oldest, was a little older than Shirley; John and Corinne were about the same age; and Mary was just older and Mike just younger than me. We had a wonderful time, and it was an important part of our new farm life. Before the summer was over, Dave Newton asked if I would like to go to his prep school. It was a no-brainer.

One of the Newton faculty members drove over the Burbee Pond Bridge to school every day – I only needed to walk the half-mile to the bridge to meet him. His son Spike rode with him. Spike, Mary & Mike Newton, and I were taught in a class separate from the prep school by a teacher named Berta. Dave Newton, whom we called Pappy, taught us English and Latin. I was 12, had nearly finished the 6th grade (we had left Springfield in May before school was finished), and found myself in a small class with very bright,

13

well-educated kids. I loved the whole Newton atmosphere, but I was in over my head academically.

In addition to this, I was also getting introduced to rural life on our new family farm, bringing in wood for the stoves, learning how to keep water from freezing, taking care of our horses (Shirley and Corinne milked the cow). The second summer at our farm I tried mowing with a single horse named Prince; Prince's mate Molly had died in the winter. Prince and I worked at it, but I didn't know what I was doing. Some things worked well, though: I managed to hitch Prince to a wagon and drive him to a store in Windham Center, and also to get sawdust from the Dutton's farm on the road to the Newton's. (I later worked for George Dutton.)

My cousin Diane sent a picture of herself at three years old, held by me as we sat on Prince. I was successful at shooting a doe in the field that summer, and in the fall I had a trap line in Burbee Pond. The pond had a backwater across the road with culverts connecting. Muskrat and mink would travel through the culverts, and I would set the traps by them. I trapped mostly muskrats, though I did get one mink. I sold the pelts to Sears and Roebuck – $5.00 for muskrats, $25.00 for mink. I learned to skin them from the tail end, turning the pelt inside out, and then stretching it on a wooden frame. I would tend my traps going and coming from school.

I'm not sure what the final blow was that pushed us off the farm, but I do remember a particular incident. We had been shopping in Brattleboro, and on the way home we got a flat tire. We didn't have a spare, so Dad drove on the flat tire up Route 30 to West Townsend, and from there headed up the steep dirt road toward South Windham and home, where we lost traction. Dad had to take the now bent-up rim off the back hub and exchange it for the tire on front, so we could make it up the hill and finally get home. This incident may not have been the proverbial straw, but it would have been close – with no money to make repairs, Dad would now have had a problem getting to work.

We sold out, losing everything but our memories, and moved to the Newton School; I think it would have been January of 1945. Mom and Dad had a room, I got a bed in one of the dorms, and I guess Corinne and Shirley would have gone back to Springfield to their Blodgett grandparents. Dad helped Mom (Mrs. Newton) with the cooking. Mother was still not well and was suffering from arthritis; later we learned she had breast cancer. I settled in with my studies and doing the regular chores of a boarding student.

When school was out that year, with the farm sold, Mother and Dad moved back to Springfield. As I think about this, I don't know how they did it, they didn't have a car and wouldn't have 'til I helped them buy one in 1948. However they did it, they rented an apartment in Springfield, and Dad got a job bartending at the Hartness House, now an inn. Anna Hartness Beardsley had sold the grand old Hartness home where Mother and Bess had worked for so many years to Treadway Inns. Dad ran the bar, which was located in the waiting area by the telescope, where I used to play when Mother cooked for the Hartnesses. If I had gone to Springfield with Mother and Dad, I would remember their situation better, but instead I went to work for George and Helen Dutton on their farm in Windham. It turned out that I never would live with my parents in Springfield again; I would live and work on different farms each summer and attend Newton during the school year. Neither my parents nor I realized it at the time, and it wasn't brought about by any animosity, but it just happened that I didn't live at home again until I got out of the Army.

As I've grown older, I've become grateful for experiencing how farming was done on the Dutton farm. George Dutton, with his daughter Helen, was farming just as he had all his life, as he waited for his son Herb to come home from the war. I got to use tools like a bull rake, a draw shave, a scythe—tools you only see today in the historical house. I learned to use them as they were meant to be used, and as a result I have a real reference point for how farming in Vermont has evolved over the last 100 years. We milked the three cows by hand. George milked two, while I struggled with one, sep-arated the milk, fed the skim to pigs and chickens, and made butter with the cream using a barrel-like churn. They sold the butter, eggs, and pork locally.

We mowed with the horses but we did a lot of hand mowing as well. I mowed with a scythe along the brook, the stone walls, the entire apple orchard, and anything else that would make hay. No brush grew on the edge of the fields, they were mowed clean, and the fields were hayed clean. We raked with a horse pulling a dump rake, tumbled with pitchforks, and pitched on the wagon by hand. Any scatterings that were left I gathered with a bull rake and dropped them off for Helen who was pitching on, and her father was building the load. On a rainy day I used the draw shave to make new teeth to replace the ones I would break pulling the bull rake. The teeth were about a foot long. I would split pieces off a block of ash and shape them with the draw shave. The only engines on the farm were in an old car and an old, single-cylinder engine that ran a saw rig, sometimes called a one-lunger because of the noise it made.

Again that summer I was able to go to dances. John Newton had his license then; he would drive by with the truck, loaded with kids, and stop for me. On the way home he would stop at Dutton's and I would jump off the back of the truck and holler "Okay!" One night he hollers back, "How about thank you?" My embarrassment was great and unforgettable.

George and his parents, ca. 1934

The Newton School, Windham, Vt.

1945-1947

"It was more than Gerald thought I was worth,
and all summer he tried to make sure I earned it."

IN THE FALL I WENT BACK TO NEWTON AS A REG-
ular prep school student. This would make my third year at the
school. The day started at 6:00 a.m. with chores: filling the wood
box for the kitchen stove, building fires in the three fireplaces,
taking care of the horses, someone to help "Mom" Newton with
the cooking and washing pots and pans, and KP. KPs set the tables,
served the food, cleared the tables, and did the dishes. For the fires,
helping Mom, the horses, or KP, you would be responsible all day.
Every night, at evening study hall, Pappy would post the morning
work sheet. Breakfast at 7:00 a.m., classes from 8:00 a.m. to 1:00
p.m. Sometimes before first class, we would have an assembly. At
some of these Pappy would teach a continuing course for the year on
either the Old Testament or Roman and Greek mythology. There
were usually seven periods with a break after the fourth period for
soup. This was called Slurp, and was held in the Slump Room.

The Slump Room had one of the three fireplaces; a second, large
one was in the multi-purpose room (dining, study, and dance hall),
and a small, old fireplace was in the more formal living room. Lunch
at 1:15, work from 2 'til 4, then a break with tea in the Slump Room,
study hall 5 to 6, dinner, then another study hall 7:30 to 8:30, bed
at 9. There were three tables in the dining room, the big table that
Pappy and Mom and Pappy's mom Gram sat at, the other two tables
had faculty assigned to them. Proper table manners were required,
as well as a coat and tie for dinner. I remember there was a time

when Gram would be a little late and arrive after everyone was sitting down. This caused the people at the big table to stand up for her. We felt this was becoming a pattern, so we got together, and the students from the other two tables stood up as well. After that, Gram was able to get to the table on time.

Pappy would put the afternoon work sheet up at lunch time. The work varied some, but it was predominately cutting and hauling wood. This was before chainsaws; the wood was cut with axes and two-man crosscut saws and hauled to the school with horses. In addition to the cook stove and the fireplaces, there were several wood stoves for heating and a steam furnace that took three-foot sticks of wood and heated some parts of the building. The cutting and hauling was done by teenage student boys unaccustomed to working, particularly in the woods. It replaced the sports they were used to. For me, the work was less of a challenge than the studies; I got a lot of Ds and rewrote things many times.

Our transportation, when the school wanted to go to dances or wherever, was a relatively new Ford ton-and-a-half dump truck with a steel platform body and two-foot wooden sides. (Years later I traded some hay with John Newton for that old dump body and used it for many years on my farm.) On Sunday mornings we'd pile into this Ford and go to church in South Windham. Pappy was church Choir Director, the Newton School students supplied the choir, and a faculty member was the organist; we would practice twice a week on the special music we were going to provide. My voice was higher at that time, I sang soprano. Sometimes the organist liked to play "Poor Jud is Dead," from the Broadway musical "Oklahoma" while the offering was taken.

Windham is known in southern Vermont just as Walden is in the Northeast Kingdom for its cold and deep snow. So it was not uncommon for the road on a winter Sunday to be snow-covered and lined with snow banks. Often the top of the snow banks would be a flat shelf that the wing of the snowplow had created by pushing the top of the bank over to make room for more snow. This offered a flat surface for skiers that were being towed by our dump truck; these skiers had to stay alert for low-hanging branches. The number of skiers was limited to two; however, there was also Shaggy Dog, an Old English sheep dog, large and furry, that had been left by one of the students and had made his home at the school. Shaggy Dog ran along with the skiers as the Ford with its load of students made its way to church.

Stanley Clay Farm

In the summer of 1946 after Newton School was out I went looking for a new farm job – they didn't need me at Dutton's, the war was over and Herb Dutton was home. I probably went first to my Kempton grandparents – my grandmother had been doing my laundry while I was at school, mailing it back and forth in a laundry case. Mom Newton would admire the patching and darning that my grandmother did. I remember very well the circumstances of my finding another farm job. I was walking down a dirt road in Reading and saw a farmer in the field turning hay with a pitchfork. I walked out and asked if he needed any help. He asked me if I thought I could turn hay; I said I thought I could; he told me where to find a fork. The farmer's name was Stanley Clay. His farm was a typical transitional farm, with equipment for both horse and tractor; his 40 cows were milked with machines. Without a doubt, the best part of this job was the team of horses. While they did what was required of them on the farm, they were primarily competition horses.

Nearly every Sunday we would load these horses in the truck and take them to a horse-pulling contest. These contests were very common at that time, and you usually didn't have to travel very far to find them. At the big meets and fairs, you weighed your team the same day you pulled them. (At the local meets there was no weighing of animals; everyone knew how much their neighbors' teams weighed. There were no money prizes, either – the farmers got together to teach their horses how to pull together, to compete, and to have fun.) You normally had three people with the team: the teamster and two hitching the evener. I hitched one side of the evener for Stanley. The stone boat had a hook on the end, and the evener had a ring; the teamster maneuvered the team around so you could drop the ring over the hook. It was important that you didn't make a metallic noise and miss the hook; if you did the team would jump ahead as if they were hitched, and the teamster would have his hands full. Each time the teams in a weight class had pulled the boat six feet or more, weight was added, and the teams would be hitched again; each time they would be more excited and more difficult to hitch. The weight classes were often 2800, 3000, and 3200, and there was a free-for-all class where teams would often weigh over two tons. We were in the 3200 class and usually won, including First at the State Fair in Rutland, where we also were third in the free-for-all. Years later my son Matt and I thought of pulling our team of horses in Danville, but we never did, and I have always been sorry that we didn't. We did work them some on the farm, but the horses just couldn't cover the acres fast enough to compete with modern farming.

Back for my fourth year at the Newton School that fall of 1946, John Newton had gone off to Princeton as a freshman, and I took over as teamster for the school. I was pleased to be given the responsibility, but it was a lot of work. On a good afternoon, I could get out two loads of pole wood and one load of furnace wood. The pole wood, from the limbs and smaller parts of the tree, was taken to a saw rig close to the woodshed that was powered by an old Farmall tractor. A three-man crew sawed this wood into stove length for all the fires except the furnace. The furnace wood was cut three feet long from the body of the tree and split, if necessary. The saw rig crew would work in the woods if they didn't have wood to buss up, and I would help in the woods, too, if I didn't have a load to haul. I was frequently loading my last load when the woods crew quit for the Slump Room break. Depending on my helper, he might quit, too. It was not uncommon to burn wood from a tree the same day it had been cut down.

Gerald Holland Farm

When that school year 1947 was over, I went back to Stanley Clay's. I was looking forward to the summer working with that good team of his, but Stanley's situation had changed, and he couldn't use me. He felt badly about it and took me to a neighbor farmer, Gerald Holland, whom he knew needed help. Stanley convinced Gerald to pay me $20.00 a week. (With these farm jobs, I always got a salary, plus board, room and washing.) It was more than Gerald thought I was worth, and all summer he tried to make sure I earned it. Gerald's farm was similar to Stanley's in that it was transitioning from horses to tractors. The problem came with adapting the horse equipment for tractors or replacing it. Gerald had a tractor, but that summer we did everything with horses; I don't think we even started the tractor. There were two teams and two mowing machines. When we mowed we used both mowers – I would follow Gerald 'round and 'round with the second team and mower. The team I used was a stallion and a mare. When I had free time I would hitch them to a manure spreader, load it by hand and spread it with the horses. It was difficult hitching them up if the mare was in heat.

The transition was taking place from a dump rake to a side-delivery rake, which is what we use today. The dump rake gathered the hay and would dump it when you tripped the rake with your foot, picking up the teeth, as you drove the horse around the field. You tried to trip it in the same place each time so you'd end up with windrows coming out from the middle like spokes. The windrows were then tumbled and pitched on by hand. At Gerald's, however – as we had at Stanley's – we raked the hay with the newer side-delivery rake and picked it up with a hay loader. The side-delivery rake leaves a continuous windrow that adapts well to a pickup head, like you find on a baler or chopper. The side rake and the hay loader were the beginning of picking up hay mechanically.

That summer I was 16, old enough to work like a man, and I did. I loaded every load of hay and mowed them all away. After evening milking I would go down to the brook to wash. The only running water in the house was cold at the kitchen sink. As the summer wore on, and it was dusk when we finished milking, I often didn't go to the brook. Late-cut hay has some kind of black dust, maybe from mature timothy seeds, that work up your pant legs making your legs black; it was not uncommon for me to go to bed that way. In late August I cut my wrist while sharpening a scythe, the cut was deep enough so I was able to see into it and watch things move, but it didn't bleed much. I think Gerald was afraid he would be responsible for a doctor bill, so he paid me off and took me to Springfield, where my parents had an apartment. He had dropped me off and driven away before I realized the apartment was empty – unbeknownst to me my parents had moved. I walked across town to my grandparents, where Dad's sister, Aunt Fran, took me to a doctor. He was annoyed that I had taken so long to get there.

This break at the end of the summer before going back to school turned out to be very beneficial for me. Aunt Fran and my grandmother Kempton were determined to get some flesh on my bones. I had grown several inches that summer, but not gained any weight. Aunt Fran also took me for my driver's license test in Grandpa's 1930 Chevy sedan.

A word about Aunt Fran. My Kempton grandparents had two children, Dad and his younger sister Frances. Aunt Fran married late and never had children; I think she was still single when she helped me with my wrist and driver's license. She made her home in her parents' house for as long as they lived, and inherited it when they died. Aunt Fran was a seamstress, working out of the front room. I remember ladies would come to be fitted for dresses she was making for them. She eventually married Andrew Martin, a carpenter; they lived in the upstairs apartment at my grandparents' house. Fran and Andrew always went out of their way to be helpful to me, and later to my wife Patty and me. Unfortunately, Dad and Aunt Fran were never close, and Dad didn't like Uncle Andy. This was always an uncomfortable awareness for me, and later for Patty, too.

The next year at Newton was my fifth year. It was in many ways easier – I was familiar with everything, was a somewhat better student, it felt like home. Jim Keeney was one of the new students that year. He worked with me on the team, and our lives have been intertwined since; we are still close friends after nearly 70 years. Every spring at Newton we had a house party. We would spend several days scrubbing the floors and getting ready for the girls to come. These were prep school girls, friends from home that the boys would invite. That year one of the guys had Eleanor Randall – we called her Randy – as his date. Both Jim and I thought she was a neat girl, and Jim and Randy married a few years later.

1948-1950

"I went to the Union Hall and got a job
working as a Gandy Dancer."

A T THIS TIME MOTHER AND DAD WERE WORKING
as butler and cook for a man named Gray in Farmington,
Connecticut. Gray owned a machine shop and met Dad while he
was staying at the Hartness House in Springfield where Dad was
tending bar. Gray convinced Dad that he and Mother should come
to work for him in Farmington. Dad was not one to ponder; he
made decisions quickly, which explains my surprise the previous fall,
when I went to my parents' apartment in Springfield and found it
empty. With the folks in Connecticut, a new world opened up for
me. It started with taking the train from Brattleboro to Hartford
during Thanksgiving and Christmas breaks from the Newton
School in Windham. The train as it headed south was filled with
kids from prep schools and colleges. We had amazing parties in the
railroad cars; I didn't know such a life existed.

I bought a motorcycle from John Newton, and during the spring
break I drove it down to Connecticut. I got as far as Northampton,
Massachusetts when it broke down. I called Dad to come and get
me; with his job as all-around handyman he had the use of the Grays'
Jeep. While waiting for Dad, a group of kids gathered, talking to me
and looking at the motorcycle; by the time Dad arrived I had sold
the bike for within $5 of what I'd paid for it.

While I hadn't been keeping track, by this fifth year at Newton,
1948, I had accumulated enough credits to graduate that June, and I
did graduate. I had no plans after graduation, but I thought I would

25

find a job in Connecticut near my parents. I found a farm job in Newington, Connecticut. The farm was part of a home and hospital for handicapped children, most of whom had Polio. I lived in a dormitory on the first floor with the kitchen help and orderlies for the hospital; the nurses and nurse's aides were upstairs. The people I lived with on the first floor were a troubled group of single men; perhaps not unusual after the war, except in their numbers. Probably the fact that the job offered board, room and some camaraderie helped to attract them, but they were an unusual group. One of these men cut his fist badly punching the mirrors in the bathroom; another man on his day off would go hang out at the railroad station; another would borrow money from me before payday, then he would pay me back and share gin with me; one guy hired out in the afternoon to work in the kitchen – he had supper, spent the night, had breakfast, and quit.

The job itself was also different than other farm jobs I'd done. We had about 30 cows, and the milk was pasteurized for the hospital. There was a big vegetable garden and a poultry operation. I worked some in the garden, but mostly did work relating to the dairy operation. I had never worked tractors, and I had a lot to learn. A couple of experiences will illustrate. One day I was spreading commercial fertilizer with a converted horse-drawn wooden spreader in a pasture that had stumps in it. I straddled a stump, thinking the tractor could get over it, and ripped the bottom out of the spreader. Another time, while mowing the back swath with a tractor, I didn't cut a corner soon enough and hooked the end of the cutter bar on a page-wire fence, breaking the cutter bar off. I'm sure the farm manager related to the CEO of the hospital what poor help he was provided. I did learn some things that didn't involve breaking anything. I learned to back up a truck with mirrors, and I learned that I needed to go back to school. If I was going to continue working on farms, I needed more education so I could get a better job, perhaps as a farm manager.

Dad and Mother had Thursdays off, and I was able to get Thursdays off as well. Mother was feeling better, she had had both breasts removed, and that had temporarily stopped the cancer. We did a lot of things together. We would go out to lunch, go shopping, play golf. We usually went to G. Fox Department Store to shop, and from there we would send care packages to mother's family in London. The Grays had a place on Long Island Sound, at Old Black Point, where we sometimes went. I put a down payment on a car, and Dad carried the monthly payment, so we had a car to share. I did, however, suffer for the first time homesickness. In the fall of that year, it hit me that I wasn't going back to school, it just hit me, I hadn't seen it coming, the Newton School had been my first real taste of home. For years after that, whenever possible, I would go back to the Newton School for Thanksgiving and for the last four days of deer hunting season.

Work on the Alaska Railroad

In the spring of '49 I took a girl to the house party at Newton and caught up with some of my friends. I learned that several Newton School boys were in Alaska, and a student there, Jake Edgerton, and I decided to drive up. Jake had a 1942 Navy Jeep—our plan was to drive to Bigfork, Montana, where Jake's aunt and uncle lived, then drive up through Canada to Fairbanks. We had a tent and planned to sleep beside the road.

I was introduced, as Jake Edgerton and I drove through Montana en route to Alaska, to open range. The area that cattle grazed included the road; there was a cattle guard across the road with fences extending both ways to keep them confined. The cattle guard was a ditch covered with pipes that were spaced apart. Cattle were afraid of the space and wouldn't cross the guard, but cars could. People used these guards on their driveways in Bigfork and fenced in their houses. Jake and I enjoyed our stay with his aunt and uncle. I thought that western Montana, with its big streams and mountains, would be a grand place to live.

We spent several extra days in Bigfork waiting for a title to Jake's Jeep, because we couldn't cross the border to drive to Alaska without a title. The Canadian government wanted to be able to remove cars that had been abandoned by Americans on the way to Alaska – we could see as we drove that it had become a problem. It was exciting as we drove up through Canada to see the towns with such romantic names – Calgary, Dawson Creek, Whitehorse. Also, as we drove, the population thinned out and the roads were poorer; in some places when you came to a river, rather than a bridge there would be a ferry. There would be a cable across the river with the ferry hitched with cables at both ends. To cross the river they extended the cable on one end, and the current pushed the ferry across. In addition to seeing abandoned cars on the roadside, you frequently saw blown tires; the mile after mile of gravel road was hard on tires; it was not uncommon for cars to carry two spares – this was before steel-belted radials.

The trip would have been more pleasant if it had rained less and if the roof on the Jeep hadn't leaked. It got on our nerves, and Jake wanted to turn around. He was thinking of the good time we had in Bigfork, but I wanted to go on, so we parted ways. We were on mile 300 of the Alcan Highway, 1,000 miles from Fairbanks and 30 miles to the next settlement in either direction. I took what I could carry – Jake would leave the rest in Bigfork – and I started hitchhiking.

The mosquitoes were furious. Two rigs went by, they waved but didn't stop. I was beginning to question my judgment. It seemed like a long time, but I doubt it was more than two hours before a car stopped. The driver was willing to give me a ride if I paid for half the gas, but he was apprehensive when he saw my hunting knife tied on the top of my bundle of clothes. (That knife is still my favorite, though I've been given many other finer ones, the latest from my grandsons with my name on it.) I would be paying for half the gas, so that was no problem, and I guess he felt I wasn't going to attack him. He was writing a story for a Minneapolis newspaper about Fairbanks and the trip up there. He was getting paid by the word, and I think picking me up gave him material to help with his word count. I also helped with the driving, and we got to Fairbanks uneventfully. The driver had a tent that we pitched on the edge of town by the river. He wanted me to drive back south with him when he finished his work, and I was tempted. Did I want to spend the summer alone in Alaska?

On the fourth day I decided to see if I could get a job. I went to the Union Hall and got a job working as a Gandy Dancer, tamping gravel under railroad ties. I was to catch a work train out to Camp Happy, about seven miles out of Fairbanks, where I would live. I was walking away from the Union Hall, having hired out, when there was Bill Bacon, one of the Newton boys, walking down the street. He said that two of the other boys, Jim Edson and Ken Perkins, were also working at Camp Happy, and that Eric Tasker had wintered there and gone back to the States. It couldn't have worked better for me.

The term Gandy Dancer is used to describe men that maintain railroad tracks. A gandy is an iron bar used to move the track into alignment, otherwise called a lining bar, or, on a Vermont farm, a crow bar. The dancers are the men with short-handled shovels, moving up and down, tamping gravel under ties that have been raised up in an effort to level the tracks. There are eight men in a gang tamping gravel in eight places under each tie, on either side of each rail, so you end up tamping gravel on both sides of the tie and the rails. There were four gangs. The lead gang, when it had finished its tie, moved up four ties, and the other gangs would follow. Jim and Ken were in the lead gang, and they got me working with them. We set the pace, the others had to keep up.

Ken and I were given another job for a short time in the middle of the summer: dumping gravel on the side of the track for the Gandy Dancers to shovel. Most of the railroad cars had doors on each side on the bottom – we would open the doors, and the engineer would shake the car to get the gravel out. But one Saturday night we got a different kind of car. This type had a scissor-like action that pushed the body part way up with air pressure from the engine, then one side would continue up and dump the gravel. On this night, one of the cars stuck, but we kept the air pressure going to it – and when it finally let go, it flipped over, blocking the tracks. The next day was Sunday, and they called the whole camp out to clear the tracks. Mostly we just sat around and watched, with everyone getting paid double time for Sunday work. The boys in the camp were grateful to us for the extra pay – now Ken and I couldn't pay for a drink in town, the other boys bought them for us for the rest of the summer. This was 1949, Alaska was still a territory. I was 18 years old. The country was exciting, beautiful, and just starting to get spoiled, an adventure that is hard to forget. Fairbanks was a frontier town; it was like an old Western movie set. The town had four dirt streets with wooden sidewalks, and while there were some stores and a bank, it seemed like every other door led you into a bar. On Fourth Street, every door did lead you into a bar where you would find ladies ready to accommodate you.

The work train was our transportation back and forth to camp, and it ran all night, but since it didn't get dark at a normal time, it was hard to know when it was your time to quit and go back to camp. We worked twelve hours a day, six days a week. Our camp had four cars on a railroad siding: Wash, Dining, Cook, and Office cars. We lived in modified tents that had wooden floors with three-foot wooden sides, ten cots down one side. There was a kind of street between the tents and the cars. What trash we generated went into a pile at the end of the street; it was common to have Black Bear or brown Black Bear working the trash pile. Another common sight was snow-capped Mt. McKinley, all 20,320 feet of it in our view.

When the gravel we were shoveling on the railroad in Fairbanks started to freeze in late October, making it difficult to tamp it under the ties, the company quit the job for the winter. Jim Edson and I took the passenger train, named the Aurora, from Fairbanks down the tracks we had been working on, to Anchorage, then had an unusual flight to Seattle. We had purchased discounted tickets, but didn't realize what the difference might be. The difference was that the plane was used for taking freight from Seattle up to Alaska, and returning to Seattle with passengers. The seats could be taken out for freight, and they didn't bother with pressurizing the fuselage, or with heat. The hostess issued us all blankets and then went up with the pilots; we didn't see her again until we got to Seattle. Several things about that trip that I remember: the yellow ice on the floor in the toilet; how, when a whiskey bottle was opened, the smell traveled through the room in that cold, dead air; and the amazing pain in my ears when we descended to land in Seattle. Car horns in Seattle sounded tinny for several days after that flight.

Cross-Country with Jim Edson

Arrived in Seattle, Jim Edson and I bought a van that had belonged to the Washington State Police. It had bucket seats with a wire barrier behind to protect the officers from the prisoners; we took the wire out and had the back open. Our first trip was to go east from Seattle through Idaho and the Rockies to Bigfork, Montana to visit Jake's aunt and uncle and get my gear. It was a fun trip through the mountains; I think we were on Route 2. Then we continued east to Mandan, North Dakota to visit a Gandy Dancer we had worked with; he had been the fourth, with Jim, Ken, and me, on our side of Gang One.

(I would like to make note here that on this trip that Jim and I made, we visited many places of whose historical significance I was unaware, Mandan being no exception. Today, on the way out to South Dakota each fall on pheasant hunting trips, driving along the Missouri River I'm reminded of how the Lewis and Clark expedition spent their first winter with the Mandan Indians. On hunting trips with my grandsons, I sometimes interrupt them as they work on their cell phones to tell them of something significant we are driving by.)

The next stop for Jim Edson and me was Logan, Utah to visit Bill Bacon, who was a freshman at the University of Utah. (You remember Bill, he was the Newton boy I met on the street in Fairbanks, he and Jim Edson were both Marine Corps veterans when they came to Newton School, both having quit high school and joined the Marines. Bill went on to have an amazing career with Walt Disney as an animal trainer and stunt man.) Jim and I had a good time with Bill, and he helped us finish furnishing our van by dropping a mattress out the third floor window of his dorm; it greatly improved our sleeping conditions.

We left Bill and drove via Reno, Nevada to Carmel, California, where Jim's aunt lived. Carmel was a very wealthy town, but Jim and I managed to adapt and had a grand time staying with his aunt. After

Carmel we really had no agenda or timetable. We spent six or seven weeks traveling, sleeping in the van and eating in diners and bars. It was a relaxed, enjoyable time, with many memorable experiences (I hope they aren't as boring as some slide shows I've sat through).

Leaving Carmel we headed southeast, more or less heading toward home. In Las Vegas I hit the jackpot on a dollar machine and was paid 150 silver dollars. They gave me a bag to put it in; the bag was empty before we left Las Vegas. We visited Hoover Dam and the Grand Canyon; I don't suppose they have changed much since we were there, except I think the dam was called Boulder then. We worked our way easterly across Arizona, New Mexico, and Texas, and one morning we found ourselves in Galveston, a sleepy port before everyone started singing about it. We were in a bar in Galveston having breakfast when I noticed a sign over the bar. The sign was all fractions and abbreviations, but when deciphered it said, "One dozen oysters on the half shell: 50 cents." We couldn't believe it, we each ordered three dozen, moved to a booth, and had a feast.

We drove along the Gulf Coast without a particular destination, as had been our practice for the whole trip, and found ourselves in New Orleans. We gravitated to Bourbon Street as if we knew where we were going, and settled there. Jim was older and more experienced than I was, having been in the Marines, and he seemed to take it in stride; but for me, a boy from rural Vermont, I still think back on that section of town and how it was a continuous, exotic party. As we walked down Bourbon Street, prostitutes would come out of doorways and walk with us, others would hang out the windows and beckon to us, I was unable to be nonchalant, Jim did better. The musicians playing outside the bars, the street entertainers: the experience was unforgettable, perhaps the highlight of the trip.

While driving north in West Virginia, we got into a snowstorm and totaled our van. We gathered our stuff together and took a bus north to Jim's home in swanky Sewickley, Pennsylvania, where we continued our carefree, though now more upscale life. I had had a shotgun with me, except for when I left it behind with Jake when I hitchhiked to Alaska, and up to this point I had found no use for it. I now put it to good use and traded it to Jim's brother for a sports jacket so I could dress more appropriately – the Edsons belonged to two country clubs, and we were frequently in one or the other. Mid-December came, and by then I think I had overstayed my welcome. Our fast life wasn't gaining in popularity with Jim's family, it was time to end the trip. I caught a bus to Farmington, Connecticut and spent Christmas with my parents.

Dave Claghorn Farm

I had planned to spend the winter in Farmington and draw unemployment compensation–this was one of the things I had learned with my new worldliness – but Mother had other ideas. She suggested that I contact David Claghorn, a dairy farmer that we knew in Perkinsville, Vermont, and see if he needed help. David's wife Connie was one of Anna Hartness Beardsley's daughters, and would have been a teenager when I was a little boy playing in the Hartness home in Springfield. I'm not sure that Dave needed any help, but he hired me, probably because of the Beardsley connection. It was the beginning of a lifelong friendship. Dave was an avid reader and talker, and I found him very interesting and entertaining. I found myself wanting to read, particularly current events so I could carry my end of the conversation. We talked about my going back to school, and Dave was instrumental in my going to the University of Connecticut. We chose UConn because my parents were Connecticut residents, so the tuition would be less.

The Korean War started in June of 1950, and if Dave Claghorn hadn't gotten me enrolled for that fall at UConn, I would have joined the Marines. Before I left for school, Jim Keeney stopped at the farm to visit, he had graduated from Newton in the spring and had no immediate plans. He ended up taking my place at Claghorn's and worked there for a year. The Newton School was failing and was not giving its students the assistance they needed to go on to college. However, with the help of Connie's sister-in-law, Peg Beardsley, Jim started at Bowdoin College in the fall of '51.

1950–1952

"I was surprised to find that I was in the two-year school of agriculture, rather than the four-year college."

I DON'T RECALL ANY PROBLEMS ADAPTING TO LIFE on the Connecticut campus, though I was surprised to find that I was in the two-year school of agriculture, rather than the four-year college. I was 19 and, having been out of school two years, I felt older than my classmates. Since I had money saved, and my tuition was low, I had enough funds. I set about my classes and college life to get all I could out of it. I had very little trouble with the academics and easily found work on campus.

George Farnham Farm

There was a requirement for Dairy Production majors at UConn to work on a dairy farm in the summer. I found this a little bit of a joke, since this was about the only work I had ever done, and I found it no problem. The school had farmers that regularly took students; one of them, George Farnham, offered me a job. I wanted to work for him and told him so, but the pay he offered wasn't enough, I said that I could earn more on a farm in Vermont. I think he was a little startled, but we were able to agree on a salary, and it turned out to be a very enjoyable, productive summer.

George's student worker usually lived with the herdsman. This summer, the herdsman's wife didn't want a student living with them, and I was fortunate to stay with the Farnhams. They were a great family with six children, the oldest was about 14. I thoroughly enjoyed their family, the conversation and lifestyle, it was a pleasant learning experience for me. I continued my interest in current events, shifting from "Time Magazine" with Dave Claghorn to "The New York Times" with George and his wife, a Bennington College graduate. They were very generous, and I had the use of their Ford station wagon to go to dances.

Toward the end of the summer the Farnhams asked me to take the Ford to Vermont and pick up their girls at camp in Fairlee, they gave me several days to do it. I visited the Newtons in Windham and then drove over to the lake in Fairlee and picked up two of their daughters at camp. (I found out later that it was the same camp Patty had been at when the war in Europe ended.) George was secretary of the New England Brown Swiss breed, and he got me a job that fall going to the national and international shows with a group of Brown Swiss show cattle.

The group was put together after the Springfield, Massachusetts show in mid-September; it was a composite herd from several Brown Swiss breeders that had shown at Springfield. There were 19 animals in all: eight cows, nine heifers, and two bulls. We loaded them in a specially designed boxcar in Springfield the day that the show there ended. The car had a second floor; we (two herdsmen and myself) lived at one end of the second floor, and there was a water tub at the other end. The tub was filled using the same spout arrangement used for filling steam engines. It was a unique experience, traveling across the country with the cattle, then living on the fairgrounds and showing the cattle.

We attended the national and international dairy shows in Indianapolis, Indiana and Waterloo, Iowa; I was gone about five weeks. We had to milk the cows by hand while traveling in the boxcar and take care of them, but I had plenty of free time, I read Tolstoy's *War and Peace* while on the trip. I got back on campus a week before mid-semester exams, and had to work hard to catch up. I was in time to drop one course without penalty and still have 15 credits. My mid-semester grades weren't very good except for an economics course in farm management; I got an A in that. That summer with Farnhams and the subsequent show-cattle trip opened many doors for me. One immediate advantage was that two farmers with pure-bred cattle hired me to get animals ready to be put in sales. They would pick me up at school, I would work with their animals, then they brought me back. I usually worked in the evening after classes.

I graduated spring of 1952, I was third in my class, and money ahead. I should have pursued a job that would have gotten me herdsman of a purebred herd, so I could have worked toward being a farm manager, but I didn't. I went back to Perkinsville, Vermont to work on Claghorn's farm and live with Dave and Connie and their two kids, Michael and Judy. There is no doubt Claghorns had become my second home, Newton being the first. Once again, my stay there was brief, I was drafted into the Army December 1, 1952. Fortunately, this allowed me time to spend Thanksgiving and the last four days of deer season at Newton.

1952-1954

"I got to race on many of the mountains
in Austria and Germany."

I HAVE NEVER WRITTEN ABOUT MY ARMY TIME, although I have certainly talked about it. I thought at the time, and I still do, that it was like two years of travel and vacation, and I got paid to do it. I might have thought differently if I had gone with my basic training company to Korea, but I was in for a better experience. After four months of infantry basic training in Camp Breckenridge, Kentucky, I qualified for two months of Leadership School; the school was on the same base, so I stayed there in Breckenridge. I had a surprise on my way across the base to the Leadership School. I found I had seven days to get there – it was called "delay-in-route"; apparently the school needed a week before they could take a new class. I wasn't just sure what to do, but decided I might as well hitchhike back East. I put my duffel bag in a warehouse, took my hand bag, I had three dollars and change in my pocket, it was around 9:00 p.m., dark, and raining in mid-April. I rode the Army bus to Evansville, Indiana and started hitchhiking.

I got a ride north toward Chicago and got off at Terre Haute where Route 40, an east-west road, crosses through. (It is Interstate 70 now.) I stood at that crossroads in Terre Haute, in the rain, watching a clock on a church spire go from 1:00 to 3:00 in the morning, once again questioning, as I had on the Alcan Highway, my judgment. A little after 3:00 a.m. a tractor-trailer, double-decked with pigs heading to a slaughterhouse in Indianapolis, stopped, and soon I was sitting in a nice, warm, dry cab. The slaughterhouse

37

was on the west side of Indianapolis; the truck driver told me that for a dime I could ride the trolley to the east side, where it would be better hitchhiking. It was good advice, Indianapolis is a very sprawled-out city. I was in uniform and, as a result, got more rides than I might have. In fact, twice I had other hitchhikers join me on the road to take advantage of the luck the uniform brought me; they returned the favor by buying me food. I traveled that day and night and pulled in to New York City through the Holland Tunnel in the early morning of the next day. The trip had taken about 36 hours.

I caught the subway up to 168th Street to Mary Newton's apartment; she had graduated from nursing school and was now working at the Presbyterian Hospital. (My future wife Patty was a second-year student at the nursing school there, though I had no way or reason to know that.) Mary gave me a place to sleep and money for a train ticket to Hartford, Connecticut. Dad picked me up at the Hartford station. I visited the folks for a couple of days, took some money out of my savings account, and hurried back down to see Mary. I had loved Mary forever and was building up my courage to ask her to marry me. I found the opportunity in the afternoon when we walked out on the George Washington Bridge; we were looking down the river into the city when I asked her. She was very sweet, but her feelings toward me were different, and she turned me down. I have experienced disappointments many times in my life, and often they have proven to be opportunities; this was no exception, as you will learn as you read on.

So the disappointed young infantryman flew back to Breckenridge for his next phase of training.

The school was more of the same infantry training, except I learned how to give classes, in the classroom as well as on the parade field. After the two months of leadership training the whole leadership class went to Korea, as our basic company had, with the exception of five men that were mysteriously pulled from the middle of the roster and sent to Austria. A soldier named Lang had a friend in personnel, and this friend was able to get Lang sent to Austria along with a Kempton, two Kennedys, and a Kuzak. The five of us were sent to Camp Kilmer in New Jersey to go by troopship to Leghorn, Italy, and then by train to Salzburg.

Since all five of us had more training, we were put in charge of the other soldiers waiting for the troopship; we waited at least three weeks. I marched the troops around to keep them busy and gave physical training classes. The parents of Jerome Kennedy, one of the two Kennedys, had a cottage on the Connecticut shore not far from Black Point; we hitchhiked up and spent three weekends there while we waited. I found that in the Army you are asked to hurry and then you wait, you get into a hurry-up-and-wait routine, I found that I never wanted to be caught without a book, others were the same way, and we traded books frequently.

When the ship finally arrived, it was a Kaiser troopship, built in the Second World War, and while I was no expert on ocean going vessels, it seemed old and worn-out to me. There were several hundred civilians on the decks above water and 1,500 troops on five decks – A through F – below water. I was on F deck, at the bottom of the ship. We slept on hammocks that were arranged in double rows of five, from the floor to the ceiling. During the day they were folded up, and there was adequate room to walk between them, but at night when they were folded down so you could crawl in and sleep, there was very little room between them, particularly with everyone's duffel bags on the floor.

The ventilation was poor, so I spent most of my time on deck. Once again, the five of us had special treatment. I was a messenger, which didn't seem to involve doing much, so I sat on deck and read all day, making sure I was first in the chow line, though there wasn't much competition for food because so many were seasick. One of the reasons for the seasickness was that the boat handled the big waves poorly; when we went into a wave the bow would go up very high and then come crashing down in the valley between waves, making the stern go up high enough so the screws would come out of the water and shake the ship, it made you wonder how much the old ship could take. As we approached the Mediterranean on our way to Leghorn, we stopped in Casablanca, an unexpected treat. We were among the few troops that were able to get off the ship and see that ancient city. We walked the streets, passing the veiled women, and through the busy markets with everything for sale, including meat hanging in the open. The sights and smells left a lasting impression.

You could say being stationed just outside of Salzburg was a dream come true, and it certainly would have been had I ever dreamed of it, but as it was, I had just expected to go to Korea. Salzburg in the summer of '53 was recovering from the Second World War, the streets were filled with strange-looking old trucks and bicycles, and many businesses were boarded up. We were liberation troops and an important part of Austria's economy. Our primary mission was to slow down Russian troops were they to attack, slow them down long enough to allow more of our forces to arrive. To accomplish this we did a lot of night withdrawals – simply put, we walked a lot at night with packs and weapons.

I enjoyed the soldiering and maneuvers in Austria, I think I adapted easily to military life, and there were many benefits that I was able to take advantage of. Qualifying for an Army ski team was certainly one of them. The opportunity to ski and spend nights in those picturesque mountain resort towns was a chance in a lifetime, and I got to race on many of the mountains in Austria and Germany, and skied, though not in competition, in Switzerland.

When the ski team was getting organized, the officer in charge, Hank Lent, took us to a glacier in Ensingerboden, Germany to see how well we could ski. We rode up to the start of the glacier in a big cable car that would have serviced the now-abandoned salt mine. We stayed in a barracks and were fed there, this was a business that the Austrians did for early season skiers. The Austrian women's Olympic ski team was there at the same time, they were staying in another barracks, and we never got to see them except when they skied down past us on the glacier at the end of the day. Our team may not have been the best skiers in the Army, but Hank was pleased with our attitude and teamwork.

We were just getting organized as a team and getting ready for our first meet when Hank had a problem with his wife and had to go back to the States. They gave us another officer, but he wasn't really interested, and I ended up taking Hank's place. I had a schedule of the meets, but I had to arrange transportation and find money for food and lodging. I spent a lot of time at battalion headquarters badgering people, and everyone on the team got good at bartering with c-rations and cigarettes and figuring out the train schedules, which of course were all in German. We developed a system where one person would find an empty compartment on a train and open the window, we would then throw our stuff – skis, bartering material, handbags – into the train. One time after we had done this we found it was the wrong train, so we unloaded everything and re-loaded it in the right train, it was a helluva job.

Our final meet was a three-day meet in Badgastein, Austria, a beautiful village situated in a valley with steep mountains on both sides. There were six of us; we had money enough for one double room and lots of bartering material. We got a double room in an inn and tried never to be seen with more than two people. We got away with it for two nights, but we got caught on the third, we must have gotten careless. I don't remember just how we worked it out, but it was difficult.

Skiing was the highlight of my "tour of duty" in Austria, but I did do a few other things of interest. I shot competitively on an M-1 rifle team; we did well enough in Europe to be flown to Fort Benning, Georgia for an all-Army meet. I also gave weekly classes to the company on current events (I was reading the European edition of "The Herald Tribune" and the Army paper "Stars & Stripes"; I could thank Dave Claghorn for that). I had a map of the world, and I attached ribbons to connect the news event with where it was happening. When it was time to ship home, the Army offered me a promotion in rank if I would stay for another year. I was tempted, but I had never planned to be a soldier and I missed home, so I sailed back home. This time I was on a newer troopship, and the voyage was more pleasant, or perhaps I should say less interesting. I was discharged mid-November 1954, just in time for Thanksgiving and the last four days of hunting season at Newton.

I was in good shape financially; I had saved money while in the Army, and also had some back pay at Claghorns I could draw. I put a down payment on a new '54 Ford Victoria, my first car, and skied and visited and tried to decide what I might do now. Mother and Dad were no longer working for the Grays in Farmington. Dad was working second shift in East Hartford for Pratt and Whitney, and he and Mom were living in Stafford Springs, Connecticut. While working for Gray, they had bought a camp lot on a lake in Stafford Springs and built a little place to come to in their free time. With Dad changing jobs they were fixing it up for year-round living. I had helped some when I was in college by paying for a well to be drilled. Now, as I decided what to do, I stayed with them and helped with other home improvements.

When I was a student at UConn, one of the jobs I enjoyed most was working in the beef and sheep barn. I now found it fun and convenient to visit my friends there, as it was only a 20-minute drive from my folks' place. Their herdsman needed a leave of absence, and they hired me to take charge and lamb out their flock. It was perfect for me; I could live at home for the first time since we were on the farm in Windham and have a challenging job as well. The job involved taking care of the beef and sheep and giving classes to the livestock majors in castrating, docking, worming, and general livestock care; a lot of this I had done while working there as a student.

When the herdsman came back in early June, the director of the Animal Science Department, Professor Al Cowen, asked me to take over their piggery. He said there were a number of experiments that needed doing regarding feeding cooked garbage to the pigs, he wanted me to supervise those experiments, and he would help me get the courses I needed for my B.S. degree. I was very tempted, it would have been a start on a new career, and I could have lived at home. I was enjoying the time with Mother and her wonderful flower gardens, but I decided not to take the job. Claghorn wanted me to go back to work for him, and I liked the life on the farm better. Professor Cowan gave me a very complimentary letter of recommendation.

Patricia Gulick in nurse uniform, 1955

George Kempton in Army uniform, 1955

1955-1961

"By the end of the weekend we had decided
we wanted to spend the rest of our lives together."

I WENT TO WORK FOR CLAGHORN FOR A THIRD TIME, it was June 1955, but this was different. This time there was no college or army that would interrupt my working there, this was what I would be doing. I settled in with Dave and Connie, they included me in their social life, and I began getting more involved. I started teaching Sunday School. The Springfield Congregational Church had a class of seventh-, eighth-, and ninth-grade boys that had become unmanageable. I had been going to church with the Claghorns, their son Michael was in the class, and I had found while in the Army that I liked teaching, so I took on the job. Discipline was no problem for me, but my background in the New Testament was weak, and I had to work hard to stay ahead of those bright young boys. Life on the farm was enjoyable, and as the summer passed by I began looking forward to hunting season. I had received a card from John Newton saying he was bringing a girl up from New Jersey for the long Thanksgiving weekend, and hoped I would be coming to Newton to hunt and to squire her around to dances.

I hadn't thought very much about who the girl might be that John Newton was bringing for the Thanksgiving weekend, but I did think it unusual for John to send me a card encouraging me to come, since he would have expected me to be there. When I met this mystery woman named Patricia, it was like a dream come true. She was beautiful, intelligent, athletic, charming, she had led a life I had only dreamed of, yet she seemed envious of my life. I had decided that life on the farm was what I liked, I was good at it, I thought I would, somehow, spend my life at it. When I told Patty this, she was enthusiastic.

We walked in the woods, supposedly deer hunting, but in reality we talked and talked, we shared our lives and dreams and found we were amazingly compatible. We had both reached that point in our lives when we were ready to get married and start a family, it couldn't have been more perfect. By the end of the weekend we had decided we wanted to spend the rest of our lives together, but I was afraid that such a big decision shouldn't be made that fast and said I would write in a few days. I wrote and proposed, she accepted, and we were married as soon as it could be put together – March 3, 1956.

Here, briefly, I'm going to give Patty's history up until she and I met.

Patricia Elizabeth Gulick was born June 26, 1931 in East Orange, New Jersey. She lived in Summit, N.J. with her parents Ivan and Mildred and her brother Richard. Ivan Gulick had gone to work after high school for New Jersey Public Service and worked there for 51 years. He went to college nights, graduating after eight years. In 1962, at age 70, he retired. Patty's mother was a homemaker. Richard was eight years older than Pat, he went to the United States Naval Academy in Annapolis and was a submarine officer. He was gone most of Pat's growing up, she complained of being an only child. Patty was able to walk to her two different grade schools as well as high school; there was also a tennis club within an easy walk. Pat has Summit High School yearbooks for all four years 1945-1949. There is no doubt that she was a very popular, athletic, academic student, as well as being active, along with her father, in the Summit Methodist Church. She formed the habit of keeping a diary and kept at it more or less throughout her life.

The Gulicks went to Cape Cod each summer, to The Pines, a family resort. They started going when Patty was a baby and went each year for 17 years. In the beginning, they would go for a week, but toward the end they would go for three or four weeks. Patty loved all parts of it, but I think particularly the sailing. When they came home, she would be bored and hang out at the tennis court hoping for a game. In the summer of '45 Patty, in addition to Cape Cod, went to a girls camp on a lake in Fairlee, Vermont. She told me about the girls "gunneling" the canoes when they heard about the war ending. I looked up "gunnel"; it is the outside edge of a boat. The girls stood on the outside edge of the stern of the canoe and bounced up and down, raising the bow of the canoe and forcing it forward.

While in her senior year at high school, Patty applied to Middlebury College in Vermont and set her heart on going there. She wrote in her diary:

March 20, 1949
This weekend has been an eventful one for me. Many things have occurred that struck sharply at my heart strings, and being restrained built up in me to a point where I had to let go of all the emotion at the same time; that broke the tension, and nothing drastic happened to me except that I have grown some, perhaps, in mind and spirit. Thursday, I received a letter from Middlebury saying that they wouldn't be able to take me. There – in that one letter was the answer to all my dreams and expectations of the past year. Of course, I was sick about it at first, but I realize that everything happens for the best – I know it does. And, I am on the waiting list, and haven't given up hope yet.

That summer, while I was riding around the country with Jim Edson in a retired police van with an old mattress, Patty was touring Scandinavia with her parents. She wrote in her diary about the flight, the people, the food, the hotels, the tours and tour guides.

Summer 1949
The first castle which we visited was Frederiksborg castle at Hillerod. It was like a dream – you could almost believe you were living in the days of the knights and glamorously romantic adventures ... I ran in the knights ballroom and the huge room where they dined in front of a mammoth fireplace ... It is tremendously difficult to describe any of the castles without taking a great deal of time and hard thinking. The most I can say is that they are truly as romantic as they seemed to us

in the wonderful stories which we have read about knights and castles and adventure...

Returning from Europe, Patty entered St. Lawrence University in New York for a year, then went to Colby Junior College in New Hampshire for her second year. By then she'd formed a plan to become a nurse, and the following fall, 1951, while I was at UConn, Patty started Columbia Presbyterian nursing school in New York City. This was the start of the amazing sequence of events that brought Patty and me together. At Columbia Presbyterian, Patty met Mary Newton, who was in her third year at the school when Patty arrived and was Patty's "big sister." Patty and Mary had a schoolmate, Jane Spross; the three became friends. Jane began dating Mary's brother John Newton, so Patty now had connections with Mary and John Newton, two of my best friends from the Newton School.

Patty graduated from Columbia Presbyterian in spring 1954 – I was in the army in Austria. For graduation her father gave her a new '54 Chevrolet; she moved home and began nursing at Overlook Hospital in her hometown of Summit. She kept in touch with her friend Jane Spross from nursing school, who married John Newton and was living in Princeton (where John had been a student). John and Jane had a 1932 Model A Ford. When they wanted to go to John's home in Windham, Vermont (the old Newton School), they would trade cars with Patty. They would take her new '54 Chevy, and she would drive around Summit in their Model A Ford. At Thanksgiving 1955, with some sort of intuition that Patty and I would get along, they brought her with them to Windham.

There was much more to getting married than I had realized, but fortunately I had very little to do with it. Patty's dad Ivan said he would give us the $2,000 he would save if we would have a simple wedding, but Patty and her mother had other ideas. I made several trips to Summit from Perkinsville that winter, where I was working for Claghorn; the trip became easier, but it was always difficult with Patty's mother Mildred – she had envisioned a very different person for her son-in-law. The wedding was in the Summit Methodist

Church, where Patty and Ivan were well loved. The reception was at a country club. Midge Jackson, Patty's classmate from nursing school, was her maid of honor, and John Newton was my best man.

The minister, Jesse Lyons, counseled us before the wedding, it was obvious he was very fond of Patty, and he questioned me very sharply. He gave us some advice that we never forgot. To paraphrase: "If you have disagreed and are angry with each other, settle it before you go to bed, never go to bed angry with one another." When we had disagreements, it was usually caused by my shortcomings, we worked it out, we didn't go to bed angry. (Patty brought a wealth of love, knowledge, and understanding to our marriage and family, you can see it in our children and grandchildren.)

After we were married we spent the night in New York City and then drove to Vermont. Patty's friend Anne Rantoule's parents had a summer place in West Woodstock and gave us a week there as a honeymoon present. We skied every day at Suicide Six, it wasn't busy during the week in March, and they would start the tow when we got there. Sometimes the workers would question why we were late, it was a perfect honeymoon. Then we set up housekeeping in an apartment in North Springfield that Dave Claghorn had rented for us, the apartment was perfect for us and close to the farm.

We had an active social life, and Patty was busy with shopping and gardening and getting ready for our first child, Sam; he was born October 1, 1956. If we had any problem it was lack of money, I didn't earn enough. It wasn't uncommon for Patty to take something back in the supermarket because she didn't have money enough, I helped a little by quitting smoking cigarettes, they cost two dollars a carton.

The Claghorn farm was on the Black River, and a decision had been made to build a flood control dam in the river to protect the machine industry in Springfield; the dam would flood out Claghorn's farm as well as Fred Knapp's farm next door. Claghorn was moving to Hudson, New York and expected me to go with him. Knapp, on the other hand, was renting a farm in Dummerston, Vermont and needed me badly. Knapp offered me the same salary I had been getting from Claghorn, plus 5% of the milk check and a beautiful house to live in. Dave was my friend and mentor–going to work for Fred was difficult for me, but I didn't think I had a choice, I know Dave was always disappointed.

Fred Knapp Farm

We moved to Dummerston on the first of April '57, our house was a beautiful Cape Cod style house with 12-over-12 windows. We moved down a month before Fred and his family moved down with the milkers, he did move the heifers down the same day we moved. The farm was owned by Ellsworth Bunker, Ambassador to India. His son had been running the farm, had left it a mess, and my job was to get the buildings, fences, and milking parlor ready for Fred's herd. The challenge would come when Fred trucked the herd down the 40 miles from Perkinsville to Dummerston, I had never milked his cows and knew nothing about a milking parlor, and the cows were as ignorant as I was. The first few milkings were chaotic, but after about a week the cows and I had figured it out, and I began to enjoy the parlor, I think the cows did too.

Our life in Dummerston was busy and fun. Aunt Fran (Dad's younger sister) and Uncle Andy stayed with us for a week or more when we first moved, and Uncle Andy did some remodeling. He made it easier to use the upstairs bedrooms and fixed up a nursery for Sam and for Jen, who came along December 14, 1957. I quit teaching Sunday School when we left the Springfield church, but we became active in the Dummerston church. We helped start a Bible study group, and we made several lifelong friends, particularly Dwight and Gladys Miller.

Other lifelong friends, Clarence and Ester Falk, who had met in India, got us involved in international politics; because of them we had two Russians stay with us once. It was part of an effort during the Cold War to break down barriers. One afternoon the two Russians visited me during milking. When I finished milking and had cleaned up, we walked out of the milk room toward my car, the screen door shutting behind us. They didn't believe that I always left like that, so casually, they thought I was doing it for effect. I don't think they ever believed that we could leave the milk unlocked and unguarded and not have it stolen.

John and Jane Newton were now living in Vermont at the former Newton School in Windham; John had graduated from Princeton, had gotten his Master's in Education at Harvard, and was teaching at Leland and Grey Seminary in Townsend. We saw them often; they had dances in the big room at the school, and we had them down to Dummerston for venison cookouts. Their family was growing as ours was. When Patty's parents visited, it was always awkward; Ivan was at ease, but Mildred wasn't, I felt sorry for Patty. My mother's cancer had become active again, and my parents didn't visit much after the first year, but we visited them in Stafford Springs (Connecticut). Mother died April 22, 1959 at age 72; my son David was nearly five months old, having been born December 4, 1958. Mother was well enough during the winter when we visited for her to be able to hold him.

My grandmother Kempton had died before we were married, and Aunt Fran took care of Grandpa until he died in February of '58. Aunt Fran inherited her parents' property, I think Dad was upset by that. She sold the house, and she and Uncle Andy bought a house in Montgomery Center, Vermont. This was fortuitous for Patty and me. In early February, before sugaring, I would get a week off, we would leave the kids with Aunt Fran in Montgomery for the day and ski at Jay Peak. We did that three years in a row, in the winters of '59, '60, and '61. On September 21, 1960 Annie was added to the family.

We had a good life in Dummerston; we had many good friends and competent young women that helped with babysitting. We had a wonderful big garden that the deer tried to get in; shooting them kept us supplied with venison. We had so many strawberries that we started a strawberry festival at the Dummerston church (in 2014 I went down to Dummerston to Ester Falk's funeral and learned that the festival is still happening). Fred's herd was milking well, he was pleased and so was I, particularly since Patty and I were still getting 5% of the milk check.

Nevertheless, Patty's dad Ivan wanted to help us get our own farm, and he watched the papers to see what was for sale. In

September 1961, about a month after Matt was born on August 8, we drove north up Route 5 to Peacham, Vermont to look at a farm that belonged to Jim and Clara Craig. Ivan had seen it advertised in the "New York Herald Tribune." That trip was the beginning of negotiations, by both letter and visits, that took place that fall. On the way back to Dummerston after our third trip to Peacham, while going through Norwich on Route 5, we decided to buy the Craig farm. For many years after, we called Norwich our "decision town."

In our visits and letters with the Craigs, Jim and I developed a unique trust and understanding of each other's needs. Jim's health was poor, and he needed to get out of farming. Patty and I wanted to farm our own farm, and Ivan wanted to help us. The farm consisted of 235 acres; 100 head of Jersey cattle, of which 62 were milkers; house, barn, and sugarhouse; three tractors; a truck; and a complete line of equipment. We agreed on a sale price of $75,000 – Ivan would lend us $20,000, and we had $2,000 of our own, giving us $22,000 for a down payment. But Jim needed a down payment of $35,000 to satisfy his creditors, this is where we get to the trust part. We agreed on a sales contract, which I will try to explain.

We would move onto the farm and assume management that January 1, 1962. Jim would continue to own the farm, pay the real estate taxes and insurance, until we could make up the remaining $13,000 of down payment. To do that, we would give him 25% of our milk income when the checks arrived on the 6th and 21st of each month. Jim would add 5.5% interest to the total amount owed, figured on a per diem basis, subtract the amount of his share of the milk check, and get a new total amount owed. I think if this agreement had been designed with the help of lawyers it might not have worked, but Jim and I had thrashed it out at his kitchen table, and we made it work because we both wanted it to. We didn't get it all covered upfront. When I bought a cow, whose was it, Jim's or mine? When I bought or sold a piece of equipment, whose was it? Who got the income from maple syrup? We worked things out as we went along.

1962

"I was going to be a Farmer."

Patricia Kempton's Farm Journal 1962-1985

MY MARRIAGE TO PATTY WAS A CLOSE PARTNER-
ship, and the story from here on is told as a partnership.
After Patty died in 2012, my daughter Jenny and I transcribed her
daily farm journal, which is given here along with my supplemental
notes. I'll introduce each year with an overview of the farm business
that year and filling in some of the details that Patty, in her busy life
as wife, mother of five, daughter, homemaker, community volunteer
didn't have time to tell.

At the end of the book is a "Directory of People Mentioned" to
help identify the many characters named.

First, I would like to say something about Patty that will be
obvious from her journal, but that I want to highlight up front. It
sums up why our marriage was a success, it was Patty's love. She
loved me for the person that I was. When she met me, I was a lousy
student and not very handsome; Patty's love gave me confidence to
thrive. Before meeting her, I never knew what Christmas was. Her
love for our family and life were the glue that made it all work – the
farming and the family; and in this old man's opinion, it continues
to operate, I can see signs of Patty's love in our great grandchildren.

Now on to the story. Patty's journal entries are in *italics*; my
supplemental notes are regular type.

When we came to farm in Peacham in the Northeast Kingdom
in 1962, we were bucking the trend: farming was in decline. There

were 26 farms shipping milk in town, but they were on the edge. Farms in this remote corner of the state had eked along during the Depression by borrowing heavily from the banks. They were in debt. Towards the end of the Depression, the great hurricane of 1938 wiped out whole sugar bushes, an important source of farm income. I believe it was the straw that broke the camel's back.

World War II came along in 1941-1945. Farms in the Northeast Kingdom were behind the rest of the country even in good times, and now in the mid-40s farmers badly needed to transition from horse power to motorized tractors. Even if they'd had the money, equipment was hard to come by during the war. When it was over, instead of having had a few years to make a gradual transition, farmers were faced with making immediate purchases with no money and no desire or ability to go further in debt. There was no incentive for sons to take over the farm from their fathers.

The local farmers were expecting failure and doubted our ability to make a living at farming here. Patty and I had a different attitude. In all the years I've farmed, I've never bought speculatively. I never asked, "How much could I make?" I asked, "What could I do if I had this land or this farm?"

We arrived in Peacham on a January morning with our five pre-school children. We knew very little about the farm we had just bought – for instance, the 235 acres were spread all over town, it wasn't contiguous, and I didn't know where much of it was. We knew nothing about the town, the townspeople, or the area. We had to learn about the schools, the supermarkets, the drug stores, hardware stores, grain dealers, cattle dealers, equipment dealers and really just an endless list. I think we were both happy and scared, but I was having a very unlikely dream come true, I was going to be a Farmer.

We soon found that many of the townspeople were related, something you had to be a little careful about, and that most of them knew who we the newcomers were. The farm was right in the village, and we found that the village was busy, with Clifton Schoolcraft's hen farm and the Peacham Academy with its boarders.

However, many of the well-preserved homes were either empty or housed only one or two older people.

With a percentage of the milk income being paid out to Jim Craig rather than a fixed amount, it was not very profitable to increase milk production. As a result, income unrelated to milk became very important to the farm business. Examples this first year: custom chopping corn and blowing it into their silos for the Harley Davises and the Ted Farrows; trucking hay for Claude Field; and renting out a room for three Peacham Academy students. The students, Bob Sorrow, Peter Herbert, and Mike Zagaradni, were bright, capable wards of the State of Connecticut who showed special promise, so the State sent them to Peacham Academy. In addition to boarding with us, they worked on the farm and helped with the custom chopping and hay trucking.

Maple syrup was another important source of income. A sugar house came with the new farm, it had a King evaporator that was 40 inches wide and 12 feet long, and there were 700 buckets. I had learned how to boil in sap by watching Fred Knapp's father Pappy on the farm in Dummerston, where I sometimes kept up the fire in the sugar house for him. I asked old Orman Hooker, a Peacham farmer, if I could tap his trees. He was willing, but doubted if there were any left after the big hurricane. We tapped mostly roadside trees those first years.

March 6, 1962
Town Meeting Day, George began tapping his sugar Maples, bright and sunny.

March 11
George boiled in our first sap.

March 17
25°-45° Gathered boiled 6 gal rather dark syrup. Roads muddy but still an awful lot of snow.

March 18
18°-42° In AM sap frozen in buckets–boiled [?] gals. Bright but windy and cold.

March 21
First day of spring 14° to 50° sap running.

March 22
30°-50° Gathered beautiful day I watched George boil for first time 6 gals a total 27 gals. Dishwasher in.

Dishwasher was a gift from Patty's parents. Patty began to notice that the families around us were getting sick more than seemed usual, she thought that sanitizing our dishes would help us ward off germs.

March 25
32°-50° Went to Burke skiing, beautiful snow, wonderful skiing, windy, cold, no sap.

March 2
Boiled 20 gals.

March 28
33°-65°.

March 29
32°-64° Sunny – lovely – Cedar Waxwing.

Cedar waxwing is a North Country bird, a first for us.

April 5
30°-50° Beautiful, Sunny, sap running very well. Sam found pussy willows.

April 6
26°-50° George boiled 'til 10:30 – Sam and Dave sick with grippe.

April 7
40°-45° Rained all day, snow going – 140 gals total – 60 B – 80 A.

April 8
43°-50° Pleasant day, no sap. Georgie off – all went to church. I took a walk and watched birds.

April 21
45°-60° Finished sugaring, about 230 gals.

April 22
Easter Sunday – partly sunny – mild. Plowed, harrowed garden. Planted peas, lettuce, radishes, carrots, spinach, beets, asters, and hollyhock. Some spring cleaning – Easter egg hunt – swings in apple tree.

April 24
32°-40° Very windy, cold, snowed a little. Dave stayed with George at sugar house and came home alone cold.

Reading this diary is an experience for me, I'm ashamed that I would let my not-quite 3 ½-year-old son walk half a mile home by himself.

April 25
Snow on the ground at 7:00, off at 11:00.

April 27
Up to 80° Lovely, started springs work. Jen – tonsillitis. – BUDS.

April 28
Up to 80° Lilac buds really coming. George spreading hen manure.

Clifton Schoolcraft, Sr. had 10,000 laying hens in the south end of the village, I bought and spread his hen manure.

April 29
Showery, cool – Planted asparagus roots.

May 3
36°-48° Cold, rainy – sore throats – lettuce, radishes up.

May 4
Mostly rainy – sun trying to come out – spreading hen manure – buckets all washed up.

May 5- 8
Cold and rainy – Mom and Dad here – kids not too well. We saw: Purple finches, Evening Grosbeak [another new bird], *Hepatica, Spring Beauty, Wild ginger.*

May 9
26°-50° Sunny but very windy – Peas up.

May 12
38°-80° (in sun) Nice breeze, but pleasantly warm – sore throats and coughs.

May 14
40°-46° Rainy – George has sore throat.

May 17
46°-100° (in sun) Kids in bare feet. George spreading, Glen [Marceau] fencing.

May 20
Hot, put up new play gym, more peas planted, lawn mowed first time, David sunburn, thunder shower in PM.

Patty's parents bought the play gym.

May 25
45°-75° Lovely intermittent clouds planted Romaine lettuce, Gr. Lakes lettuce, parsnips and North Star corn. Leaves almost fully out now. Peas doing very well, other things all up.

June 5
45°-68° Corn up, also lettuces, eating radishes, manure pile gone.

That would have been the pile between the barn and the church parking lot that I had built through the winter. I realized that if we kept a manure pile there in the warm months, that would be the end of milking in that barn – although no one ever said a word to me about it, I knew that the church would not put up for long with the run-off into its parking lot. I began trucking the manure to the Hardy lot behind the Historical House and spreading it there.

June 7
45°-70° Started mowing, planted tomatoes.

June 11
Very warm, humid, showers alternating with sunshine, boys putting up pea fence, finally took off storm windows.

June 15
Increasingly warmer and dryer, haying in full swing, but garden drying out.

June 18
Lovely dry, 1700 bales of hay in barn, everything in garden up, went swimming.

July 3
We've had mostly nice summer weather, finally got some rain, haying is about finished, our garden is excellent, we've been eating lettuce and radishes for quite a while, peas are almost ready to pick.

July 4
We went for a picnic on our upper wood lot, found where there are lots of blue-berries. Baseball game, chicken barbecue, music in church, fireworks. There was a slight sprinkle of rain, then clear again, we need rain.

July 5
Cold, windy, Picked and ate peas.
Cool summer, very little swimming, much harvesting, 45 qts peas, 100 qts beans.

During these years, Patty's diary stops after about July 4 and doesn't resume until the next winter. I think the summer was just plain too busy for her.

Sam gets a haircut on George's first workday off since he was 12, Dummerston, Vt.

The Village Farm, Peacham

1963

"My Daddy died."

PATTY'S FATHER IVAN DIED SUDDENLY IN JANUARY of a heart attack a few months after his retirement. Patty's mother Mildred couldn't deal with it and went into the hospital. Patty's brother Dick would have handled the arrangements, but he was in the hospital with the mumps. So it was left up to Pat, and we found the experience sad but in some ways very fulfilling. Ivan had worked for the same company for over 50 years and was loved and respected by hundreds. They came to the viewing by the bus load. They lined up and waited to talk to us and tell us about Ivan and their relationship with him. It was a moving and rewarding experience, particularly for Pat, and tragic that Mildred had never met any of these people. I took advantage of my free time there to set up the depreciation schedule for the farm, cattle, and equipment; as I write this I wonder if I should have, since, at this point, I didn't own them.

In March, David broke his leg – Patty didn't write how it happened, I expect this was because I did it. We had bought Sam a better pair of ski boots, and they had disappeared; we looked all over for a couple of weeks and couldn't find them. When we did find them it turned out that David had hidden them. I was very angry, I picked David up, hollered at him, and put him down too hard. I don't think I was aware at the time that I had broken his leg, I think I just stormed out and went tapping. Patty somehow handled it all, did something with the kids, got David in for an x-ray, admitted him to the hospital with his big cast, and in all likelihood, came home and cooked supper for everyone. When I started this diary, I hadn't anticipated facing so many of my transgressions.

Extra income this year included ski instruction; I was paid by Peacham Academy for coaching, and I had started a ski school. Before we moved to Peacham, the Stevens Valley Men's Club had set up a ski hill north of town on Philo Robinson's hillside on the Bayley-Hazen Road. There was a rope tow and a warming hut with a kerosene pot belly stove, where candy bars, popcorn and hot cocoa were provided. Sometimes we made sugar-on-snow. The tow operated Saturday and Sunday afternoons. A season pass for a family cost $35.00. All of our kids skied there. I would set up slalom courses for racing. Sometimes I would set up our Case SC tractor to power the rope tow. Sometime around the mid-1970s Philo Robinson sold the land, and the ski tow was closed.

Already I started getting involved in town activities; because I taught the ski team, I was involved with Winter Carnival, and I joined a town study committee that was looking at a broad range of things relating to the future of the town, from replanting dead and dying trees to whether we should have zoning.

On the farm, we increased our herd with seven Holstein heifer calves that I bought from Ken McPhee for $365, this was the start of our Holstein herd (Craig had Jerseys). Because local farms were going out of business or cutting back, there was a lot of land available to rent. Farmers had been renting land around town, but they couldn't keep it up. They asked me to take it over, and I did. For extra income, we continued to truck hay for Claude Field during school vacation when Peter Herbert and Bob Sorrow were with us. We sometimes had Peter and Bob, Glen Marceau, and Frenchie Powers, another farm worker, at the supper table, Patty would get two suppers, one for the kids and one for us after evening chores.

Dec 31 [1962]
30 [people] in house, broken pipes, frozen everything. Annie and Jen chicken pox, Sam had it over Christmas.

Jan 3, 1963
Warm today 20°+ Dec 30th thru Jan 2nd were bitterly cold with severe winds, down to 25° below.

Jan 26
My Daddy died.

Jan 28
Sam, Jen, Dave, George, and I went to Summit.

Feb 2
Committal & Memorial Services for Daddy.

Feb 3
Drove back home.

Feb 4
26° below at 7am.

Feb 5-7
Mild pleasant.

Feb 8
26° below again at 7.

Feb 15
Teddy went to the hospital to have his leg amputated.

Teddy was a Border Collie, I had trained him in Dummerston to work cows. He had been hit by a car and lost the use of his leg. Our vet John Stetson said we should amputate it or else it would always bother him. We did, and he got along on three legs very well.

Feb 16
We've had more snow so you can hardly see the house.

Feb 25–Mar 1
Winter carnival time, cold, clear, bright, wintery, John Ashford [Road Commissioner] funeral, Mother sold her house, on the way to Virginia.

Mildred moved into an apartment close to Patty's brother Dick in Norfolk.

Mar 4
Weather has been warmer 25°-35° mostly sunny, a little more snow. Sam slight case of flu, Dave has been uncomfortable with what may have been a broken collar bone.

Mar 5
Town Meeting Day, springy although not too warm, George on town Study committee.

Mar 6
20°-30° Rain & Snow. Sam back to school.

Mar 9
David broke his leg, he is in hospital with big cast. Springy weather, George began tapping out, Sam and Mike [Zagaradni] helped. Pete [Herbert] broke his leg skiing.

Mar 10
Cold again, snow, wind, very wintery, lots of people have the flu.

Mar 13
Temp. 20° Foggy at 7 AM, yesterday George set 100 buckets on Hooker run. David was happy as a lark last night, really having fun in the hospital. David discharged from hospital.

Mar 16
George set more buckets in sugar bush, Matt not feeling well.

Mar 21
20°-30° Sap running slightly, pussy willows.

Mar 24
18°-42° Cow died, John [Stetson] and George did a PM, last stages of peritonitis. Sap running some.

Mar 25
20°-50° First really warm day we have had, now it promises spring.

Mar 26
Made out Will with John Swainbank. Erica [Randall] had baby boy. [Aunt] Frannie and Andy [Martin] came. George made first 1963 syrup, fancy. Boys [Bob Sorrow, Peter Herbert] moved out to new dorm.

The new dorm was at the newly-built Kinerson Hall at Peacham Academy; our dorm students (and rental income) moved there, but Bob and Peter continued to spend vacations with us and became part of our family.

Mar 27
40°-50° Started out nice but got cool and raw. Saw a Woodcock, Frenchie [Powers] saw a robin.

Mar 31
18°-50° Claghorns visited, had picnic on Sugar House Hill, gathered and boiled.

This was the first time we had seen Dave and Connie Claghorn since we had left them in Perkinsville to work for Fred Knapp in Dummerston seven years before. It was very nice of them to come.

April 1
18°-60° Tapped more trees, gathered, boiled, made about 48 gals Fancy in total, I started spring cleaning.

April 3
Midge [Jackson] arrived.

April 4
Cold, windy, some snow, slippery roads. Went to town, Dave's cast checked, Midge took kids to Museum.

April 5
Sunny, terrifically windy, lunch with Doris [Stetson].

April 6
Wind died down some, Midge and I walked, boys cut wood.

April 7
Midge had to leave, nice day, took kids gathering, Stetson's for popcorn and sugar on snow.

April 8
24°-35° Started out nice but stayed rather raw and windy, George boiled all day, we had picnic at sugar house.

April 10
Bob Bean's house burned down. They and the McGills [?] lost almost everything, Thresher tub lost.

They were boiling sap in the woodshed.

April 13
Nice day, sunny, windy, Newtons came [John and Jane Spross].

April 16
Beautiful day, up to 60°, George pulling buckets, some crocuses peaking through, some in town in bloom.

April 19
Cool windy, planted peas.

April 20
Ditch dug and pipe put in to carry sewerage beyond garden etc.

April 22
George finished up with some sugaring tools and got started moving manure pile.

April 28
29°-60° Nice day, George took Jen and Sam fishing with Frenchie and they picnicked at Foster pond.

May 1
George spreading hen manure, rainy in the 40s, David's CAST OFF!

May 4
George planting #4 night pasture to seed, finished spreading it with hen manure. COWS OUT!

May 6
Frannie and Andy came, Andy to go to Vet's hospital. Peas Up!

May 10
Snowed.

May 12
Snow almost gone, George butchered heifer, went for ride with kids, found trillium and Myrtle.

May 20
50°-60° Rainy until about 6 PM when sun broke through. We have planted lettuce, beets, etc, and some corn. Peas are well up and asparagus, also saw trillium, Jack in the pulpit, violets.

May 23
32°-45° Snow flurries.

May 24
32°- Lovely, getting corn land ready.

July 4
First Peas to eat.

1964

"We lost all our corn in the field."

THIS WAS A DIFFICULT YEAR, MILK PRICES THAT had been up to $6.00/hundred pounds (CWT) in previous years had dropped to $4.00/CWT; for two months they were below $4.00. Many farmers were selling their cows. In addition to the low milk prices, we lost our corn crop and our home garden to a bad hailstorm in July. It was the worst I have ever seen; it hailed and rained very hard for a long time, destroying everything. Bob Sorrow and Peter Herbert had become part of our family and worked hard at everything I could think of to bring in extra income. They were a big part of our making it through that year, and of course it was the home and love that Patty provided that made them want to be part of the family.

I traded the plows and $535 for new three-bottom plows, and the Farmall Super C tractor with a Brocken axle for an older Farmall C and $600.

1964
Early winter brought some very cold weather, but in general this has been (so far) a mild winter with not too much snow. We have skied a lot, however. Sam is doing very well and David and Jenny have improved a great deal.

Mar 3
Beautiful, warm, water running down the road. Town Meeting, at which there were various unpleasant circumstances particularly

involving the tax collector and funds in his hands. Our 8th Anniversary. We went out to dinner and had a lovely time, very special.

The tax collector hadn't turned the taxes in. The selectmen and auditor tried to cover it up by borrowing the money, two selectmen – Ken McPhee and Ken Bean–quit, Maurice Chandler stayed on.

Mar 4
Frannie and Andy came, began tapping out.

Mar 5
Heavy rains thunder and lightning, flash floods around Vermont, Hardwick and White River especially.

Mar 7
George and boys tapping, Sam found Pussy Willows, also Daffodils up several inches.

Mar 8
George, boys, kids tapped.

Mar 9
Dave, Ronnie [Craig]*, Matty, and I helped George tap, rainy, cold, miserable.*

Mar 10
Snowed about 8 or 10 inches.

Mar 21
Today is lovely but up to now it has been rather cold, windy, etc., last week George made 20 gallons of syrup.

Mar 26
George boiled, kids, (Sam, Jen, Dave) had supper at the sugar house had a great time. He made 13 gallons, mostly in pints.

April 1
12°-45° Started out bright and sunny but became cloudy and finally rained, George and Frenchie gathered, we had a chimney fire all day but not salted, George boiled tonight.

Some people believed that pouring salt down the chimney would put out a chimney fire. I never tried it; in fact, I have always let chimney fires burn themselves out. Glen Marceau was drafted into the Army in October 1963, and Frenchie Powers took his place as a fulltime worker.

April 8
17°-45° Buckets full, gathered, sent out syrup orders, entertained Gov. Hoff at Library, John Stetson's sister died, his mother died a few weeks ago, George boiled made 25 gals, A.

April 11-12
Below freezing at night, warm days, during last week George boiled late at night several times. Sunday the family had a picnic at the sugar house while daddy boiled.

April 13
22°-64° Frannie and Andy came, I'm back in my barn chores, George, David and I gathered the Hooker run, crocuses, daffodils, tulips up a bit.

Patty in the spring often washed the milking machines for me so I could get out sooner.

April 18-19
Warm pleasant weekend, finished sugaring, about 175 gals, Clarks [Jean and Don] visited, something chewing my tulips.

April 22
Rainy, David had ear ache, big tractor stuck in mud.

April 26
32°-70° Lovely day, planted peas (freazonian), lettuce, beets, chard, some carrots, sage, basil, dill, sweet peas, foxglove, poppies, asters.

April 28–May 3
All summery days, kids in shorts, getting dusty in the roads, George planted oats in #3 pasture, putting fertilizer on other pastures, radishes and swiss chard are up.

May 11
Rain, transplanted some plants from JoAnne, Blackie had one baby.

Blackie was "JoAnne" [Joan] Churchill's young cat.

May 18
Transplanted more from JoAnne [Joan Churchill] also from Mrs. Little.

May 24
Hot day in 80s, Did grounds work, Peas up 10 inches, Manure pile almost gone.

May 28
Cool in 40s, some rain, eating our own lettuce, still some asparagus.

May 30-31
Tom and Reene [Atkinson] came for weekend, lovely time, Frannie and Andy came Sunday.

June 4
Rain last night and today which is welcome, Bob [Sorrow] arrived, kids out of school, corn almost all planted in fields, Mrs. Smith [?] gave me chrysanthemums.

June 15
Still not much precipitation, everything up in garden, we looked at field corn, and it looks spotty like last year, we hope and pray it will come along.

June 24
Some rain, but mostly good hay weather, lots of hay in.

July 2
Mom and Dick arrived.

July 3
Dick flew home, we had a terrible hail storm and lost much of our garden, and [?] of our corn in the field. It was AWFUL; all we can do now is wait and see how much will come back.

July 4
Pleasant day, went swimming in the morning, watched Little League in PM, older kids went to fireworks.

July 7
Big truck broke through ramp with a load of hay, no one hurt.

1965

"About 40° in the house..."

EVERY YEAR THE GERMINATION OF OUR CORN WAS spotty; I finally realized the split-boot planting shoe on my old planter, that had been designed for horses, was worn out. The fertilizer was too close to the seed and was burning the seed, particularly if it was dry, as the fertilizer would attract moisture and then the seed would go to it. The newer planters put the seed and fertilizer in separately. Replacing equipment was a problem; Jim Craig was willing for me to upgrade things, but I had to have the cash. Milk prices remained as low as they had been last year. I was able to get a new chain saw for $200; traded the old manure spreader and $850 for a new, bigger spreader; and bought an old Studebaker truck for $250.

1965
We had a good summer and fall [1964], all three kids in school, health so far very good, had 33° below in Dec.

Jan 27
Haven't had very much snow this year, but we have had neat skiing, all five kids on skis, today it has snowed some, 6 inches.

Feb 15
Beautiful full moon at 5 AM, lovely day, Academy working on snow sculptures.

Feb 22
12° above, snowing, a few days ago we had temperatures about 15°
below zero and it stayed cold and windy for several days. Last night we
saw several owls flying across the road when we were on the way home
from Littleton, bringing Steve Clark here.

Feb 23
8° below, about 40° in the house due to the wind etc.

Feb 25
20° above, snowed a bit, rained a lot, hailed some, and there was
thunder and lightning in the late afternoon.

Feb 26
20° above, Nice day, icy, Joan and Cub [Snively] came.

Feb 27
Racque's house burned.

We were all at a meeting in the church when news of the Racque's
fire came. We couldn't save the house. A log house was later built
there, it is now owned by Margaret and Bruce Maclean.

Feb 28
20° above, I went sliding with the kids on the road over to Churchill's
and we had a great time, real neat crust.

Mar 2
20° above, It looks like a real sugaring day, Sue O'Brien did not go in
as school Director, Elmer Taylor is back for three years.

We were very disappointed to see Sue lose and Elmer go back
in as Director.

Mar 3
30°-40° Our anniversary, springy, water running down the road, cut up 2nd quarter of beef, tastes quite good. Roy Randall died.

Mar 7
Started tapping.

Mar 9
20°-40° Gathered, George boiled 'till about 10:30. Made 3+ gals of beautiful fancy syrup.

Mar 16
12°-32° Sap not running, Erica and Donny [Randall] moved into the Roy Randall farm.

Mar 19
30°-40° Snowed during the night, sunny and warm in AM, sap running, gathered almost all the buckets, not much sap.

Mar 20
George boiled, brought home about 9 gals in small cans.

Mar 21
0°-25° Went to visit Andy and Frannie, found when we came back that Vernon Roby had not come to work also that he had stolen beer, etc.

Mar 22
6°-28° Told Vernon he had to quit, he acted completely innocent. We felt sorry, but could not trust him, we had been told similar instances concerning him. Snowed 2 or 3 inches.

April 6
24°-50° Lovely day, George, Matty, Annie, and I went gathering, then Bernard [Churchill] came to help, Sam helped Frenchie do chores.

April 15
26°-55° Lovely day, George boiled, I went to town to look at washing machines, rained last night, snow almost gone.

April 18
22°-40° Easter, snowed a bit last night, Ike Thrasher [Thresher] working part time, Reene and Tom for dinner, Easter egg hunt, David and Sharon [Craig] won, sap running like mad.

April 19
25°-52° Frenchie and George gathered, sap running, George boiled.

April 20
27°-60° Lovely day, we gathered, everything was full, running over, George boiled, we've made about 135 gals now.

April 23
32°-45° Spread fertilizer yesterday, pull buckets today.

April 25
Jamie [Craig] boiled all the sap in, about 200 gals, George harrowed the garden and we planted the early things, peas, carrots, lettuce, etc.

May 2
Mostly 30ish at night and warm during day, children have colds/earaches, George working very hard to get land ready for seeding and corn.

May 10
58°-80° Rainy this morning, George has about half the manure spread.

May 22
Last night I planted daffy bulbs which Mrs. Wallace gave me, planted 2 peace rose bushes in front of fence. Last night George built a fence for me from old pieces of split rail fence he found up in his big field. The fence was a surprise for me and it looks beautiful. Asparagus is finally

up and will cut some today. Yesterday the cows got into Mr. Field's yard and he is suing for damages.

Mr. Field lived in the old farmhouse just west of the firehouse on Mack's Mountain Road. He was nearly blind and had strings throughout his flower garden to guide him, the cows tangled everything up, we were very sorry.

May 26
George started planting corn, looks good, well covered, etc.

May 29
Corn all planted and rolled.

May 31
Set out tomato plants, cooler on bulk tank quit, George had to take milk to Maclam's tank, Ham Strayer arrived.

June 7
Bulk tank still not fixed, still no rain, went swimming, Andy and Frannie came yesterday for dinner. Hired Minister yesterday, saw corn up George's field, he plans to plant more rather than seed the lower Berman piece.

June 8
Weights: Sam [?], Jen 70, Dave 57, Anne 38, Matt 35, Mom 155, Dad 153.

June 10
Finally we have had rain in several showers the last few days, our garden looks beautiful, George's corn looks spotty but seems to be germinating.

June 23
The corn was burned by fertilizer due to strength and drought, George had to replant more than half of it. Finally got bulk tank repaired, now we are haying. We have had lots of rain, 4 or 5 inches, also some beautiful weather for fun and haying.

1966

"We paid Craig off ..."

1966 WAS A TURNAROUND YEAR FOR US, I HAD always realized that it was, but until I read Patty's last journal entry, where she talks of "doing things her own way," I hadn't realized the effect it had on her. The major event happened in February, when we finally reached the $35,000 down payment on the $75,000 that we owed Jim Craig for the Village Farm. We went to the Danville bank, took out a $40,000 mortgage, and paid Craig off; we now had credit. We traded our rusted-out Ford wagon and $4,700 for a new VW bus; our baler and $1,900 for a new 268 New Holland baler; our side rake and $730 for a new New Holland rake; and bought a bale buncher for $110. The monthly payments to the bank were similar to what we had been paying Craig, but in addition we now had to pay the insurance and taxes. But milk prices were up to about $5.50 per hundred and we were able to make it. Glen Marceau had returned from the Army, and not only did the cows benefit from having a good cow man in the barn, but it took a big load off of me.

We were becoming more involved in the town and school. Elmer Taylor resigned as School Director, and I was elected to finish his term. Clifton Schoolcraft, son of the Schoolcrafts with the hens, had decided not to seek reelection, and Sue O'Brien was elected to replace him. Frances "Frank" Randall was on the board, and the three of us served for many years together and did a lot of things that I'm sure will come up in Patty's journal. Patty got involved with putting on plays and was the town tennis coach. Because she had nurses training, people began coming to her for shots and diagnoses. We were raising money to pave the town tennis court, where we played a lot.

1966
Again I haven't recorded anything for several months. In September or late August David broke his left arm using a skate board. He started off the school year in a cast and had quite some problems with it. We had snow in October and hardly a thaw since Thanksgiving Day when George took the kids for a long ski hike.

Sunday before Christmas Sam had a bad accident at the ski tow. He got caught in the rope and got dragged up into the pulley. His head was cut open and minor cuts and bruises to body and face. He spent 4 days in the hospital but recovered very quickly and had no complications. He had 20 stitches in head and 3 in face, now he is back skiing and all set again. Christmas was very happy.

Jan 19
Music class this morning, 14 children, Mrs. Rowe died yesterday.

Alice and Ed Rowe were a prominent family that lived on a farm on East Hill. I believe Patty was talking about Ed Rowe's mother.

Jan 27
Albert Bradley's home burned this morning.

The house was at the junction of Penny and Ha'Penny Streets.

Feb 5
We had a young kids ski meet which was great fun. Sam took 2nd place in his class, 9 to 12 yrs, and David 1st in his, 0 to 8 yrs.

Feb 27
We had 10 to 15 inches of snow, lovely skiing, kids all improving, Sam has new skis, Dave has his old ones.

March 1
Town Meeting Day, almost a touch of spring with the mud in the road until it turned cold and started to snow. George elected School Director.

March 2
Snowed and blew all night, now it looks almost like we are snowed in. Matty was uncomfortable with an ear ache all night. School closed, George started tapping.

March 5
Weather gradually becoming warmer and today it's raining again, George gathered a full tub of sap, our seed starting kit arrived.

March 11
Larry Taylor has mumps, had to scramble around to find a replacement, which we did, Carl Powden, flower seed sprouted.

Carl replaced Larry in a musical "Danny the Dark Green Dinosaur" that Patty was putting on.

March 12
Had a dress rehearsal and later gave "Danny," had a big crowd and it was quite successful.

March 13
Dave has mumps, Sam, Jen, and George skied in afternoon.

March 15
2° above Wind blowing, George finished up with indoor improvements, $105 collected so far for tennis fund.

March 17
40°-50° David sick with high fever, 104, in bed flat all day, must be flu, George tapped more and gathered some.

March 18
28°-50° Davie sick during night vomiting and diarrhea, weak, stayed feverish during day, although he did begin to eat and feel a little better, George tapped and gathered.

March 19
George off but boiled all day, children with him most of the afternoon, David much better.

March 20
George boiled and canned up about 24 gals, went to ski hill for sugar on snow and skied a bit. We prepared syrup orders including a large order for a Wells River Grocery, we had just enough.

March 23
Doris [Stetson] and I went to Norwich and had a nice lunch with the Wallaces, they took us to see pianos and I picked out a nice used one.

March 24
Mild day, no sap, George boiled in about 35 gals yesterday, we have orders for almost all of it.

Patty had developed a good syrup mail order business with Summit friends as customers.

March 25
Did not go below 30°, David and Jen vomited, Sam not feeling well, George and I went to Norwich to get the piano, we took Matty, had a nice time.

March 27
We all went to church and then after dinner cut boys hair, and George and mine too, pleasant day at home.

March 29
5°-35° Matty looks mumpy, doesn't feel too bad.

March 30
20°-33° Matty is very swollen, feels terrible, has a fever. Peter [Herbert]
arrived today, and will stay for several weeks probably.

Mach 31
20°-35° Annie mumps, George and Peter cut some wood and
gathered sap.

April 1
Frenchie's B-day, 21 Yrs, George gathered and boiled in about 12 gals,
Matty better, Annie felt bad all day, fever 103, vomited several times.

April 2
30°-42° Annie's temp up to 104 last night, still vomiting. I judged
one act plays last night, Cabot won over Peacham and Danville. Sap
flowed well today and boys gather quite a lot. Annie sick all day, called
Dr. Farmer for advice, even following his advice the temp never went
down below 102 and every so often the vomiting would start again.
When I put her to bed it was 103 but I didn't dare give her more aspirin.

April 3
28°-40° Frenchie has mumps, Annie woke up at 5:30 feeling better,
had cold water and went back to sleep, temp 102. George and Peter
did chores gathered and boiled, chores again and up after chores to boil
again, big sap tank has a small leak. Annie had fair day but fever not
all gone and she is terribly weak and exhausted. She did eat and drink
some and kept it down, Frenchie feels awful and looks awful.

We joked about Frenchie's short, thick neck, how the mumps
were first on one side and then the other side and then the other
side and then the other side. With Frenchie sick it really added to
my work load.

April 4
25°-40° George boiled until 1 AM, Annie better today, Frenchie about
the same, George has made about 135 gals fancy syrup. Robins.

April 5
25°-40° *A little snow cover this morning, George boiled in about 25 gals, Frenchie is much better, Daffys, Crocuses, and Tulips are up.*

April 6
Looks like beautiful spring morning, George boiled all day until late at night.

April 7
20°-45° *Sap flowing, George boiled has about 215 gals fancy syrup.*

April 8
George gathered and boiled. Report cards came home, all the kids improving, Sam got As in all his academic subjects, Cs in social behavior, etc. David had no Ds, and a B for the first time, Ethel Case does mark hard.

April 9
Snowing, ground all white again, colored Easter eggs, went to Frank Green's for dinner and bridge.

April 10
29°-40° *Easter, there were more people in church for a Sunday than I have ever seen. After dinner we had an egg hunt and flew kites, we had a nice day.*

April 11
30°-44° *Snowed again, sap not running, George began tearing down bull barn to use wood for sugaring and get ready for building in summer.*

April 30
It has been a cold week, frost at night etc., yesterday was warmer and today looks as if it would be lovely. Thursday George had an accident with the big tractor, he started it while standing behind, it had been left in 6th gear with the throttle wide open, it bounded into the barn and crashed through the floor. It looked like a dreadful situation but

by noon today it was all fixed and back to normal. Ham Strayer was visiting and left the tractor in gear, Peter is in Texas.

May 1
Yesterday was beautiful, we planted lettuce, etc., and I transplanted pansies and carnations to my border garden, George put up fence all the way down to wall.

May 10
Cold yesterday snowed, snow still on ground today, had to buy hay from Randall's.

May 25
Very warm, mostly fair days, gardens coming slowly, first 12 tomato plants look poor, planted 2 more. George will finish corn today.

June 1
Last few days have been cool with light frost at night, no rain, the garden looks good except tomatoes, Tom Atkinson sick in hospital.

June 15
Lovely summer weather, went to Newton's Sunday in our new Volkswagen Bus which we got Thursday we had a lovely day.

July 5
I am having a wonderful summer, doing things my own way. We have been swimming a lot, sometimes twice a day. Our garden is doing very well, children swim a great deal better now, Matty and Annie almost have it, Matty dives, so do the three older kids.

Family supper at the Village Farm, Clemens Kalischer, 1967

The Sugar House, Village Farm

1967

"Leo told us that our offer for the old Lanctot house was accepted."

THE PRICE OF MILK WAS UP AS WELL AS PRODUC-
tion per cow. The increase in milk production was brought on
by a number of factors; the most important was an improvement in
genetics. We had sold Craig's bull early in the first year and started
breeding artificially, also the Holstein heifers I had bought in 1963
were now milking with their second calf, and having Glen Marceau
back helped, though he wasn't fond of the Holsteins. Things
improved to the point where we bought a tenant house for Glen
(the Lanctot, or Brooks, house) and seriously considered buying
a neighboring farm. This was only one year after we reached the
downpayment on the Craig farm and bought it. We also sent three
kids to summer camp.

We made three equipment purchases: an old 1955 Ford truck
for $650–we went through a lot of old trucks–new 10-foot John
Deere KBA transport harrows for $575, they were beautiful, I got
a good buy from a dealer that was going out of business; and a new,
but had been demonstrated, Heston mower-conditioner PT 10 for
$2,000, this was a new type of mower that I had seen demonstrated
in Dummerston when I was working for Fred Knapp. We still use
a mower of the same principle today, it revolutionized haying. It
mowed and conditioned the hay at the same time, it eliminated
bunches so the hay would dry faster, and it could windrow as well
as leaving 10-foot-wide swaths, three feet wider than my old mower.

Feb 9, 1967
We finally had snow for Christmas and then some good skiing later in
January, there was a big thaw, lots of sickness etc. This week the cold has
been extreme, down to 20° below, the Kimball's house burned. This is
winter carnival week. The photographer Clemens Kalischer has been
taking pictures of Peacham for two weeks now for a book to be pub-
lished on New England. He selected our family to follow in particular.

The Kimball house was a two-family house located in South
Peacham just past the Mill Trace toward the village, Jamie and
Sandra Craig and Steve and Marcia White lived there. A small
house has since been rebuilt. Kalischer took many fine pictures
of Peacham and our family that were published in a coffee-table
type book.

Feb 19
Lovely day, has been cold, 10° below for week or two.

Feb 24
Six or eight inches of snow in last two days, Wed. the Conners visited,
yesterday the Millers came, we had fun, Becky [Newton] stayed over-
night Wed. and Thurs.

Feb 28
It stayed cold until yesterday afternoon, up to 30°. Last night a little
snow fell and flurries continued today. We had a wonderful weekend
of skiing, Sunday morning we went out cross country, it was lovely
in the woods. Went to Hanover and purchased equipment for the
Academy ski team, jumpers, cross country skis, also quite a few items
for ourselves (mom sent a check to buy kids skis), we bought jumpers for
Dave, cross country skis and boots for Sam, new downhills for Annie
and Sam, boots for Dave, George bought a touring outfit for me as an
Anniversary gift.

Mar 8
We've had several inches more snow and it has been quite cold, wonderful skiing last weekend. Town Meeting yesterday was very pleasant, we took a poll vote on the school and people were for a new masonry building.

Mar 10
Yesterday George started tapping, it was beautiful, I skied cross country to Powden's with Birthe [Filby].

Mar 13
12°-30° Saturday was warm and springy. The Newtons [John and Jane Spross] were here and we had a good time tapping, skiing, and Powdens and talking.

Mar 14
Rain, power off 5:45 to 9:00.

Mar 20
The past few days have been cold, 15° below at night, never got above zero. Yesterday it was sunny and much warmer during the day, had sugar on snow and a perfectly beautiful day at the ski tow. The kids are really looking good on skis, David has improved tremendously.

Mar 24
20°-38° Sap has not run yet. David home with bad cold. Dave's fever up to 103, sap ran just a bit, sunny but windy.

Mar 25
20°-35° Sap not running, wind blowing, Annie and Matt sick with David's bug (flu?).

Mar 26
20°-37° Beautiful Easter Sunday, Annie, Matt, and I stayed home, I have bug now, sap flowing. I have lost 7 pounds, 167 to 160.

Mar 28
30°-40° George boiled in about 10 gals, Matty and I feel worse again, Jen down.

Apr 1
32°-70° Kids have been sick all week, fevers up and down, etc., finally this morning they seem better.

Apr 10
Past week has continued varied weather, quite a lot of wet snow, Uncle Andy spent weekend, Frannie and I went down for him Friday. George has been backed up with sap, made about 125 gals, thunder showers last night.

Uncle Andy Martin is staying at the Veteran's hospital in White River Junction.

Apr 12
It has been terribly windy and cold for two days, George has about 175 gals fancy syrup, my weight 158.

Apr 16
George has boiled all week, fortunately Steve [Clark] was here and Bert [?] working, have made over 200 gals fancy, Crocus blooming, planted Sam's tomato seeds.

Apr 18
30°-40° It has been wet and cold several days with the temps staying around 30°, rain, hail, sleet, snow, sap ran yesterday, 240 gals syrup.

Apr 20
More snow yesterday and day before, sap running over in buckets, Boardmans [Jean, Howard, and family] up.

Apr 21
20°-55° Nice day for a change, 298 gals fancy and A.

Apr 27
Last two days have been beautiful, sunny, cool, but warm in the sun, George finished boiling yesterday and began pulling buckets. First tryouts for operetta.

Apr 28
Finished tryouts, Mark Powden, Hansel, Cathy O'Brien, Gretel, Patty Chandler, witch, Sam, Father, Kathleen Pierson, Mother, Sheriden Lane was so disappointed. Planted first peas.

May 1
Discovered that milk check ($1377.00) had not reached the bank, called NEMPA [New England Milk Producers Association] in Boston to report this and talked to a very nice man who said they'd send a new check unless ours had been cashed. Nice days, raked yard and cleaned up, Sunday planted lettuce, beets, chard, etc.

May 8
Several inches of snow, all over, ugh.

May 11
It has stayed cool and wet all week. We were issued a new check. Leo Berwick told us that our offer of $6500 for the old Lanctot house had been accepted, now we'll have to start planning.

The Lanctot house, also referred to as the Brooks house, is on the Bayley-Hazen Road at the north end of the village. It became our tenant house for 50 years.

May 14
30°-70° Yesterday and today have been lovely, sunny, cool. Kids started to paint scenery at the Academy.

May 15
Cool, rainy, many colds, all the kids in the operetta have colds except for Sam.

May 19
Humid, a little sun, showers, Sam has found quite a few wild flowers, he saw a Rose Breasted Grosbeak. Rehearsed with principals, scenery finished and it looks beautiful.

May 20
Dress rehearsal fair, Hansel and Gretel beautifully done, very well received.

May 29
Yesterday was nice and today is lovely, but all last week we had cold, wet weather, leaves are still not out, our peas are up and other small things, no sign of corn.

June 7
Finally it has become summer the last five days have been increasingly warmer, up into the 90's. The leaves are pretty well out, the lilacs are coming, apple blossoms out, everything is growing like mad. Our early garden corn is up several inches. Yesterday ended school for the year, report cards good, David improved a lot.

June 10
The garden is coming up beautifully, early corn is several inches high, we've been eating asparagus, field corn planted, wt. 145.

June 19
Georgie had weekend off, we realized the Hooker farm had not sold and they still hoped we would buy it. We went to see them about it Saturday and actually made an offer. They wanted $37,000, we probably could give them $8,000 down and then small assignments twice a month. We went over Sunday, took the Boardmans and walked around the place. George took the kids fishing Saturday, we all went swimming Sunday, quite a weekend.

Orman and Sue Hooker were selling their farm on Worcester Road.

June 23
Hectic week, last weekend we looked at the Hooker farm with intent to buy, house for us to live in, and land to complement our farm. Everyone is very excited and it would be wonderful in many ways, but there are some drawbacks, mainly that it would put us pretty deeply in debt. The Brooks house is still tied up in probate court and when it is free we will have to decide. George cut hay Monday and it has rained these last several days.

July 3
Mother is in Bradford and we have visited twice, lots of hay baled and in the barn, kids finished Bible school and enjoyed it, still haven't decided about Hooker's, it's a bit frightening. Bob Daniels, who owned the West Barnet store, shot himself in the head and died tonight.

July 13
Sunday evening we went to see the Hookers ready to put $1,000 down to bind the sale on their farm, we to buy it for $36,000, $2,000 down, the rest in assignments to them, $150 per month. They told us they wanted the whole amount at once. We went home and talked, we realized this was impossible and perhaps the whole venture was too much for what we actually got out of it. We'd be under such a weight of debt that life might not be a joy. When I told the Hookers of our decision they wanted to come to our terms, but strangely enough George and I felt the answer had come to us somehow and that we should not do it.

July 19
Warm, humid summer days, more than enough rain, it seems to be taking ages to get the hay in, garden thriving. Things ought to come through on the Brooks house for Glen [Marceau] this week. We still feel we made the right decision on the Hooker property.

July –
Sunday, Mr. [Walter] Severinghaus called and asked George and me to come over. They wondered if they could do something to help us take over Hooker's, like they buy the house and we buy the land. We

really were amazed at turn of events, but we still felt we had made our decision.

July –
Tuesday we got our loan and bought the Brooks property for $6500, now we have to fix it up.

July 20
Drove to North Hero on Lake Champlain to take older three kids to camp for two weeks. It was a lovely day, nice drive etc, the camp seemed very nice, friendly staff, pretty view.

Aug 14
Busy summer, we went to Boardman's to a dinner party Thursday, Friday we drove over to get the kids at camp, arrived home at midnight. Saturday we planned to stay over at the woodlot, asked the Boardmans to join us for supper. Loren and Donna Farmer and darling girls stopped by, so they came too, we had a grand time, we seven slept out. Sunday George hayed, I served punch after another wonderful concert, at supper time the Kalischers stopped by and then stayed overnight.

Mother is not enjoying herself much, she doesn't want to spend any time here, and it is hard for me to go off all the time so....I don't know what the solution would be.

Aug 23
Last Wednesday George, Davie, and I drove to Dummerston, went to [Dwight and Gladys] Miller's for supper, then to a party and over night at Crockett's, we had a wonderful time. Saturday we were invited to a party given by the Westerns at the big house in Windham. We took all the kids and drove down. Mary expects a baby soon. John and Jane [Newton] together but not happy. Mike Newton was there also some other old friends of Georgie's.

The "big house in Windham" would be the former Newton School.

Aug 31
George's Dad and Mata [Kempton] were here Sunday, Jim Keeney came Saturday, had a picnic at the wood lot, and stayed through Sunday dinner. The boys all stayed overnight at the wood lot, Annie, Jenny and I went to a shower for Anne Petrie. Tuesday Jim, Randy [Keeney], Ben [Keeney] and Mike Newton came over and spent the night, the Keeneys are considering buying the Hooker farm.

Oct 18
Much has happened, we finally bought the Brooks house and have fixed it up for Glen and Ruth who married on Sept. 15th. Glen almost quit before that, but decided to stay. He doesn't seem particularly happy about the job. The house looks very nice.

The Keeneys, same date as above, did buy the Hooker's and we are renting the land. Bob [Sorrow] and Anne were married Sept. 17th, George was best man. All five children in school now, I have the days alone, I am always very busy. It seemed a bit sad to see little Matt go off to school and at first he didn't like it much, but it all seems to fit together.

Nov 15
Snowing, school seems to be going well, report cards all good, David needs to work hard on spelling and reading, he loves his new teacher Gretchen Bond, who is also our neighbor, living in Nancy Bundgus' house next door. Her husband [Duncan] teaches at Danville High School, we like them a lot.

Nov 18
More snow, wonderful for tracking deer. Birthe [Filby] shot at a big buck two days ago, missed. I have seen deer, but no horns.

1968

"Duncan is George's Campaign Manager."

A S THE KIDS GREW AND PATTY HAD MORE TIME, she began to write more, filling in the blanks, it is becoming quite a story. Everything was expanding. The School Board–Sue O'Brien, Frank Randall, and I–sold the three remaining one-room schools in Peacham and built a new K-6 school. We remodeled a shed attached to the house, giving us the family room we needed as the kids got bigger.

We remodeled the bull barn and built a shed on Keeney's barn to accommodate heifers, allowing us to milk more cows in the village barn. We purchased three labor-saving pieces of equipment: a silo unloader for $1,355, so we didn't have to climb up into the upright silo to pitch the silage down by hand; a gutter cleaner for $1,887 to save me cleaning the barn with a shovel and wheelbarrow; and a dumping station for $575, a stainless steel pot on wheels that pumped the milk through a hose to the bulk tank rather than our having to carry it to the tank. We also bought a Hawk-built spreader for $1,870 that handled sloppy manure better.

Our good friends John and Jane Newton divorced, but this is a story that will continue, as will my drinking too much at parties and my venturing in to politics.

Patty mentions how cold it was in the winter. The village farmhouse was heated with a combination wood/coal furnace that didn't have a blower, and we were burning poor wood that was green besides. The Craig farm came with two woodlots, one on Mack's Mountain Road and one near Foster's Pond – neither one was very convenient. I cut down trees along the side of the road for firewood. Around Christmas I would break down and drive my truck to Ide's in St. J to get 5-6 tons of coal, we would be warm for a couple of months, and Patty would smile.

1968
The Christmas holidays were busy and nice. The Keeneys were in their big house [Hooker farm], Boardmans here, Hummons visited, Hamiltons [acquaintances from Conn.] here over New Years. There were several parties and get togethers, lots of fun. George and I had a trauma New Year's morning, we haven't had many in our marriage, I guess it won't do us any harm. We've both thought a lot and maybe understand each other better.

Jan 8
30° below zero, windy, house cold, inside AM 40°.

Jan 9
35° below, no school.

Jan 10
30° below, today we got a load of coal and immediately the house was warmer.

Jan 11
25° below.

Jan 30
25° above, the extreme cold lasted almost two weeks. Now for a while it has been reasonable and we've had a little snow. George bought a silage unloader, farm business is going along quite well. Rev. Jerry and Kathy Buckley are leaving Peacham in March, they have not liked it here. He doesn't seem to be able to get "with" people and has cooled people off toward himself and the church.

Feb 19
Two weeks ago we drove down to Greenwich to visit the Hamiltons. We went into NYC by train and then went up into the Empire State building, we all enjoyed it. It was fun seeing the Hamiltons in their home and area. On the way back we had a close call with a car crossing in front of us unexpectedly. We felt blessed to get home safely.

Feb 26
The weather has remained very cold, with night time temps often 10˚ below or colder, most days have not reached 20˚ above. During vacation last week we went to Burke one day and got terribly cold skiing, there were quite a few frost bitten noses and ears.

Mar 2
For several days it has been mild, even up to 40˚ one day. Yesterday and last night the wind has been blowing like crazy, the barn roof began blowing off.

Mar 3
Our 12th wedding anniversary, George has the duty so we will celebrate later.

Mar 5
Town Meeting Day, cold, sunny, George unanimously re-elected to school board, Ken Goslant replaced Leo Berwick as Selectman. Sam and Jen went to Hanover with the Bonds and bought new XC [ski] equipment.

Mar 8
0˚-34˚ Jim [Quimby] brought closet for our "cloak room," it's nice. We asked him about renovating our shed. Went XC skiing, I used hard Red [wax], it seemed to work pretty well.

Mar 9
24˚-50˚ Beautiful spring day, skied.

Mar 10
30°-50° The Bonds and all of us, except Annie and Matty, went on a XC tour on the ridge behind Keeney's, picnicked, it was fun. Then we skied on the Historical building hill because the tow broke down, had cocktails at Slaight's and the Bonds came to our house for pancakes.

Mar 12
5°-12° Started snowing 3 PM.

Mar 13
Hung a few buckets, snow accumulated to about 8 inches.

Mar 14
0°-25° George and David Field washed buckets, David will work for us until he goes in to the service.

Mar 15
0°-34° Kids had half a day, so all three boys went with George and David and hung 300 buckets or more, sap was dripping. We had Stetsons, Crismans, and Hendricks for dinner, good time.

Mar 16
25°-50° Beautiful day, tapped, got sugar house ready, kids and I skied, it was fun but very slushy.

Mar 17
38°-40° Rained most of the night and some of the day, Boardmans up, Buckleys last Sunday.

Mar 18
33°-45° Gathered, started up rig, no syrup yet.

Mar 24
25°-30° Snowed, blew, George boiled 10 gals.

Mar 27
30°-60° *Sap running like mad, George boiled, Bill Lederer spoke at Fellowship, 60 people.*

Mar 28
25°-55° *Gathered, boiled, George opened bids on school, lowest $200,000.*

Mar 30
Warm nice day, lots of company at sugar house, Boardmans all up, Hummons up with friends. Powden's house burned, they got a lot out, not a total loss.

Mar 31
25°-65° *Heavenly day, tulips, daffeys up, sap not running for some reason, George boiled in between chores, have made about 100 gals. People ran the road to see Powden's house, many helped to bring things down to Yankauer's place where the family is going to live now.*

Apr 2
23°-50° *School board met with lowest bidder.*

Apr 3
30°-50° *Beautiful day, sap running, George boiled, canned 20 gals grade B, finally got it back up to grade A. Big party for the Powdens with gifts.*

Apr 4
Dr. Martin Luther King assassinated in Memphis.

Apr 5
Boiled, Bengie Blankinship very ill, in Brightlook [St. Johnsbury hospital].

Apr 6
12°-15° *George cut wood.*

Apr 7
24°-60° Lovely day, Ski tow sugar-on-snow party, gathered with David Field and Bonds, have made about 150 gals.

Apr 8
30°-55° George boiled, Peter [Herbert] arrived to stay about 3 weeks.

Apr 9
45°-55° Syrup is grade B, but we canned 25 gals.

Apr 11
36°-60° Beautiful day, George started other projects, getting out manure, clearing out for gutter cleaner, planted some peas.

Apr 12
24°-70° Unbelievable day because of the warm weather, Sam shot a woodchuck, also found coltsfoot. Sap not running well. Total eclipse of the moon, kids stayed up to watch it, then fell asleep on the porch on blankets.

Apr 13
45°-80° Hot day, quit sugaring.

Apr 14
45°-85° Easter, beautiful day, very warm again. We all went to church and then had an Easter egg hunt on the sugar house hill, George put up two rope swings.

Apr 15
Rained most of the day, cooler.

Apr 16
34°-50° Jim, Shelby, Peter and Chris Baker [Cape Cod friends] arrived.

Apr 17
Lovely day, had such a nice visit with the Bakers, Peter is going to come and work this summer.

Apr 18
Another lovely day, the kids, Peter [Baker], Joanie and Bennie Blankinship went to town with me. Sam took some flowers to the museum, went to dinner at Bonds with Randalls [Susan and David] and Peter.

Apr 19
Out to dinner at Martland's.

Apr 20
Poured cement for the [corners for the] gutter cleaner, Craig Marcotte decided not to work this summer, Peter [Baker] left.

Apr 29
Lovely day, windy, more cement for gutter cleaner, Sam visited academy.

Apr 30
Nice day, George taking out manure, David Field finished working Saturday.

May 1
My hair is below my waist but I plan to have it cut tomorrow.

May 2
Had my hair cut, the hairdresser really didn't want to cut it.

May 5
George Sunday off, boys fished, played softball in afternoon, gutter cleaner working.

May 8
25°-60° Lovely, manure pile all spread, asparagus up.

May 11
Warm beautiful day, Boardmans with Barb and fiancé, Bond's had Duncan's brother and wife, party, very gay etc.

May 25
Hooker auction, we bought quite a few things.

We bought a small set of harrows and the contents of the second floor of the horse barn, which included a brown ash crook (left over from making sled runners) that Jim Quimby made into a coffee table for us.

May 28
Warm beautiful day, George finished planting corn, lots of asparagus.

June 3
Westerns, Hamiltons, Boardmans all up for the weekend party Saturday night here. The Westerns stayed here and we had a wonderful time. Several hard showers yesterday, mostly rainy, early peas are up.

June 4
George cut hay, Annie sick with virus.

June 5
Senator [Robert F.] Kennedy was shot and seriously wounded after making a victory speech in California. The gunman was a young Jordanian Arab.

June 6
Senator Kennedy died even after surgeons operated to remove the bullet and bone chips from his brain. It is like a nightmare, it shouldn't be real.

June 7
Senator Kennedy's funeral, National Day of Mourning.

June 13
Went to Greensboro and bought some lilac and honeysuckle bushes for here and Glen's [Marceau's] yard. The man who owned the nursery was especially nice and interesting.

June 14
Fireplace is finished, we had a fire in it to try it out.

The fireplace was in the new family room were adding at the Village Farm.

June 25
We have had a day or two of partial sun otherwise rain. It makes certain work impossible and it's depressing. Jim [Quimby] started work on our shed yesterday, Keeneys came Sunday.

June 29
Mother arrived in Montpelier by plane, one suit case was missing.

June 30
We had a beautiful day for George's day off, played tennis, went swimming, picnicked and visited. The day was beautiful but we did have hard thundershowers at night.

July 2
Another beautiful day, George put down a lot of hay, I went to town saw mother.

July 10
We have been having mostly lovely weather with occasional rain. Jim K[eeney] has been working with George on haying, with a huge crew of kids. It has been busy, yesterday Judy and John Lane came from Dummerston for the day with their children. Jim Quimby is progressing beautifully with our "shed room."

July 13
Yesterday was another busy hay day. I went to town to do many errands, took Annie and David and met mother. David saw Dr. Toll for apparently another strep infection.

July 15
Warm weekend, no rain, got in some hay at Keeney's. David is not improving, I postponed his week at camp. Mother very unhappy at the St Johnsbury house.

July 16
I took David to the doctor, evidently he has a complication from strep, like rheumatic fever or arthritis, joints swollen and sore, general malaise. He can hardly walk, we have to wait 'til Friday for a definite diagnosis and plan for treatment. I feel so bad for him, no activities, no camp.

July 22
The past two days have been beautiful, we had a storm Friday which cleared the air. David seems a little better, I worry a lot about him. The girls slept at the wood lot last night, with Dorigen Keeney, Sally and Becky Newton, and Kate Peck. John [Newton] brought his girls [Sally and Becky] up Saturday to stay a while. He and Jane are separated and getting a divorce.

July 26
Yesterday I had to rush Becky [Boardman] to Dr. Toll with a sure reaction to a bee sting. She was here alone for a few days, she had to go to the hospital to be treated. David is better and allowed to do more but the disease did have a cardiac effect and he is still restricted.

Aug 5
We are just back from 4 days vacation to Cape Cod and the Bakers, then to Norwell, Ma. where Duncan Bond's mother lives, then to Sharon, Vt. to take Jen to camp, and stopped in Tunbridge, Vt. to see George's folks. We had a grand time. David saw the Doctor before we left and was given a nearly clean bill of health.

Aug 20
We have been busy, taking kids to camp and bring them back; company,
parties, Mom, trying to get work done in between things. George and I
both have bad colds and we're exhausted. Now George is trying to get
a second cutting in.

Sept 16
The summer busyness is finally quieting down. We had two parties last
weekend including people we had been wanting to get together with.
The new room is all done and beautiful. Loey Ringquist has been to
visit twice, once with Judy Claghorn. [George's] Uncle Andy died.

Sept 30
The days have been getting back to daily routine, which is lovely.
Charlie and Stephanie Metz were here over the weekend painting the
Martland's house, which they bought. We had a nice party Saturday
night and the Metzes stayed overnite.

Oct 3
It has continued mild and beautiful, Sam had a nice birthday, George
took him bird hunting, George got one partridge, yum. George is run-
ning for the State Senate.

Oct 5-6
Rained during the night, snowed in Walden, roses, corn, broccoli,
squash, etc. still growing, may stop now.

Oct 30
Nice weekend, cool but nice, Metzes here, George watched a 6 point
buck for 10 minutes while bird hunting. We are seeing lots of deer.

Oct 31
George has spoken on the radio and had ads in the paper, Duncan
[Bond] is his campaign manager.

Nov 8
George did not win his campaign, votes were: Kitchell over 5000,
Morse over 5000, George 2700. He did not expect to win, but was
disappointed. Snow today.

Nov 13
Birthe got her deer, lots of snow.

1969

"All three boys made the little league team ..."

1969 WAS THE FIRST YEAR WE HAD ANY DISCRE-tionary money since we had left Knapp's at Dummerston. This was due mostly to our putting up better quality feed and therefore increasing milk production, and a better price for milk. Keeping our older heifers at the Keeney farm also helped by freeing up space in our barn to milk more cows. We traded the old Farmall C for a new Case 430 with loader and $3,900, and we traded our old Case chopper for a new New Holland chopper and $4,000.

Jan 1, 1969
We have had snow and cold in the extreme right along. The snow depth is tremendous, a lovely base for skiing, but hard to get around, have skied quite a lot. Peter [Herbert] here for Christmas; Baldwins visited [Dummerston], Loey [Ringquist] and Judy[Bruno], Peter Baker. Lots of parties, Metz, Powden, Crisman, Stetson, Bond (New Years). Mother has been sick over Christmas.

Jan 9
The snow continues to build up.

Jan 12
We had a slight Jan. thaw this past weekend, it warmed up to 35°, rained a little but not seriously, skiing is still great. We had a fun race at the tow, Sam, Dave, and Matt won their classes, Chris Marcotte, Bobby Blanchard, and Albert Goslant won theirs. Took kids to see "Westside Story."

Jan 23
Sunny days, went to Burke Tuesday and had a great time.

Feb 9
Snowing all day, began to blow at night.

Feb 10
20°, blew all night and many roads are drifted full. Sam and I fought our way over to feed the heifers at Keeney's, it was really wild. No schools open for miles around, people were stranded all the way south to Conn, NY and Boston closed.

The Keeneys didn't live in their Peacham house in the winter and the road was drifted full, we skied over every day for a week, about a mile each way.

Feb 16
Pleasant days, cool, good Winter Carnival races last Friday. Sam raced and did okay, placed fifth in slalom. Randalls and Metzes having an awful mess, Stefanie [Metz] and David [Randall] are "in love," both want to divorce their present partners to marry one another, the children all know, everyone is unhappy.

Feb 20
This has been vacation week, beautiful weather, sugar weather. Charles Edward Metz had a bad fall and broke his leg at the hill today, George and I weren't there, we had gone to Montpelier to Crisman's for dinner.

Feb 22
20°-50° Weather heavenly, really hot in the sun, have done some XC skiing, it's lovely. Barkley Stetson got caught in the rope at tow, the safety gate worked alright, but the men turned the tow back on before Jenny and Kyle [Lewis] got Barkley untangled. It could have been very serious but the girls held him and he only sustained rope burns.

Feb 25
Another great snow storm, 33 inches in St. Jay, fortunately no wind and temperatures mild.

Mar 1-2
George set some plastic tubing on the sugar house hill.

Mar 5
8° below – Yesterday was Town Meeting Day, it was an interesting meeting, Charles Morrison replaced Sue O'Brien on the School Board, the board got money they asked for. We went out to dinner to celebrate our anniversary with the Bonds. This morning is very cold but bright, it seems like the snow will never leave.

Mar 22-23
Cool at night, springy in day, sap flowing.

Mar 26-28
Some rain, some snow, tapped more trees, rough work with all the snow.

Mar 30
George boiled, Doris and Dave Hummon [son] arrived for a few days. Betsy [Boardman] and Julian [Smith] here on honeymoon, haven't seen them yet. Judy Claghorn visited with a friend.

Apr 8
20°-50° Gathered, boiled, around 100 gals, found crocuses next to pile of snow in front yard, Redpolls.

Apr 12
22°-50° Lovely day, boiled, had a young college boy stop who said he was a hitch hiker, knew the Lederers, was looking for a place to stay. He hadn't been here long when the State Police, John Emery, stopped here looking for him, some complaint about drugs.

Apr 16
40°-60° Hot, roads dry in many places, crocuses blooming, daffys up,
George boiled in all the sap, made 270 gals.

Apr 24
Mostly cool and rainy all week, George boiled like mad, but the first
syrup after the warm spell was dark and smelly, then he got it up to
B but according to some authorities it may be "buddy." Peter rode a
10 speed bike over here from Stowe. Started pulling buckets, indoor
seeds sprouted.

Apr 26
New English bikes, Dave and I, Weekend off, harrowed garden, played
baseball, George and I went out, dinner and dancing.

May 6
George finally got leads on big Case tractor and got it about fixed,
radishes up.

May 7
Cool, some showers, George plowed and harrowed, had dinner at
Lederer's, met a Greek Consul and his wife who were very interesting
very nice. George fainted after martinis, dinner and a cigar. I was
scared to death, I thought he had a heart attack or stroke. Afterward
he was very puzzled as to the cause for this, never having passed out
in his life. We even wondered if Bill could have slipped some drug in
his drink or something. Bill is so strange and once threatened George
because he thought George was flirting with Corinne, actually Corinne
was doing the flirting.

May 8
Rained, mild, George harrowed, Peter picked stones, the three of us
had dinner at Sue's [Randall] with Duncan and Gretchen [Bond],
Randalls are legally separated, David at his folks.

May 13
George is spreading manure, some snow, some rain, Bill Lederer told
me that Corinne had to be operated on for breast cancer. I feel very
badly, though I know it can be completely removed, which I'm hoping.
Jimmy and Dorigen [Keeney] arrived for a few days to plant their
garden and plan about the house.

May 25
Mostly lovely day, children's Sunday at church. Boardmans up, George
played tennis, Corinne home from the hospital. Mother cat had three
kittens, now with the baby the kids brought in from the barn, we
have eight.

May 26
George started planting corn, I planted more peas, caul., broc., parsnips.

May 27
George finished one field, white frost.

May 30
Hard showers in early AM, George could not plant corn so we all went
to Memorial Day meal and ceremonies, sun in PM.

May 31
40°-70° George's B-day, pretty day, eating asparagus, kids swam at
lake with Hamiltons.

June 1
Warm day, Reene [Corinne] and Tom [Atkinson], Aunt Frances
arrived, had a nice time, Franny staying a while.

June 7
45°-70° Rather cool rainy week, field corn up. Kids finished school yes-
terday, Baccalaureate last night. Frances has been sewing a lot, went
to town twice, she gets depressed, ready to go home. Boardmans here,

Betsy and Julian leave for trip to India Wednesday stopping at Scotland, England, Switzerland, Italy, Greece, then India.

June 10
45°-90° Beautiful day, George cut more and baled a little. I drove Aunt Frances home to Richford, Birthe went with me, also Jenny, Annie, and Matty. We drove through Stowe and Smugglers notch, it was a lovely trip.

June 11
Beautiful warm day, George baled 500 bales, I took the kids to the lake. Mrs. Barber has returned her contract and I feel badly because I have complained about her religious teachings as much (more) as anyone.

Mrs. Barber was a Peacham Elementary School teacher who had very conservative views.

June 12
Beautiful day, tried out New Holland chopper on grass. Swam, all three boys made the little league team, even little Matty, they brought home uniforms and were very excited.

June 17
Had a lovely weekend off, the little league played its first game, beat Barnet's 2nd team, 10 to 2, Sam 1st base, Dave 3rd base, Matt relief pitcher, good job.

July 7
Beautiful hay weather, George finished Claude's big field. Dad and Mata [Kempton] here yesterday, left this morning, they don't seem to want to stay long. I guess what [George's aunt] Frances says is true.

I'm not sure but Mata may have felt that I thought she married Dad too soon after Mother died.

July 17
Finished haying Keeney's in time to go swimming and visit Stetson's summer house on Harvey's lake, Peter arrived with fiancé, Judy Bruno.

July 30
Rainy, it has been rainy for a week, now it is a little depressing, finished haying last week. Yesterday we all went down to visit the Newtons, John has remarried a 20 year old [Jane Greenwood], very nice, pretty, capable. Becky Newton's prognosis is extremely poor. Jane Spross Newton is in Woodstock working. Jim and Randy [Keeney] went to Detroit yesterday.

John and Jane Spross Newton's daughter Becky was fighting a Hepatitis C complication.

July 31
Yesterday, we drove through areas of Weathersfield and Springfield where rain had washed out bridges and roads. It has been declared a disaster area.

August 1
Beautiful day. George took Sam and Dave in the truck and went to Windham again to get a dump truck body from John [Newton].

The dump body was from an old truck of Newton's, we converted it to a dump trailer and used it for many years.

August 2-4
Muggy, hot, showery – the garden looks like the tropics.

August 7
Some sun, some rain, warm. Matt's birthday – Church Bazaar. Mom arrived on Tuesday to stay at Rabbit Hill.

August 10
Still has been rainy. George, Noreen Powers, and I took Sam and Vaughn [Powers] to camp on Lake Bomoseen. It rained all the way over and then cleared for a while in the afternoon. After leaving the boys, we went out to the Covalt's [Rutland friends] for supper; we had a lovely time.

August 12-13
The Westerns came with their family. It's been beautiful weather, we played tennis, swam, etc.

August 15
Drove to Hampton Falls, NH where Peter [Herbert] and John [?] have been living, went out to lunch, then drove to Providence. Dinner out with Judy's [Bruno] family that night.

Peter Herbert and Judy Bruno were getting married; we drove to Providence for the wedding.

August 16
This morning we had breakfast in a little coffee shop and then walked around the city which was fun, they have made several city streets so that only pedestrians are on the streets – very nice just to walk around without the traffic. Had lunch at Bruno's then the wedding – cocktails at five and dinner afterward. Very fabulous meal served to 180 people! The Brunos are very nice and we enjoyed them.

August 17
Left after coffee and buns – got to [Dwight & Gladys] Millers at 11:30. We had dinner and visited there until 5:00. Gladys is pregnant again. Got home at 8:00 – found out Teddy [our dog] had been hit by Paul [Hooker] in our truck and is at the animal hospital. Sam came home. He had a good week at camp.

August 22
All week has been lovely weather. I guess Monday and Tuesday there were some thunder storms and one hail storm. After that the air cleared. Had dinner with Mom at Rabbit Hill on Wednesday. Today went to the Caledonia Fair.

Sept. 2
This past weekend was beautiful – hot and sunny. We did a lot of tennis and swimming. Saturday was the dedication of the new [elementary] school with an Open House. It was well attended and very nice. Peter and Judy are at Claude's [Field] but have found an apartment in Lyndonville.

October 21
SNOW! Poor mother is supposed to leave tomorrow and she was sure it would snow. I told her it never snows in October. We have done some bow hunting. I had one good shot at a doe but missed. David has his hunting license this year and has done some bow hunting.

Oct. 27
This past weekend we drove to the Boardman's in Newton Center [Mass.]. We drove all around Boston that afternoon and then put Georgie on a jet for Chicago – Denver. Sunday I went to Church with Jean [Boardman] – kids walked around. After dinner we followed Jean out to Melrose to pay a short visit to the Westerns – trip home was a bit tense – had dinner at Birthe's.

I was flying to Denver for the annual meeting of the Congregational Church's Board of Homeland Ministries, I served for six years.

1970

"Played lots of tennis all weekend and also swam."

1970 STARTED WITH THE LONGEST POWER OUTAGE we have ever experienced in the 50+ years we've been farming, 54 hours. Our house was heated with a wood furnace that didn't have a blower, and we had a woodstove in the kitchen. The water in the village, as well as for our heifers at Keeney's, was supplied by gravity, so except for poor lighting, we got on quite well. We cleaned the barn and fed by hand, the problem came with milking the cows and cooling the milk. We had a petcock on the intake manifold of the old Case SC tractor and could run a hose from it to the vacuum pump that ran the milking machines in the barn. The tractor supplied vacuum enough to run two milking machines, we used lanterns when it was dark and carried the milk to the bulk tank; what we couldn't do was cool the milk. We survived quite easily compared to some farms, and although we had to dump the milk we couldn't cool, a newly formed milk co-op called Yankee Milk, which we joined this year as charter members, paid for the milk we had to dump. Yankee Milk later became Agri-Mark, and we remain charter members, with our milk going to Cabot.

We traded our VW Bus and $2,550 for a new one, we also traded the Case SC tractor for a new John Deere 2520 tractor and $6,650, and we bought from "Bunker" Kitchel the Grim 5x14 oil-fired sap evaporator for $1,300. I have looked through the records and can't find where we spent more, but in addition to the evaporator, we bought a six-barrel gathering tub that is still our best tub, an 1800 gal stainless steel milk truck body for sap storage that will last forever, 400 sap buckets that are used every year, and several miles of used plastic sap tubing with spouts. That fall and winter we sold our old 40-inches-wide x 12-foot-long evaporator and installed the five-foot-wide x 14-foot-long oil-fired rig, and we started putting pipeline in the Keeney bush with the 1800 gal milk truck body at the bottom to catch the sap; with the additional buckets we had 1500 we could put out. This started a major sugaring expansion.

To give you an idea of what was happening with the cows, in 1963 we shipped 478,720 pounds of milk, and our gross milk income was $27,361 or about $5.70/cwt. In 1970 we shipped 677,149 pounds of milk and our gross milk income was $51,143 or about $7.65/cwt.

We finished building a lean-to shelter in a woodlot that we owned on Mack's Mountain Road, that had come with the Craig farm.

January 29, 1970
32° snowed and rained last night. Up until the last few days the weather has been constantly cold often below zero for about a month. The weekend after Christmas it snowed then rained and froze and we lost our power for 54 hours. George was on that weekend and it was quite a struggle.

Feb. 7
10° Foggy. Last week we had a real thaw – then cold again, another thaw – now cold again. No snow.

March 3
Town Meeting Day – 10° Sunny, Bright, beautiful! About 10 days ago we had temps 20° below.

Ted Farrow replaced Ken Goslant as selectman, Lorna Quimby replaced Frank Randall on School Board, town voted to buy K. Goslant's garage as a Town Barn. Went out to dinner with Jo and Ron [Crisman] to celebrate our Anniversary.

March 17
15° Blowing snow flurries. We had a beautiful weekend of skiing, both xc and downhill. George has about 500 taps out pipeline and buckets but no sap yet.

March 19
20°-52° Beautiful, sunny, lovely, sap running.

March 20
Nice day – Two gallons Syrup.

March 21
27° Snowed, very wet.

March 24
27°-37° Sap ran – George has made about 20 gallons. Jen has lost 5 lbs. Hopes to lose 15 more.

March 26
20°

March 30
0°-34° George boiled several more days last week has made over 50 gals. Yesterday it was quite cold and we all five skied. George went to see Doug Kitchel Jr. about buying an oil fired sugaring rig which had only been used a few years. He also looked at other sugaring equipment.

April 2
25° SNOW – Gathered boiled in about 25 gallons.

April 3
22° Still snowing, blowing.

April 5
18°-33° Chores, skied. Glen [Marceau] & Paul [Hooker] gathered not much.

April 6
15°-40° Nice day. Georgie boiled in about 20 gallons.

April 7
25°-40° Nice day. Canned.

April 8
25°-60° Beautiful, warm springy, sap really running.

April 9
28°-60° Girls overnight at the leanto!

April 10
28°.

April 13
25°-45° We had a nice weekend worked and played. Made a tennis practice court on the hardtop. Kids on vacation.

April 14
25°-60° Beautiful, warm. Gathered boiled. Boys went to leanto overnight. Snow on road up to 4-5 feet deep! Crocuses.

April 16
25°-65° Lovely day 201 gallons syrup.

April 17
38°-50° Nice day. No sap. Cleaned around yard. Annie, Meg Powden, Dorigen [Keeney] to wood lot.

April 18
38°-50° Greenup Day in Vermont. Cool.

April 19
20°-40° Cool pretty day George on for weekend. Glen & Paul gathered, Sugar on Snow at ski tow. Boardmans here.

April 20
24°-34° Cold, Raw, Rain, Snow, Hail. Had my hair cut.

April 21
Similar day. George not able to pull syrup grade back up to A. Have made 201 gallons. Fancy and A.

April 23-24
Rainy and cool. 250 gallons syrup – all finished sugaring.

April 25-26
Family all went to Montreal for the weekend. We stayed at the Laurentian Hotel and drove around, walked around the city. We had a marvelous time! Mild lovely weather.

April 27-29
Temps 45°-80°! Beautiful–George spreading manure. Glen fencing, Paul washing sugaring things. I planted some vegi seeds. Kids raking etc. – fishing!

May 3
Warm (Hot) – All week temps up to 80°-90°. Last night it's cooled off and rained. Buds on apple tree, leaves starting to come out on big maple.

May 4-5
Cool nights, warm days. Lovely. Radishes are up, Larry Filby back from Guam.

May 6-7
25°-45° Cold, raw, rainy, snowy, blowy.

May 11
50° Yesterday we spent the day fishing up the brook by Penny Street. Pete and Judy [Herbert] came part of the time and had a picnic with us. It was fun. The kids all swam in the brook. It was very hot. Rained at night.

May 16
Pleasant weather, all week – <u>George planted some field corn</u>. We ate
a small amount of asparagus. All bulk fertilizer and manure spread.

May 21
Good weather has prevailed; George has half the field corn planted; our
garden is doing well, corn is up; we've been eating asparagus. Finally
made a deal for a new Volkswagen bus $2,550.00.

May 26
Nice weekend, tennis, gardening – kids even swam at Harvey's – came
home frozen. Apple blossoms in full bloom, lilacs almost. George is
hauling gravel for our sewage field – hopes to get it done – this week.

May 27
28° Rain/ New Red VW Bus.

Not many people had Volkswagens at that time, mostly Fords and Chevys, our VW bus was unusual. Since it had an air-cooled engine, there was no heat; I would make everyone take off their coats to let their body heat warm it up, this was not a popular rule.

May 29
Frost last night. George is finished with sewage field.

June 1
The weekend was sunny, hot, beautiful. On Georgie's birthday Pete &
Judy came, we played tennis, swam, Loey [Ringquist] and friend came
– Had a party in the evening – Mills, Stetsons, Filbys, Powdens, Bob
Hendricks, Penny had her foal when we got up on Georgie's birthday.
It's a lovely little Filly.

June 4
Having hot humid weather with occasional showers. Georgie's corn
came up well.

June 9
Last Friday George and I went on David's class trip – a campout at Groton Forest. We stayed over Friday night. It was lots of fun. Saw hundreds of ladyslippers on top of Owls Head. Pete and Judy stayed with the Kids Sunday, we climbed Owls Head again with Pete, Judy, Ben, Kyle and the family. George started to mow yesterday but the Heston broke down. Sam stepped on a terribly jagged piece of glass at the lake and cut his foot.

June 22
We've had good weather mostly and have gotten some hay in, but this morning it's raining and there's a lot of hay out – the forecast indicated not rain so soon. Saturday Dad and Mata were here. Yesterday Boardmans and Hummons – all played tennis – Friday we had a dinner party – Filbys, Crismans, Keeneys, Packards, Boardmans, later.

June 30
Mostly good weather but two days out of the past week we've had heavy rain. We really needed it. The garden looks great. We are already eating small beets and carrots, head lettuce. Georgie gave me a metal tennis racquet for my birthday. It's very powerful and should enhance my game.

July 4
Rainy & humid most of the week. George has been working on the sawdust bin ripping away rotten parts and rebuilding for horses and heifers.

July 6
Very busy weekend. Party at Crisman's Friday night. Tennis, thundershowers people in and out Saturday. Little league game rained out. Barbecue okay, but slow so people had to wait a long time. Just got the fireworks done before more pouring rain. Visted Keeneys and Shapiros after that. Sunday a good tennis match Howard [Boardman] and I against Georgie and Phil Carruth. Results: they won. 0-6, 6-1, 7-5. Lunch with Phil and Boardmans here. Visited with new neighbors – Cohns. Hamiltons arrived.

July 7
Beautiful day George mowed a large amount of Claude's [Field] field.
Baled some. Ballgame – Peacham 6 – Monroe 9. David hit a good one.

July 10
Beautiful, hot. We got in about 2,600 bales in the past two days.
Finished Claude's. Ruthie [Marceau] and I worked some. Kids all had
physicals yesterday. Everyone is fine.

July 13
Busy weekend. Mike Z's [Zagaradni's] friend and another friend came
Thursday nite and stayed till Saturday. People in and out Saturday
and Sat eve. Square Dance at the Keeney's. It was very nice, kids had
a marvelous time. John and Jane (Greenwood) Newton and Pete
[Newton] and Jim [Newton] stayed here overnight and until after
lunch Sunday. Boardmans had dinner with us. Gary Schoolcraft was
in a very bad accident Saturday night. He was hurt critically and Peter
Randall's navy buddy was killed. It was Peter's car. Peter not in car
evidently. Gary is in Hanover with a serious skull injury I think the
whole Village must be praying for him to make it.

July 20
Yesterday we took Jenny to Rock Point Episcopal Conference and Dave,
Matty and Annie to Camp Ingalls. It was a beautiful day and they
seemed excited. Then George, Sam, and I went up and visited Aunt
Frannie for a while. Garden is lush. We're eating peas. David was
chosen on the all-star little league team.

July 27
Tuesday we drove to Baldwins [Dummerston] and stayed til Thursday.
The Crocketts were there and one night the Browns and Faulks also
came for dinner. We had a most wonderful time – played tennis, swam,
and talked. We found those friends as dear as ever. One day George
went up to Rupert to talk with Bill Meyer who is running for Senator
on the Liberty Union Party platform. He wanted George to fill the
Governor slot. George grappled with that idea several days and finally

decided it was too much and might be detrimental to our family life. Thursday we went up to the Newton's to visit and pick up Sam Western. We found ourselves feeling depressed. All week was sunny and hot. Saturday night dinner at the Rough's.

We were depressed about John and Jane (Spross) Newton's earlier breakup and the disruption it had caused in their wonderful family of five children. It was a monumental rift in the ideal family that the Newton clan and the Newton School had represented for Patty, me, and our family life.

July 31
All week has been hot and humid, more like N. J. and south than Vermont – even nights have been hot – uncomfortable. Wednesday Jean [Clark] drove to Burlington with Annie and me to get Jenny at camp. We had fun. That same day, however, we found Teddy dead and that upset everyone very much. We don't know why he died. George buried him on top of the Sugarhouse hill.

August 10
Had some rain which cooled our weather a bit, but basically still hot and beautiful summer days. Lots of tennis and swimming, kids taking turns staying at Pete and Judy's this week. Yesterday Dave's all star team played a northern team at Lyndonville and won 9-6. David didn't get to play.

August 17
Very hot all last week again. Very unusual. Sam bought a border-collie, Scotch collie pup named him Nicolas. He's awfully cute. Played lots of tennis all weekend and also swam. Pete and Judy came for dinner last night to celebrate their anniversary and we all had a lovely time.

August 18
The weather changed finally. It should have rained yesterday but did not, evening.

August 22
RAIN The Ketchams stopped to visit us.

August 25
I drove to Boston to pick up Mom at the airport with Annie, Jen, Matt. We had a good rip.

October 30
Mom only stayed about two weeks, three perhaps, and we all drove her to Boston that time. Then we spent the weekend with the Westerns which was lovely. Went to the beach and picnicked, some swam. Came home through Marblehead [Mass.] which was interesting.

Corn is all chopped. Last Thursday the family drove to the Hummon's in Montclair, NJ. We spent until Sunday there, went to Summit and looked around, visited the Faulkiners. Saw cousin Minta in Nutley. Saturday we drove into New York to see Barb [Boardman and her husband] Bill. Had lunch, drove around, walked around, shopped, even had a tour of the hospital where Bill works, Roosevelt. Sunday George went to Baltimore with Serge [Hummon] to the UCC [United Church of Christ] Corporate Board meeting and the kids and I drove home. We had breakfast at Nancy and David Andrews that was lovely. We had wonderful weather this week. Cold at night (20°) Warm in the day 50°-60°.

1971

"We felt badly because he had been here
the day before wanting work."

THIS WAS A YEAR FILLED WITH EMOTIONS, GOOD and bad. On the bad side, we had the untimely death of Frank Ryan, the tragic suicide of Paul Hooker, and a suicide attempt by Aunt Fran. Patty took charge of the situation with Aunt Fran and got her rehabilitated and into an apartment in St. J. She then assumed the responsibility for Aunt Fran's welfare. Also on the bad side, two more of our friends' marriages broke up, Jim and Randy Keeney and Larry and Birthe Filby. While a divorce is obviously difficult for the couple involved and their family, it is also difficult for their friends.

Finally, Patty didn't mention it in the diary, but Peacham Academy closed in 1971, dealing a major blow to the village and town. The Academy had been the center of education for the area from the beginning and provided employment for many.

On the good side, Sam and Jenny, at 14 and 13, showed their ability to step up when needed and handle responsibility – Sam milking the herd two nights in a row while I planted corn, and Jen keeping house and preparing the food for the family and the help while Patty was away. A lot can be said for the opportunity that farm life offers for young people to build character.

Jan 18, 1971
We had a busy happy holiday season. The first snow came in early December and there has been quite a lot. We've had a lot of very cold

weather day after day 10˚ to 20˚ below. The Stetsons went to the Virgin Islands after Christmas, and while there had a very bad auto accident. John has his Knee in a cast and Doris is in Brightlook with a badly damaged leg and will have to stay for several months.

Jan 26
Days have been beautiful and mild, Skiing over the weekend was excellent. Sam competed in a XC meet at Madonna Mtn. [renamed Smuggler's Notch in 1973].

Jan 31
Nice day, ski races, Matt took both Jr. slaloms with Annie close behind.

Feb 1
20˚ below again, I had a complete physical with Dr. Farmer, every-thing apparently okay except for overweight. I spoke to Mens Club on Risk Factors in Coronary Heart Disease.

Feb 3
Jim Quimby working on our front hall, putting in two closets, paneling walls, he and Buddy [McLam] are going to redo our bathroom also.

Feb 7
Yesterday and today temps went up over 30˚, it was warm and sunny. Sam raced XC in North District Meet, he came in 18th out of 70. David and I skied XC to ski tow, Jenny has a bad sore throat.

Feb 8
12 to 14 inches new snow, no school, kids skied.

Feb 22
We've had various kinds of weather, none very cold. Sam went to Brattleboro with the ski team to compete in the State Meet, the Caldwell boys cleaned up in the XC and did well in other events. St. J placed fifth in combined four events. They waxed poorly and placed eighth in

XC. Work is still going on in our hall and bathroom, Marilyn [Petrie] comes to paper hall today.

March 2
Town Meeting, nice day, George off School board, Burn Page took his place, party at Powden's in the evening. Tom Atkinson died Sunday.

March 5
Yesterday and today we have been having a huge snow storm, snowing and blowing, half day school yesterday, today none.

March 6
Lovely day, skied in deep powder, very successful square dance.

March 8
Snow started again yesterday morning and stopped sometime during the early morning today. It's beautiful but what snow, our windows in the new room are covered.

March 10
25° Beautiful day, George and Paul [Hooker] started hanging tubing. New flooring in hall, kitchen, and cubical room, hall is all finished now, wallpaper, paneling, woodwork, and new closets upstairs and down.

March 18
Pete [Herbert] and Carl Powden have been working some this week doing odds and ends and helping to tap, it has been cold.

March 19
10°-35° Mostly raw, more pipeline up, had dinner with Anne and Gordon Mills with some very nice friends of theirs.

March 22
Good but tricky skiing over weekend, we had the duty at the ski tow. Today I walked over to Doris Stetson's to visit, it was fun, took me about an hour, I could walk on the snow part way.

March 25
10°-30° I walked to Powden's for a visit this morning.

March 31
Last weekend we had a picnic on Saturday at the top of Packard's field where we had pipeline. It was beautiful and sunny, afterwards the boys helped George and Matt and the girls and I walked home, the girls went riding. Sap did not run much. Sunday we all skied and it was the most beautiful spring skiing I've ever enjoyed. Yesterday George gathered the first sap and today boiled some, not enough to make syrup.

April 7
23°-36° Snowed 4 or 5 inches then cleared, State forester visited, Georgie made 23½ gals fancy.

April 10
Gathered, boiled made 19 gals. Last night had Ryans, Crismans, and Mills here for dinner, lively evening. This night house is filled with teen-agers, Bobby B[lanchard], Craig [Marcotte] and June [Hendricks] came first, then a group after a hayride in the snow.

April 11
Easter Sunday, family all went to church, then girls rode horses, boys gathered, skied in the later afternoon, fun spring skiing. Kids on vacation, Craig Marcotte here for the week.

April 12
Gathered, boiled, have made 65 gals. Kids skied, Jenny, Kyle, and Kathy [O'Brien] went to the leanto for overnight, beautiful evening with a full moon and stars.

April 16
George butchered a Holstein heifer at Keeney's, found he had made a mistake and butchered a bred one rather than an open one, he felt awful.

April 17
Gathered sap in afternoon, lots of kids came along. Ham Strayer with Marilyn Chase, square dance at night.

April 18
This noon we heard on the radio that Frank Ryan died, He died in Boston, we don't know much about it yet.

April 20
Went to the funeral home and saw Frank, it just doesn't seem possible that he is dead. We talked to Peggy, she is in a daze of unbelieving I think. Visited Peter and Judy [Herbert].

April 21
Frank's funeral service in the Catholic Church. Church was full, many tears were shed, it was a lovely service. Spring is finally coming, snow going, but as Fred Mold said, spring is not as joyous this year with the loss of Frank.

April 25
Yesterday was beautiful day, temps 28° to 60°, gathered sap, cleaned around garage etc. Square dance last night, George boiling today, Craig and kids gathered.

May 1
Green up day, the weather has been rather blagh, cool, rainy. George finished boiling, 192 gals, pulling buckets, Sam found yellow violets.

May 10
Yesterday was fun, we had egg hunt and flew kites on sugar house hill, lots of kids showed up, and everyone had a good time.

May 19
Hot days, leaves almost out, peas up. Last night we had a meeting of concerned citizens to discuss the disposal of the PA [Peacham Academy] property. We came up with three proposals for the trustees to consider. 1,

Town assume all debts and own all property. 2, Town assume responsibility for $38,000 Kinerson Trust Fund and own Gym. 3, Town have first option to buy.

May 26
George has planted one corn piece, we have eaten asparagus twice.

June 1
George got the field corn all planted by Sunday. We planted more in the vegetable garden. It was beautiful and the kids worked some and played at all sorts of things. SAM MILKED ALL ALONE two nights, because Glen was off, and George wanted to get his corn in. He got along okay except he was very tired. Birthday party for George's 40th birthday was gay last night. Pete and Judy were here and Bobby Blanchard and some other of Craig's friends came in.

June 7
Yesterday Georgie took our kids, Craig, Bobby, Peter, June [Hendrick], Kyle, to Mt. Washington, to Tuckerman's Ravine. They had a wonderful time, I stayed home and worked and rested.

Eleven of us with skis and boots in the VW bus to Tuckerman's.

June 14
David drove with me to Boston last Wed., we stayed at the Western's and had a nice visit. Thursday we met Mother at the airport and drove to Rabbit Hill, had dinner, then home. Jen made the meals, etc., while I was gone.

July 9
Ate peas, Gretchen and Duncan [Bond] were here for a full week with their darling daughter Jessica, and we had a lovely visit.

Aug 1
Ate corn, busy summer, Aunt Frannie stayed one week, very good time. Birthe has been back and forth, Larry is leaving her for another woman,

and she is trying to get a job and come back here. David got "Most Valuable Player" trophy for little league and made all stars. Matty visiting in Maine for a while, Youth Center had successful public supper.

Aug 21
This week has been hectic with getting the final hay in from Priesters, Dawsons, Randalls, Packards, and then some rowan [grass] from Seavers and Bermans and ours, perhaps finally we're done. Yesterday when Paul Hooker had been missing in his woodlot all Thursday and overnight, while some people were organizing a search party, Chris, Carey, Candy, Carl, Casey [Marcotte] drove up into the woods with tractor and trailer to search and in a short time found Paul dead of gunshot wounds, self-inflicted. It was a tragedy, we felt very badly because he had been here only the day before wanting some work.

Sept 1
George was pallbearer at Paul's funeral last week. Jim and Randy [Keeney] are having a difficult time right now. Jim is edgy about his job and also is involved with a blind girl whom he feels he needs to help, awful problem for Randy. We keep having break downs, motor in the truck broke down and no one would fix it, so George and Craig are fixing it. Arnold Nunn is fixing the baler, haybine, rake, we've lost two cows, one by lightning, and one got very sick and we sold her before she died.

Sept 12
We got most of the equipment fixed and now we are ripping up the building over the front porch, Craig is still painting the house; Les Page is coming to reroof the house. Randy went to Wisconsin for a week and left Dorigen there. June and I got up this morning early, Randy had called and asked us to meet her in Barnet at 6AM. June waited and I worried, she never came, it turned out that Jim knew she was coming at 4:00 instead.

Oct 28
It has been very warm and beautiful, almost all month, we have not used the furnace yet, and most days no heat was needed. The corn is all cut and George is plowing, Craig is back painting the house. Last Friday we got a call that [Aunt] Frannie was in the hospital having tried to end her life, we went up. We went again Tuesday with Peter and emptied her apartment, she can't go back there. She's physically okay, but very depressed, it is very sad. George called his dad, but he isn't interested in doing anything, so the responsibility remains with us.

Nov. 15
Now Frances is in the St Jay Convalescent Centre, she seems okay, is sorry for what she did, and now feels she is ready to get back in an apartment around here. The weather is now wintery, we've had several inches of snow, and this morning it was 9°. This is opening weekend of hunting season, and all of the boys have been out, but no luck yet.

Dec 17
We had no luck hunting, loads of snow and beautiful skiing. Frances is settled in an apartment in St. J, seems fairly content. Jenny got on honor roll at SJA [St. Johnsbury Academy].

1972

"I feel lucky to have this life."

Ten years in Peacham

I HAVE ALREADY MENTIONED THAT THE STEVENS' Valley Men's Club built the ski tow on the Bayley-Hazen Road north of town and ran it for many years. The club met once a month in the basement of the library. We cut the wood to heat the Congregational Church, as well as put on an oyster stew supper. Our main fundraiser was setting off the fireworks on July 4, I would help do that.

The Christmas Ball Patty mentions this year was a grand occasion and a good example of how social our lives had become in Peacham. Not only did we attend a lot of parties, but we gave them ourselves and helped organize many town events. Jen and Annie were among the principal workers at the Christmas Ball.

We were beginning to learn how to use the maple tubing; this year we made 590 gals of syrup compared to an average of 235 for the last three years. We bought a set of three bottom plows for $1,094 and a used, four-row corn planter for $590 – this was an improvement but it still wasn't great – and a 15-KW generator for $927. I took a night class in welding at St. Johnsbury Academy and put the generator on a trailer along with an electric welder, giving me a portable welder I could use in the yard as well as a generator to run the farm with – milk the cows and cool the milk when the power went out. We use the same system today for outside welding, though most of the welding and repairs are now done in our most adequate shop.

In 1972 a group of teachers began thinking of starting Peacham Academy up again, after it had closed the previous year.

Jan 5, 1972
Our Christmas was really special. We had Christmas dinner on Christmas Eve and all exchanged gifts, it was one of the nicest I've ever known, Frances and Craig were with us. We also had a great holiday week, skied, visited with the Dawson family; Jean, Don, and Margie Clark spent a few days; Jen had a New Years Eve party; Youth Centre had a supper New Years Eve night which was marvelous.

Jan 9
Georgie gave me a pair of Fischer Superglass skis as a late Christmas present, they are really great. Barb [Boardman] and Bill [Hoffman] were up all last week. Barb and I went out XC skiing one day and had a nice time. Keeney's car was out of commission all last week so we had to transport. Saturday Sam raced in a XC meet in Lyndonville, placed 10th, and 3rd on St. J team, he wasn't pleased.

Jan 23
The weather has been like a roller coaster as Fred Mold says, at the moment it's warm and rained last night. There is a real epidemic of flu and strep. Every family around has been affected. David has had trouble getting rid of his respiratory infection and has also had quite a few bad boils and abscesses. George and I went to Dummerston and went to see the Millers; we stopped at the Hackett farm auction on the way down. The man that owned that huge operation was killed while loading corn, the pile was so big that the upper part fell on him.

Jan 26
Yesterday it rained and the temp went up to 40°, then the wind came up and it blew like mad and the temp dropped to 10° below 0 last night. This morning the milk room was frozen and the bulk tank wasn't working.

Feb 7

The winter has stayed a little more constant lately, quite cold and a great deal of wind. We had a big meet at the ski tow yesterday, Tri-State Girls special slalom, there was lots of excitement. I finally got the bug and I've been sickish for several days. The kids still don't feel tops.

Feb 22

It snowed 6 inches or so over the weekend and then turned cold and blew. The Clarks came to visit and to ski but we didn't get in any Sat. or Sun., very good square dance Saturday night. Yesterday was a nice day and we ran the tow and had a good turnout and real fun skiing. David took a bad fall, lost both skis and hit a tree. He was unconscious for a short time and really scared George and Craig. Luckily Dave Dawson was there and he checked him over twice. An hour after the accident Dave's color was back and Dr. Dawson poked and squeezed and decided nothing was broken. We were lucky he hit the muscled part of his back. George has been setting out maple tubing for a week now.

Feb 23

26° below zero, the wind blew like crazy again yesterday. I went to a luncheon at Virginia Bentley's with some others, it was very special. There was a fire in Barnet and one in Danville yesterday. Last night there was a bad fire in Peacham out at Martin's Pond that took the life of a SJA [St. Johnsbury Academy] boy, Awful.

Feb 28

It snowed several times in the last week and the skiing has been beautiful. I took Matt and David to Lyndonville one day to practice jumping with the SJA team. They enjoyed it and now Sam wants to jump. Dave, Matty and Annie were on vacation last week and had a good time.

Mar 1

Yesterday Sam, Dave and Matty jumped at Lyndonville with Al Eaton coaching, they did well, Matty got in a few beauties. Today the family all went to Montpelier and Ron Crisman took us on an excellent tour.

We listened to the legislature and the Senate, and then we had dinner at the Crisman's, a very nice day.

March 2
Rained and froze last night so it was very icy this morning and all schools were called off. Better weather tonight so we all went to see Dr. Zhivago.

March 8
Busy weekend. Older kids out of school Mon-Tues (Town Meeting). Meeting lasted till 4:30 then went out to dinner with Peter and Judy (an anniversary gift). Craig seems unhappy. Talked to him today – he feels he needs to get away and have a change so he probably won't be working much longer. I had to scold Kyle [Lewis] yesterday because she tried deceit with me again I was very angry. What she really needs is her own mother [Corinne Lederer].

March 13
Started tapping. Weekend was fairly warm. Skied at Burke on Sunday (Peter and Judy's Christmas gift). Last week we had some extremely cold weather.

March 14
8°-35° Watched a pileated woodpecker off and on all day yesterday right in the side yard. 170 lbs – started exercise class.

March 15
20°-30° Started snowing last night at 8 and continued until midday today – 8-12 inches. It's beautiful but! Craig plans to leave at the end of next week, so we'll have to find a new man.

March 16
17°-45° Lovely spring day. Craig and George hung buckets on Sugar House Hill, they had to go up on snowshoes, pulling buckets on a toboggan. David Magnus, Bill Rough, Duncan Bond, Bill Marshall, and John Conover have a plan for reopening Peacham Academy. They

are very enthused. *There will be meetings next week for the public. One
Act Plays.*

March 17
31°-37° Rain all day

March 18
*29°-34° Rain turned to snow – sap dripping. Good skiing – cleared in
the afternoon. (Planted early tomatoes and peppers in pots.)*

March 19
12°-30° Bright sunny morning – Good skiing.

March 20
*30° PTG [Parent Teacher Group] meeting with David Magnus pre-
senting ideas about Peacham Academy. <u>Frank Miller started working
part time.</u>*

March 21
*20°-40° Old Fairbanks Morse plant [St. Johnsbury] burned. It was in
flames when I drove the kids to school. Lovely sunny day.*

March 22
29°-40° RAIN.

March 23
More rain.

March 24
*Colder, snowed a bit. Gathered. Craig left. Bobby [Blanchard], Candy
[Marcotte], [Aunt] Frances, and Judy [Herbert] came for dinner.*

March 25
*20°-30° Working on pipeline. I had a long talk with Corinne about
Kyle's situation and her own.*

March 26
20° Quite nice day. All skied. Mark [Powden] here.

March 27
8°-20° Putting up tubing.

March 28
18°-24° Putting up tubing.

March 29
28°-45° Putting up buckets. Sap running.

March 30
28°-33° Snowy – "Miserable" – made syrup.

March 31
28°-46° Snowy – then sun came out and it was beautiful – sap flowing – syrup cooking. Mr. [Ed] Rowe's funeral.

April 1 & 2
Sap flowed all weekend. Gathered, Boiled, Skied, sold syrup – had lots of visitors. Have made about 100 gallons. Carl Powden worked.

April 3
25°-40° (or more).

April 4
20°-40° Later in the day snowed and rained, Sap ran. Carl and Frankie [Miller] worked. 167 lbs.

April 5
15°-40° Gathered Boiled.

April 6
15°-40° Gathered. 220 gal. 140 Fancy.

April 7
4°-33° Snowed last night about 4 inches. Hamilton Slaight in hospital with coronary attack – critical. Heard from Bonds that they'll stay over there [Austria] another year. Also another baby girl Rebecca Erin.

April 13
Judy, Annie, Jenny, and I went to Montreal Tuesday and Wednesday and had a really good time. Today we went to start A & J on orthodenture, I'm still not happy about it.

Patty didn't care for the work the orthodontist was doing on the girls' teeth.

April 19
33°-55° Sunny in the morning then showery and cooler. Walked to Reeve Brown's with Susan Ross. Democratic Caucus, George Chairman.

April 20
31°-45° Snowing miserable in the morning. Cleared in the afternoon. George and I went to Lyndon State to hear Peter Brown, Bob Rachlin, and Ray Anderson play a chamber concert. We went with the Mills and on the way home stopped to see Gordon's [Mills] plant that makes insulation for transformers.

April 21
22°-37° Visited school this morning. Teachers want to coach an operetta again this year. Annie did exceptionally well on achievement tests.

April 22
29°-50° Nice day gathered boiled. Birthe and kids came for supper.

April 23
30°-45° Snowed. All white at 6 am. Partly cloudy day. Ryans came for early supper and afternoon.

April 24
32°-44° Beautiful morning, then rained in afternoon. Walked 4-5 miles.

April 25
22°-45° Cool. Sap flowing well.

April 27
22°-40° Beautiful morning.

April 28
30° Such a lovely day and increasingly warmer. The snow is finally going – still a pile in front and on the garden. Kids played tennis. The temps up to 65°. I sat on the hot deck. Kids sleeping on deck.

May 1
38°-70° Warm, dry, and dusty. George finished sugaring made 590 gallons. Frannie spent the day.

May 2 & 3
Rain thunder showers. Still patches of snow.

May 4 & 5
Rain.

May 6 & 7
Lovely days. Green up for Peacham and ourselves on Saturday. Sunday we had our Spring Egg Hunt and Kite flying on the sugar house hill. Peter, Judy and Aunt Fran came out and stayed for dinner. The Marcotte family plus some O'Briens and Wasons and Lederers came to the Egg hunt. We had a wonderful time. Snow is mostly gone except in the woods. Still have not planted the garden. Erica [Randall] is in the hospital with a nervous breakdown and Saturday Gib Randall had a heart attack.

May 10
Planted peas, early corn, and small stuff. Had a nice day. Georgie took time to plant with me and also worked with the horses and girls. Boys are taking down pipeline.

May 12
Week has been mostly cool and windy – some rain. Planted 50 strawberry plants. Erica and Hamilton [Slaight] home. Gib had another attack.

May 15
Nice weekend. Frannie out. Girls painted house where Craig left off. Planted 20 raspberry bushes and some shrubs. Boys finished washing, pipeline. Peter graduated from Lyndon College. They had dinner with us last night. Friday the girls and I had a nice trip to Greensboro to get the bushes.

May 17
Rainy. Warm. Gov. Wallace shot Monday not killed. Asparagus and lettuce up.

May 23
Nice weekend. Planted more corn. Tennis, went to the lake. Jen and Dave swam – Water icy. Dinner at Peter and Judy's to celebrate Pete's graduation. Summery weather. Loey came with her husband. Married last week. They stayed overnight and we really had fun. Corn up.

May 25
All week the days have been beautiful – sunny, hot – summery. George has planted two cornfields and is now preparing the others. We've eaten asparagus twice.

May 27
Two more nice days. David and I drove, yesterday, to Hanover and New London to visit Joanie Snively and to find Georgie's birthday gift – cross country skis. It was really beautiful and we had a good time.

May 29
Memorial Holiday. Days are still hot summery – getting very dry. Sweet corn growing fast – Asparagus patch is amazing this year. Hummons and Boardmans here last night. Lots of summer people up.

May 30
Another beautiful day. Yesterday was so great we all worked until 11 then went swimming at Harvey's lake. It was beautiful. Water refreshingly cold – then we played tennis and watched the Memorial day parade. Peter, Judy and Frannie were here – had a chicken barbeque and played games in the yard. It was such a wonderful day and weekend I feel so lucky to have this life and the family I have. We celebrated Georgies birthday.

June 2
We have had 3 days of rain and very much need it. George still has corn to plant, but that which is in is growing well. Matty is taking recorder lessons and likes it very much. Little League has started and Matty has played several positions in practice. Annie had two teeth out yesterday to begin the straightening program.

June 6
Annie began to get braces on her teeth. We started practicing for a Mary Poppins musical play to be given at school June 15th.

June 12
The week was very cool and got down to 32° on Saturday night; the wind blew so things did not frost, luckily. Matty had a bad Strep throat Friday and missed the school trip to Granby Zoo.

June 16
The children gave "Mary Poppins" it was wonderful. Also the last day of school, Weds night Annie and I attended Dave's eighth grade graduation. The program was okay but it seemed ridiculous to go through all that. Matty has played in two L L games, he played center field in one and third base in the other.

June 19
Played tennis in the morning then we all went to N. Springfield to a reception for Loey and Nathan [Grey] at the Ringquist's. We paid a visit to Herman Young on the way home, it was a nice day.

June 21
This week we started our "Share Your Talents" program and it is getting off to a good start. Yesterday I had the "day off" and it was really great. I did what I wanted to do and the girls got all the meals.

July 4
Beautiful day, but cool, 45°. Matty pitched the L L game against Barnet which we won. The Dawsons came for a picnic supper and then we went to the fireworks which were really good, George and David Randall set them off. Last week it rained most of the time, Sunday it was lovely and we got hay in. Monday was very rainy all day, so we were lucky to have such a beautiful fourth.

July 21
We still have had a lot of rain but at least it is warm, we are gradually getting hay in. We are on David Field's big field now. We have been swimming every day this week or so. Loey and Nathan came last weekend and we had a wonderful time. The kids played their last L L game Monday. Matty went in to pitch after a tie in the 7th inning but could not pull them out. He has been selected to play on the All-Star team.

Aug 4
Just like a Sept. day, clear and cool. Still trying to get in 1st cut hay. We've eaten corn, tomatoes, beans, pulled up peas because they were finished and planted more as an experiment.

Oct 15
25° Today it is snowing and blowing, it also snowed a little on Monday. It's too bad I let so much time go by without writing, because lots of things have happened. Jenny, Annie, and I flew to Virginia in August

and stayed with [brother] Dick's family. The flight was really beautiful and exciting and easy and we had a wonderful visit with Dick's family and Mother. It was a really good thing to do because now, we have a relationship with the Gulicks and we can picture their home and the places where they work and play. I was hoping it would bring mom closer to them, but it didn't seem to.

Oct 20
12°-37° One of the things that happened about 3 weeks ago was that Frenchie quit. Donna was unhappy living in St. J and I guess other factors figured in. He gave us only a few days notice, right in the middle of corn cutting. Fortunately Peter wasn't too tied up and worked steady for 1½ weeks, then Glen and George finished because Sam was home a few days and could milk.

Oct 29
George has manure all out at Packards and Keeneys, Glen and George have been doing outside work while Sam milks and Dave and Matt do chores. Three or four weeks ago we brought in a baby kitten from the barn. We weren't planning to keep her, but she's adorable, and everyone loves her, she seems very smart.

Nov 3
Rain storm with thunder. Boys have still been doing chores, George asked David Bradley if he'd like to work part time, starting on Glen's weekends.

Nov 5
4 inches snow, the boys worked this weekend so they could have the first weekend of hunting season off.

Nov 6
Visited Diane O'Boyle with Anne Mills. They moved here from Westchester County, four young children. They completely remodeled the house and it is very plush. Jenny has been riding Schilling and

Annie Penny. We bought a new harness for Schilling and a lovely little sleigh and an express wagon.

Nov 7
Tom Salmon won the election for governor, 2ⁿᵈ Democrat to become gov. in 100 years. Nixon won by a landslide, Brenda [?] lost.

Nov 11
MATTHEW SHOT A 4-POINT BUCK ON THE SUGAR HOUSE HILL.

Nov 13
Jen had two teeth out getting ready for straightening.

Nov 28
We had a wonderful Thanksgiving, the Hummons were with us for 3 days, Phil Carruth and Aunt Fran joined us for the dinner. Georgie took Friday off to go with the weekend, so we had a little vacation; no more deer.

Dec 17
Last night George and I went to a party at Bob and Pat Schwartz and later to a party at Ross's, they were both fun. Sam and David are both practicing for the ski team, they ride home with George Blanchard.

Dec 30
The days preceding Christmas were very busy primarily due to the great preparations for the Christmas Ball which the youth centre has been planning for weeks. They sent invitations about a month ahead to every person on the [voter] check list. The Ball was a kind of dream of an old fashioned formal occasion, and it turned out beautifully. The kids spent many hours making decorations, fixing up the downstairs of the church, and baking, shopping and planning. Many people came to the ball and they thoroughly enjoyed it.

Our Christmas was very nice, Peter and Judy and Fran spent the afternoon and Christmas Eve with us. We had a special dinner and then opened gifts. The Wasons had an open house on the 29th and the Clarks are here for a few days. Drove Sam and David to Lyndonville for practice, Jean [Clark] went too, it snowed all the time. We showed slides in the evening.

Dec 31
Rainy and warm, Dawsons all came over for indoor games and lunch. After lunch Georgie took out the sleigh and gave some people rides. A few skied, a few went on sleds, all had supper except Georgie and I because at 8:30 we went to Mills for a New Years Eve supper party. The Fuehrers were also there with his parents, it was very pleasant. Felt bad about leaving the Clarks, but it was all planned.

Hut at Philo Robinson's ski hill, Patty & kids, ca. 1966

Membership Card, Men's Club

1973

"... gathered sap like mad..."

T HE YEAR OF THE AMAZING SAP FLOW — 925 GAL-
lons; last year had been our biggest year so far at 590 gallons.
Dorigen Keeney, Carl Powden and Frank Miller helped with gathering, and although we had a good system in place, it was still unusual
to have made 600 gallons of syrup in eight days, 100 gallons in two
of those days; this was done without pipeline vacuum machines,
reverse osmosis machines to take water out of the sap before boiling,
or syrup pumps to strain out the niter, as are common in today's
sugaring operations.

In March last year, David Magnus, Bill Rough, Duncan Bond,
Bill Marshall, and John Conover started holding meetings to try
to re-start Peacham Academy. The plan evolved into an alternative high school that they got started this fall in the old Academy
building in the village. Sam and Jenny transferred there from St.
Johnsbury Academy, and David, Annie and Matty would attend
the new school as they became high school age.

We planted a locust tree in my mother's memory this year. My
mother had died when Pat and I were living in Dummerston on the
Bunker farm, and Dad brought us her ashes. Across the valley from
the Bunker farm was a hill that made a very pleasant view. The top
of the hill was open except for a clump of locust trees; we enjoyed
the spot and would sometimes picnic there with our young family.
One time we took a shovel and Mother's ashes; we had a small service with the kids and buried her ashes there by the locust. So we
planted a locust in her memory in Peacham.

Glen Marceau left to take over another farm; he had been an important part of our farm team, and until we got a replacement the kids stepped up to do the work. It is hard not to be proud of their work ethic. They did jobs that were difficult, sometime unpleasant, and often repetitive, and did them with a good attitude. I think the loving fellowship that Patty brought to our home was responsible for their attitude. Now, as I sit here writing, an 85-year-old widower and great grandfather, I believe our children have passed this work ethic on to their children.

This year we traded our old manure spreader and $1,390 for a 205-bu. New Holland spreader; our old Hessen mower and $2,422 for a New Holland haybine; and we bought five Jersey cows for $285 each. We built two sheds for $2,192, one for dry cows and one for equipment. With this new housing for dry cows, and the heifers being housed at Keeney's, and also with the remodeling of the bull barn, we were now able to milk 80 cows in our barn. When we bought from Craig in 1962 we had stalls to milk 62 cows.

Jan 1, 1973
I will be writing in my new Gibran Diary that Matty gave me for Christmas, except for possibly the weather here.

I have not been able to find the Gibran diary, so we are missing January and February, but she seems to have returned to this journal on March 5[th.]

Mar 5
Yesterday it rained and was warm, today is bright, sunny, springy, George tapping in Keeney's sugar woods.

Mar 6
Town Meeting Day, SAP FLOWING.

Mar 8
Rained during the night, finally cleared by 3 am, then lovely and sunny. George took all the kids and Ben [Keeney] and began tapping and

hanging buckets, they did the Sugar House Hill, across the field, and Keeney's driveway.

Mar 9
Beautiful day, the family tapped the Hooker Road, and up the [Mack's] Mtn. Road part way. Sap not running much.

Mar 13
28°-38° The sun shone and made a very nice day, sap flowing, boys gathered.

Mar 14
25°-40° George boiled, made about 40 gallons, sap flowing, boys gathered.

Mar 15
31°-35° Cold raw windy, some rain, George boiled and canned syrup, Boys gathered and put up more pipe line. There is still snow, but the fields are getting bare, made 64 gals total.

Mar 19
27°-32° Snowed a little last night, roads very slippery, raw, windy, wet today, the boys gathered all taps, George boiled, made 37 gals.

Mar 24
22°-47° Sap flowing, Frank, Carl [Powden], and all the kids gathered like mad, all tubs full, George boiled all PM, made 45 gals.

Mar 25
24°-50° Beautiful morning, sunny, afternoon overcast but nice, George said yesterday's sap run was the biggest he's seen since we've been in Peacham. We have 2200 taps of our own and we are buying sap from 900 taps of Cary's [Marcotte] and Shane's [O'Brien]. The Bulk tanker body at Keeney's was overflowing as well as many buckets. Last night when George stopped boiling all holders were full, including Carey's on his trailer, 80 gals today.

Mar 26
Rained, George boiled all day, cleared in the afternoon, Frank and Carl gathered, Sam, Dave, Matty helped, and Ben in Sugar House. George came home for supper and then went back up with Frank and Carl. The boys helped George at the Sugar House and then got a load of sap at Keeney's; George came home at 2:30 AM.

Mar 27
21°-34° George boiled all day and until 11 PM, bulbs up, tulips, crocuses, and daffys.

Mar 28
18°-46° George boiled all day until 11 PM, sap is still flooding him.

Mar 29
22°-40° George boiled all day, came down for supper, and back up 'till 2 AM, Frank took 9 drums of syrup up to Newport.

Mar 30
28°-55° Sap is running some, George is catching up finally, but he is awfully tired.

Mar 31
Amazing day, George finished boiling in sap, have made over 700 gals.

April 4
Snow mostly gone again, George boiling, the boys gathered yesterday and today.

April 5
28°-38° This morning there is a blanket of snow, 6 to 8 inches.

April 10
28°-32° Another Blizzard – George boiled and did some canning, Billy Lee Langford came to work for us.

April 11
20°-32° Cold windy, George hauling sawdust, Ben, Billy Lee, and Glen working on sawdust bin. Ronny Cochran asked for Glen's job and will start July 1ˢᵗ, and it is all settled.

April 14, 15, 16
Beautiful sap weather, boys gathered, Glen and Billy Lee fenced.

April 17
50°-70° Beautiful, boys gathered and pulled buckets, George boiled, 925 gals total.

April 18
Pulled buckets, cleaned sugar rig, harrowed garden, Sam found Spring Beauty and Hepatica.

April 19
Beautiful day, boys washing buckets, taking down pipe line, I planted peas, some small things and some corn, George started spreading manure.

April 23
Lovely day, things are getting green, more sugaring things cleaned up, kids are finding wild flowers.

April 24
George spreading manure, boys cleaning tubing, Billy fencing with Glen.

April 25
Lovely day, cows out to pasture today.

April 26
George finished spreading manure, radishes up.

April 28, 29
Rain all weekend, this is Glen's last weekend working for us, he will take over the Churchill farm. George is planning to have two milking crews, he and Billy in the morning and Sam and David in the afternoon.

April 30
A bit of snow on the ground, finally cleared and nice sun in the after-noon, first day without Glen, things went pretty well, peas up.

May 1
Plowing, picking stones.

May 8
Jen and I planted 8 more rows of corn, early corn and asparagus up. Things are going somewhat better with Billy Lee, he is a slow learner, Sam's crew is doing great.

May 12
Peacham Green up day, everyone working hard and enthusiastically, we ate asparagus with hollandaise.

May 13
We planted Locust tree in memory of [George's mother] Grandmother Kempton.

May 14
George started planting corn.

May 15
Light frost, the early corn we planted in our garden doesn't look like it would survive.

May 24
It has been very wet, but George finished planting corn.

May 30
Nice day, we checked the field corn and found a few stocks up. Billy Lee is doing better but he doesn't fit the job very well, he is depressed, since we put in the pool table, he has something he likes.

June 1
George decided to let Billy Lee go, we've had so much tension here with his poor work. We gave him a week's pay, now he will go back to Randy [Keeney]. The family will now do all the chores 'til Ronny [Cochran] comes.

June 4
Beautiful day, we are managing with the work load, but the kids are tired, corn is up but spotty.

June 5
New Haybine is here, ready for the sun.

June 6, 7, 8
Mowed.

June 9
Sprinkled a little in the morning but got the hay from the first field anyway.

June 10
George mowed another piece, the weather was excellent and the new mower was helping dry the hay faster, George had to bale two pieces unexpectedly. As a result, David and Matty milked and Sam led the hay crew, Jen, Kevin [Lewis] and Kyle Lewis.

June 11
Very hot day, temperature 110° in the sun, 80° in the shade, the kids got in all the hay that was out, Bobby Blanchard came to work for us. There was a very severe electrical storm, Sam and Jenny were at Harvey's lake, and they came home fast, they were really scared.

June 12
Hot sunny day until about 4 when we had a bad thunder storm again (not like last night though), quite heavy rain. The power went out and we had to use the generator. Bobby and George started cutting some spruce at the upper wood lot. The garden looks great, the early peas are blossoming.

June 16
Poured rain all day, cold, around 40°, Bobby told us he had another job, that was disappointing.

June 21
Very warm and humid today, George tried to bale hay but it wasn't dry, he went fishing in the afternoon, then did chores, it rained in the evening, we've had over 5 inches this month.

June 27
Beautiful day, good drying until about 4:00, it sprinkled, then rained, we had a lot of hay out, it's really too bad.

June 28
Nice day again, Sam raked hay, then it rained again, our garden is absolutely lush with growth, hard to keep the weeds down though.

June 30
Rained very hard during the night and again this morning, there has been bad flooding all over the state, especially in the Winooski valley. Even in Peacham several bridges were almost washed out and some of the roads are impassible, the road from here to Marceau's, just before their farm was badly washed, we went to look and it was a big gorge instead of a road.

July 3
The weather still hasn't straightened out, it is still hot and humid and once in a while a shower. It is really oppressive, my legs ache most of the time and we both have trouble sleeping.

July 5-10
The weather changed, excellent for haying, lots of hay went in the barn.

July 12
The garden is profuse, but the peas aren't doing that well due to the heavy rain and inadequate fencing. Our strawberries have been lovely but are almost over, the peas are still good.

July 25
The big push for haying is almost over, we have finished everything including Keeney's. We've pulled the peas and are harvesting green and yellow beans, summer squash is coming.

July 30
The weather has been very good, some rain, mostly sun, the job on the house is coming along fast.

We were converting a woodshed into a living room at the Village farmhouse.

Sept 11
Almost all of August was hot, enough showers to slow up haying, but really great summer weather. The upstairs is finished except for plumbing, electricity, and painting.

Nov 27
It is too bad I have neglected writing for so long. In the meantime, we hired Cary Marcotte, who boards here, and Kirk Sinclair who lives with his wife Pinky in S Peacham. Kirk is interested in a farming venture of his own eventually and he wants experience, he is a very nice person. Since we had extra help George has gone ahead with the two barns he wanted to build in the summer. One is a shed for dry cows, so we have more room for milkers in the barn, the other is equipment shed, the dry cow shed is done. We've had alternating weather with some snow, the ground is bare right now. Sam is in Boston having a

city experience with the Peacham [Alternative] School. The school is
going along quite well and the kids find it very exciting.

Dec 3
We had a very nice weekend, Thursday and Friday nights the School
put on the play, "David and Lisa," it was a huge success, Excellent,
Terrific!! The kids had their cast party here Friday. We went to the
PTG bazaar, George and the girls went horseback riding twice, long
rides across the fields, there is very little snow, just enough to sled.

1974

"I somehow thought I would always live here."

T HE MILLER FARM IN GREEN BAY, PEACHAM HAD been for sale for a couple of years, from the field that we call the Lower Johnson Piece I would look down on that farm and think to myself, "I need that place." Richard and Eloise Miller owned it, it was 350 acres with 73 acres of open tillage and some sugarbush. The Millers wanted $350,000; we had zero. Patty and I decided to offer $145,000 for the farmhouse and barns and 103 acres. Richard wanted us to have the farm, and he accepted our offer, agreed to carry the mortgage, and we celebrated around the kitchen table at the Village Farm drinking dandelion cordial that Jenny had made. We would put $40,000 down and pay Richard and Eloise $6,000 every six months for 15 years.

To help finance this purchase, we began selling parcels of land that had come with the Village Farm; as soon as we put the word out, people started contacting us. Without question the building of Interstate 91 along the Connecticut River from the southern border of Vermont to the northern border was responsible for the interest in these lots. Interstate 91 made Peacham accessible to people from the south looking for a vacation home in Vermont. There wasn't a lot of land available in town, we were able to take advantage of the opportunity.

The Millers were very cooperative about the transfer of their farm and allowed us to start renovating their barn in fall 1974 even though the purchase wouldn't take place until January 1975. They had an auction in the summer of 1974, and we bought 13 of their heifers and wintered them in their barn. At another auction we bought a milking parlor and the dividers for the free stalls, which we worked on installing that winter in the basement of the renovated barn, as well as pouring cement for the parlor. We purchased a John Deere crawler loader for $8,160. Ben Berwick was very handy with it and was also a great help with the basement renovation. We traded our old baler and $550 for a new John Deere baler and $2,000.

As usual, I am reminded as I transcribe Patty's diary of my short-comings. During this year of huge change and challenge, my lack of understanding and my ambition led to two breakdowns. The most obvious was David's mental breakdown; as I read the diary I can see how I left it all up to Patty and I was involved as little as possible, and as she pointed out when we admitted him to the hospital in Hanover, it wasn't hard to see "contributing factors and past symptoms."

The other breakdown I didn't see until now as I read the diary, how Patty stopped writing of events as she had been, probably she was no longer able emotionally. I had been blind to the hesitancy she had for moving to a new home, the Miller farm, taking on a big mortgage, and how much extra work and responsibility it was giving her. This was added to David's sickness and concerns about our daughter Annie, as well as all the other things going on with the family. I just kept plowing on, she deserved a better husband.

We rented the Frye house (since torn down) two houses down from Peacham Library on what is now Old Cemetery Road. We needed it to house Ben Berwick, whom we hired this year. Ron and Anne Cochran would move into the Village Farm. We now had two very competent hired men – Ben and Ron – and they had great fam-ilies. Two of Ben and Jean's children, young Ben and Janice, helped on the farm, as did Ron and Anne's son Andy. We were poised for a major expansion.

January 1974
My recording in this and the other diary has fallen behind. This year I will just record in this one. We had a good Christmas and a big New Years Eve party which was fun. No skiing until the 2ⁿᵈ weekend in

January. We had very cold weather on the 17th and 18th of Jan., 18 to 25° below but it didn't last long.

Feb 1

The wind started blowing yesterday in the afternoon and became worse and worse along with diving temperatures. We went to the movies to see "Mash" (everyone except Sam) and including Betsy and Julian [Boardman-Smith]. At about 2:15 AM Sam came into our room woke us up saying the fire alarm had rung and there was a fire at David and Anne Randall's, he and Cary went right down. At 4:00 AM the doorbell rang and Burns Page asked me to look at Mike Wright's arm which they thought was broken. I agreed and they took him right to the hospital. The fire was terrible because of the dreadful wind and ice on the ground all around the house. They were not able to save it. Today the kids from the school went all over collecting clothing and money and food for the Randalls. I started with a sore throat Thursday night and today Sunday I still have it, it was bad Fri and Sat. I'm staying in bed today to try and get well to start the week.

Feb 6

The sore throat has continued and also stuffiness and a bad cough. I haven't been anywhere except to Gretchen's yesterday. I do feel better today. The weather is cold and clear, 0° and below. Finished reading "A Thing of Beauty" by A J Cronin, it was very good.

Feb 7

Snowed about 6 or 8 inches, finally a beautiful winter day.

Feb 8-9

Lovely weekend, the skiing was good although we could use more snow, George and I took care of the tow this weekend. Saturday evening we had dinner at the O'Boyle's with the Magnuses and the Randalls, it was very nice.

Feb 11-13
*Peacham played Cabot in basketball, won handily, also the faculty
played, theirs won by one point, very exciting. Girls finally got to the
orthodontist.*

Feb 16
*Peter, Judy, and Elizabeth [Herbert] came to visit for the day, it
was fun. Lori Laird is staying here all week with Jen because we are
going away.*

Feb 18
*Sam, Annie, and Matty went on a school trip to Canada with five
other kids and Jim Kenary. David went with Duncan [Bond] and
other kids to Washington DC. The gas problems [nationwide gasoline
shortage] are extremely critical and we hope they won't have too much
trouble. Jenny's concentration week is being in a one act play, she will
be home with Lori working, cooking, etc.*

Feb 19
*Georgie and I are leaving today to visit the Westerns and the Newtons
[Windham] and to stay at an Inn somewhere and ski.*

Feb 25
*Now everyone is home from trips and vacations, even Kirk [Sinclair].
David had a fine time in Washington, Sam, Matty, Annie were excited
about their trip to Quebec City, George and I had a wonderful vacation.
A good visit with Mary [Western] and with John [Newton] (although
Jane had just left him) and a little skiing at Bromley. We had a beautiful afternoon of skiing at Suicide Six, sunny and lovely. We then drove
to Stowe, stayed in luxurious accommodations at the Green Mtn. Inn,
dined well, and walked around in the rain the next day (Friday) and
looked at the nice shops, had lunch at the Swiss Chocolate Pot. In mid
afternoon we drove to Peter and Judy's and stayed there for a very nice
dinner. Saturday David arrived home from Washington having had
a very good time and Sunday night Sam, Anne, Matt, arrived home
all excited from their trip.*

Mar 1
Wed thru Fri the kids and George set up the whole pipe line system on Keeney's.

Mar 2
Sam, Jenny, Chris [Marcotte], started off hitchhiking to Quebec City, in the afternoon, George's sister [Corinne] arrived to spend a few days.

Mar 3
Our 18th Anniversary.

Mar 4-5
Rain and Mild, there are washouts in various places, the boys have done some tapping now and sap is running. Town Meeting, no special concerns, the town voted to appropriate money fairly generously.

Mar 6
Sam and Jenny got home safely and had a good time. School begins again today. George is hanging buckets on the sugar house hill. Kirk and Pinky are back, but Kirk is planning to go back to school.

Mar 8
20°-25° Cool, breezy, Corinne left by bus, Sam's band played in the Catholic Center.

Mar 9
10°-25° George fired up the arch to thaw out the sap, he was worried that the flues might split, Gretchen [Bond] and I walked.

Mar 10
Snow flurries, increasingly windy, miserable cold, this kind of day makes me very depressed. Pete and Judy came for the afternoon. Cary had to shoot his horse, Lady, because she was dying, it was very upsetting for him, naturally.

Mar 12-13
Continued very windy and cold, made a body feel like it had to fight the weather all the time. We went to the kids evaluation tonight, all were doing pretty well except Matty. Matt is fooling around and not trying at all. Jenny and Frank Green came over for a while afterward, it was fun.

Mar 14
Continues cold, the two one act plays were given for the first time, Jenny played the lead in "Infancy," it was fair, Jen was very nervous. "Zoo Story" with Jeff Skoller and Bill Ranch was great.

Mar 15
Plays were given again, everyone said they were excellent. We also held a square dance at the Rec. Center which I seemed to dub up in every way, the last thing being no piano, we had to borrow Bob Dimick's organ. The dance was okay, but not too well attended. This was Cary's last day working for us.

Mar 16
Warmer, snowy, Jen fed pizza to the band before they went to Blue Mtn. to play for a dance. It was an awful night, snow, rain, but I guess the dance went very well, and they were asked to come back again.

Mar 17
We had the biggest snow storm of the year.

Mar 18
Cold windy, to Montpelier for orthodontist.

Mar 19
We went to town to shop for a pickup, we tried a Chevy V8, with power steering and a Ford with everything standard, both were $3200, we preferred the Ford and got the salesman to come down on the price. We went to see Infancy again along with Cabot's play, the first stage of the contest, Peacham's play was done super well and they won.

Mar 20
The kids are alternating doing morning chores now that Cary's gone. George and the boys tapped more trees along the pipeline, sap not running again yet.

Mar 21
We had about a foot of snow, it is beautiful but not just what we wanted NOW. We heard this morning of two dreadful things that happened in our area: 1 The Elkins Tavern was broken into and everything inside smashed and wrecked, an estimated $10,000 worth of damage. 2 A young man in Barnet was murdered. We all feel sick about it.

Mar 22
I got the new pickup truck.

Mar 23
Lovely day, George and Matty and Annie went horseback riding, later they all skied, and Georgie and I snowshoed up into the Keeney's sugarwoods to check the pipeline. It was fun, I thoroughly enjoyed it. We went to Magnus's for pot luck supper.

Mar 24
It was raining when we got up this morning, then it gradually became colder. Fran spent the day, Gordy [Gorlay] did weekend chores with Sam. Dorcas Gill (Spencer) came over this afternoon and we discussed at length the mess made down at the tavern. She and Bob Camarra felt that it was young kids from the area but he is having a hard time getting information. George and the boys gathered some sap which George boiled in, he has made no syrup yet.

Mar 25
George sent the kids off to Burke to ski today because it was a beautiful day and no sugaring work to do. The day ended badly because the kids stopped at the Drawing Room [a tavern under the Portland Street bridge in St. J that Jim Keeney had started] and had supper which they hadn't planned to do. They did call at 7:00 but supper

*here was waiting for them, also the Drawing Room was not a place
we liked them to hang out. Sam came home with Cary, and David,
Jenny, Annie, Craig [Marcotte], and Chris [Marcotte] had our car
and we didn't know where. We were terribly upset, fortunately they
came home soon and we spent several hours hashing over the whole
thing, causing crying and tears at times. Actually in some ways it was
good because we all got thoughts out that should have been out before.
We talked a lot about the Marijuana situation and came to a pretty
good understanding on that. I think I feel really sorry for Sam because
he felt responsible for everything and the other kids had kind of used
him. We also thought that if the Marcotte boys had not been along, the
problem would not have occurred.*

*Mar26
Fair day, Jen took her driver's test and flunked.*

*Mar 28
Sam told George he had asked Kathy Murphy if she knew anything
about the vandalism at the tavern. She said she had been there along
with Debby Kimball and some boys that were friends of Soderholms.
Then today Debby told him it was just a story. This afternoon Helen
Wason told me that [her son] Peter had heard kids bragging about
taking part in the vandalism, she plans to encourage Peter to tell Bob
Camarra about it. I wish I felt I could take both of these things to
him myself.*

*Mar 29
10° below 0 to 20° above, I took Gretchen to town and did my shopping also Fran.*

*Mar 30
A little snow this morning, Peter and Judy came so that Judy could see
Infancy with us in Lyndonville. We took Betsy and Julian, Judy, Annie,
David and Anne Randall. On the way I asked Anne if she knew any-
thing more about the vandalism investigation. She was very silent a
moment and then said, "It was Jay [her stepson]." I felt absolutely sick*

for her, she has had so much trouble. She did talk quite a lot about it on the way to Lyndonville. There were other children involved and all have been found out, and will have to go to court and receive sentence.

April 1
Today the kids came home from school saying that Jay, Douglas Jamieson, and Daniel Bradley had been the vandals. There was a short article in the paper giving no names, but I'm sure our community will all know and they should. It's really a shame after all the Jamiesons do for the kids, it is sad and awful.

April 2
24°-37° Some rain and freezing in the morning, some schools closed, hung more buckets. Pinky and Kirk have moved out and will be going to Bermuda, I will miss them, Kirk is going back to school this fall.

April 3
BEAUTIFUL DAY, I saw a flock of Snow Geese today, at first I heard them while hanging clothes and I looked all around and finally saw them right over head, not too high, absolutely beautiful. I don't know when I've seen such a beautiful sight. The kids at the homestead saw them too.

The homestead was a place in our woods where the school was building a camp of sorts.

April 4
Anne Randall had a nervous breakdown and is in the hospital for a few days. George boiled the first syrup in, the outlook for the season is not very good.

April 6
Boys put up more buckets, the Peacham School Band played for a dance at the Rec. Center.

April 7
George canned 48 gallons of A, the Magnuses and their kids, and Gretchen and Duncan, came for pot luck supper and sugar on snow, It was fun.

April 8
Matty home sick with sore throat and fever.

April 10
Matty still home, Jen home.

April 13
George boiled, lots of sap, made about 50 gal.

April 14
Easter Sunday, many people in church, George boiled, Annie, Molly [Dawson], and I gathered with Sam, had a good visit with the Dawsons, Molly is here for a few days.

April 15
Gathered and boiled, Jim Keeney working this week.

April 17
22°- 62° Lovely day, Annie, Molly and Matt went horseback riding, George and the boys worked at various things. When they went gathering down at Packard's, the Case 8000 broke through the middle of the road and got stuck. They had to come home and get the John Deere and it took a lot of work to get it out. They didn't find much sap either. Annie and Molly went to the woodlot to sleep after they did their barn chores.

April 18
George, Jim [Keeney], and Ron did some fencing and put dry cows and horses out back. They went gathering in the afternoon, but didn't get much, decided to start pulling buckets tomorrow. I put Molly and

Matty on the bus, Molly to go home and Matty to go to Hartford to visit Aunt Corinne.

April 20
22°-60° Lovely day, gathered sap, all except Sam who had to do chores also go to St Jay to practice with the band for a dance at the Candlelight. The Bonds and George and I ended up at the dance, we had a great time.

April 23
Warm, some showers, George and the boys started pulling buckets, got stuck again on Ha'Penny. Sam bought a motorcycle, paid for it, but doesn't have it yet.

April 24
Snowed several inches, Sam got the Case 800 stuck on Academy Hill, George helped him get it out, Sam was on the way to Keeney's to get some cedar poles for the Homestead.

April 25
24°-45° Went shopping, all went to PTG chicken pie supper and entertainment, was very well attended and very nice.

April 26
31°-40° Fair day, Jen, Sam, Kyle, went to Burlington for the weekend, the rest of us saw "American Graffiti."

April 27
31°-40° Lovely day, Annie and I did house work in the morning, boys in the barn. We played some tennis then we planted seeds in the garden, Lori [Kimball], Annie and I did the planting.

April 28
40°-70° Lovely day again, Crocuses blooming, I drove in and picked up Fran and brought her out for the day. We played tennis again, planted more seeds, Jen, Sam and Kyle came back having had a great time.

April 29
50°-72° Some showers, went to town with Lori, Matt, Shane [O'Brien], and David, Matt bought a 10 speed bike. Nixon spoke on TV for 35 min. about Watergate. He is offering transcripts of the tapes that were subpoenaed from him.

May 2
20°-50° The girls have been riding the horses a lot lately, it's nice.

May 5
Very cool and windy, Jen and Kyle set up their tent on the sugar house hill and slept out Sunday night. Planted potatoes, onion sets, herbs, nothing is showing in the garden yet.

May 6
We heard the news today that Hannah Sleight died Sunday of a stroke and heart attack, very surprising.

May 7
Jen went to Dr Toll today because she had a back pain on one side. He said it seemed muscular although she had a slight infection in the urine. JEN PASSED HER DRIVING TEST.

May 8
Nature class meeting at Parkers on field day.

May 10
Saw the movie "The Sting" with all the family and the Bonds, it was fun.

May 11, 12
Cool and some rain, about two hours of sun on Saturday, Gretchen and I went to Greensboro to the Nursery and Willy's Store. PEAS UP. Girls gave me a pretty vase for Mother's day.

May 14
Nice day, leaves still trying to come out.

May 15
Beautiful, David seems really up tight these days, I don't know why.
Open house at the school.

May 24
Mostly cool and dry until yesterday, it rained most of the day. This has
been a rough week. I don't really feel like writing all the details and
I'm sure I will remember anyway.

David lost his way coming home from the Hanover bike trip and rode
25 miles extra arriving not here but at the Churchill's in a state of
exhaustion and severe anxiety. All week he has been upset/up & down,
with very paranoid fears about people plotting to kill him. Although
I wanted to hospitalize him Saturday night and called Dr Toll, he
discouraged me and we tried to deal with the situation until finally I
took him to Toll Thursday and today we took him to Hanover to the
Mental Health clinic and after some preliminaries he was admitted to
their wing. I was very thankful for this because we were not able to help
him. It's a wonderful center and I'm sure he will get good care. It's very
sad to see someone suffer the way David has been, it makes us think
back over everything in the past, and it's not hard to find contributing
factors and past symptoms.

May 25
Rainy, some sun in AM, asparagus finally up and in a few days can be
cut. Jean [Boardman], Becky [Boardman], Betsy and Julian [Smith]
are here, we went up to Shangri-la [summer house in village] to the
Wason's auction together. In the afternoon David called and was very
insistent about coming home. It upset and frightened me a lot. We went
out to dinner with the Bonds at Phil's drive-in. I was too worried to
enjoy it a lot. I talked to the nurse at 10:00 and she said he had slept a lot.

May 26
Talked to David and he seems somewhat better. Boardmans came
down for potluck supper, it was really nice. I called Dave, and Jen and
Matty talked to him. Jenny went to Stowe school.

May 27
Mostly cool, wet, depressing, Monday the Boardmans visited Dave and later Annie, Mac Parker, and I went down, he was doing pretty well. Tuesday Lori visited him, he's getting lots of cards and phone calls.

May 30
Still cool, Jenny left at 4:15 AM to go with Mike B[ussiere], Jeff S[koller], and Joe LaBerge to the Boston area to look at schools. Annie and Matt did chores and then finished preparing for their trips. Annie and Sam went with Jim [Kenary] and a group to the White Mts. to hike and camp for 7 days. Matty went with Dave Magnus and a group to bike to Greensboro, fish and camp. Poor David missed his trip to Nova Scotia, which he had been looking forward to for so long. Lori [Laird] and Duncan took that group, Lori was dreading the long driving part.

June 4
David came home over the weekend, I went down Saturday afternoon and brought him. He had a good time and seemed very much better. He played tennis a lot and planted his pumpkins. I took him back Sunday and had supper with him. The weather was good finally, Monday I planted more seeds and worked in the garden. Tuesday George and I brought David home from the hospital. He is better but he has a long way to go, I think, to get himself all together. He doesn't seem to remember well or be able to concentrate on things or stick to anything very long. The garden looks good, most things are up, peas growing really well, some early corn up, eating radishes. The last few days have been warm and summery.

June 14
The past week has been warm and lovely, sometimes hot, things are growing like mad. We are in a summer schedule now, kids working part time. Sam is living partly on the sugar hill and partly here, not working regularly. David doesn't feel he can cope with work or responsibility here, however he is doing odds and ends. Yesterday George asked him if he wanted to rake, he did want to try and did pretty well. Jenny has moved to the sugar house hill with Nancy [Wason], and

working part time here. The Bonds moved in to their new house and are very excited.

June 21
The summer is busy, Annie went down to Concord [Mass.] to visit Molly [Dawson] for a week, Matty went to Skollers for two days, David is doing Annie's chores. George hired two fellows who are staying at Martin's pond this summer, they are working part time.

Sometime last week George told me about a plan he had for expansion and improvement of our farm. He would like to buy the Miller farm and build a milking parlor there with a free stall set up. He talked to the Millers and they seemed interested. The kids seem to approve. If we did that we would sell Ron's [Cochran] house and they would live here. I somehow thought I would always live here so it is a little hard for me to picture changing.

June 27
Last weekend we (Sam, Matt, Dave, George, and I) went down to Dummerston to a party which was given by the Baldwins and others, it was fun, we saw many friends. We have been over to the Millers with the kids now and they seem quite excited with the idea of buying the farm and living there. We went to the bank and we can get the down payment of $34,000 and their support but they do think it's quite a risk to try to keep up with the payments. David and I went to Hanover to see Dr. Gallagher. He is going to try a lot less medicine as Dave has been getting along quite well.

July 7
We've been trying to hay it seems to rain when we get anything down. The kids spent some time at the three day Banjo Festival at Burke this weekend. Annie, Jenny, and Sam went Friday and came back Sunday, David went up Friday for a while, they really enjoyed it.

It's been really hard trying to decide about buying the Miller farm. I'm happy here and the pressure of all those payments is scary, but the idea of building a parlor there and using that farmland is challenging and

George has been very excited about it. Beth and Dave Dawson this weekend both pointed out to me that a big change is often very good for people stimulating their lives in many ways. They gave me a little different outlook and a little courage. So George asked Richard if we could buy about 100 acres, 70 tillage, and 30 woodland with house and barn for $145,000. Richard said he would take a day to think about it.

July 8
Eloise and Richard Miller came over here tonight and said they had agreed to sell to us at the price George had suggested: we gave them $4000 as a binder with the down payment to be paid in January. We drank some of Jenny's dandelion wine and toasted to each others happiness. It sure is scary but exciting and challenging.

July 15
Busy days, we have had people contacting us to buy land already and one outfit ready to sell us a milking parlor. Phil Carruth is dying for the piece of land on Ha-Penny Street and we'll sell it to him if Hummons don't mind. We finally got some hay weather and we were able to get in a lot of good hay. The whole family worked very hard also Jim Keeney. The garden is growing very well we've had Peas several times.

We sold Serge and Doris Hummon the land they built on, which adjoined the piece Phil wanted.

Aug 2
Many things happen and I neglect to write them down. Sammy has been gone for two weeks now with Cary Aiken hitchhiking to the west coast to visit Ben Keeney in the Portland region. He has sent a number of postcards and seems to be having a good time.

Aug 6
Sam called last night, he is getting slightly homesick, he leaves today to come homeward. Jim Keeney is sick, Ron is on vacation, so we are short handed. David is now working full time and seems to be getting along okay. Saturday George went to a farm auction and was fortunate

enough to buy a milking parlor for $2000, which is a great buy as long as everything is in good shape, a new one would cost about $14000. Today we all go over and pick up parts of it.

Last week Matthew's all star team played in the Lyndonville tournament. Matty pitched the first game against Lancaster. Rick Phelps from Ryegate pitched most of the second and Matt finished it against Lyndonville and they won it. In the finals they played Newport, Matty pitched 6 innings and Newport beat them in a close game, 7 to 6. I felt bad that Matt couldn't be the winning pitcher, they played well and were good sports.

Aug 7
Georgie and I went to town today to pick out a new refrigerator, also did birthday shopping for Matty. Saw Bobby Blanchard at the Danville store and he is looking for a job. He is coming over tomorrow to see about it. We had a really nice party for Matty. The Boardmans and Hummons and Aunt Fran were here. We had steak cooked on the grill and ate at two picnic tables.

Aug 8
This was a big day, President Nixon resigned. The news was filtered through the day, but it was not really definite until tonight at 9:00 when Nixon made his speech. The speech avoided all mention of guilt or criminality. He said he was resigning because he no longer had the support of Congress. He was doing what he thought was best for the country.

George hired Bobby Blanchard who will start next week, he will work 8 to 5 mostly on the milking parlor and free stalls. We just interviewed Ben Berwick for a full time farm job. We would have to find housing for him for the coming year until they could use the tenant house when the Cochrans move here. He and his wife [Jean] seemed very interested but didn't give us a definite answer.

GERALD FORD SWORN IN AS PRESIDENT

Ben Berwick Sr. came to me and said his son Ben was not happy with his job on a farm in the Newport, Vt. area, and he would make me a good man. Ben turned out to be an excellent worker, particularly intuitive and handy with equipment and a very nice person to work with.

Aug 9
Jenny left early this morning to drive to Montreal to meet Kyle and Kevin [Lewis] at the airport flying in from Hawaii. Chris Marcotte went with her. They plan to all stay overnight and come back tomorrow. They want some time to have fun in Montreal.

Aug 12
This was a beautiful day weather-wise but weird in some ways. Jen called Saturday from the border on the Burlington side saying they had been caught with Marijuana hidden in the car. They couldn't bring the car away until George went up or signed a statement saying he knew nothing about the drug being in the car. They got a ride home with friends of Kevin's, Jenny also lost all her money, $70. I was very cross because I thought Jen's freedom had really been abused, it could have been such a great weekend.

Sunday morning after Matty and Matt Skoller came down from the woodlot, having camped overnight, they started down to the So. Peacham brook to swim. Matt S fell off the bike and came back to me with what looked like a broken arm. I called his family and we met at the hospital. It was broken. Also yesterday Ben Berwick called to say he'd like to come to work for us. Now we have to find housing. It really makes me feel nervous to think of providing a living from this farm for a whole second or third family, it seems our milk checks won't do it.

Aug 14
Monday Jenny and Chris went up to get the car. Pete O'Boyle signed the statements and notarized them. Jen got the car and didn't have to

pay a fine after all. This morning Tiggsy [cat] had three small infants, we thought she was ready yesterday. In the middle of the night Jenny left with June Hendricks and friends to go to a concert in N.J. I was not too happy about it but I let her go.

I traded Pete O'Boyle a set of small harrows I had bought at the Hooker auction for straightening the mess out at the Canadian border.

Aug 15

I showed land yesterday to some friends of the Dawson's, it was strange since I have never done that before. They were very interested in the land below the Bond's, they would not build in the Bond's view, I'm pretty sure, and would not build anyway for a while. I looked at the Frye house in hopes to rent it for the Ben Berwick family. The Hummons have not gotten back to us and Phil is getting edgy and so am I. Jenny got home late last night. Sammy called from Syracuse and said he would be home soon.

Aug 27

Again so many things have happened I should have kept up better. Sammy got home, he'd had a very interesting trip. He was glad to get home. I was able to get the Frye house for the Berwicks. Dick's family, Dick and Vivian [Gulick] and daughters Robin and Wendy arrived Tuesday and stayed 'til Sunday. We did lots of things and enjoyed them very much. I hope they had a good time. I was disappointed in Jen and Annie's attitude however, I thought they were not too hospitable.

Friday George took the boys to the White Mts. camping. It was too bad they left when Dick was here but it was the only time they could do it. Jen took them over on Friday and picked them up Sunday. They had a wonderful time. Saturday I took Dick's family to Stowe through Smugglers Notch, we had fun. Sunday I showed land to friends of Dorcas Gill's, they loved the land below Bonds. They were really nice people. Gretchen is very upset that we might sell that land.

Aug 28
*We took Sam over to UVM [University of Vermont] and he got settled
in his room and we looked around campus a bit. Then we went off to
a picnic and went to cocktails and dinner with many other parents of
freshmen. It was an excellent affair, well run with superb food. The
president of the college gave a short speech, we saw Sammy afterwards
and he seemed really happy, I hope he will be.*

Sept 2
*Labor Day. We've a lot of blackberries and have made jams and pies.
Wednesday afternoon we, all except Sam, went to Maine for two and
a half days. We stayed at the Fuehrer's cottage on Orrs Island. The
weather was poor but we stopped one day at LLBean, Portland Stove
factory, Bass Shoes, etc., had fun and bought some things. Friday
morning we did get to a beach, Popham Beach, and everyone except
myself went swimming. It was very cold and everyone got numb, but
they had fun. We came home Friday afternoon, went up to Boardman's.
We are bringing our land deal with Phil [Carruth] to finality very
soon. The Dawson Friends [Sidney and Anne Wanzer] are very serious
about the land below Bonds and the Boardmans want the Lower
Johnson piece, so we might just finish with land transactions for a few
years if all goes through.*

*Sam came home with a friend from UVM yesterday. It was fun to have
them, the friend was very nice and Sam seems extremely happy.*

Sept 9
*Yesterday we all went over to Lafayette camp ground and from there
hiked up Mtn. Lafayette. It was very hard going for me but it was beautiful and we had a picnic on the top looking out toward the Presidential
Range. There were a few clouds and some mist but you could see about
everything. We had hoped Sam would be home to go with us but he
didn't come home.*

*I guess mom is definitely coming to Vermont soon to stay in an apart-
ment in the science building for a while. We want her to do this and
hope it works out well. This last week Julie Clark has been staying*

with us to enter the Peacham School and find a place to board. So we have seen Jean and Don [Clark] and had a little time to visit. The Boardmans finished their vacation last weekend. Corinne has a job at the Middlebury Inn and will start Sept 15th.

Sept 24
Last week mom arrived, Jenny and I went down to meet her plane in Lebanon. On the way down I asked Jenny why I had heard Diane O'Boyle refer twice to Annie and Craig [Marcotte] and Jenny said they had been going together since last winter and she told me quite a lot about it. I was really shocked at the information and also that I could have been oblivious of it for so long.

Mom has not been to our house yet. She likes her apartment and is enjoying herself except she has had a cold. We have had a really good garden, I think, Saturday and Sunday we harvested our potatoes and onions and squash and yesterday I brought in tomatoes and peppers, I have not canned tomatoes but we have been eating them since early Aug.

Dec 8
It's too bad I let things go by so long without writing but it seems so busy.

1975

"There are so many things that happen that
I wish would never go out of my mind."

THIS YEAR OF 1975 WAS A VERY BUSY, DIFFICULT,
emotionally draining year, the worst thing was that Matty had
a bad accident while gathering sap; he broke both legs. It was hard
on everyone but hardest on Patty. With her professional training
she took the lead and then was never sure that the help that Matty
got was as good as it would have been in Hanover or some other
hospital, and so she worried and felt responsible herself that the
bones wouldn't knit well. As with last year, I was never aware of the
pressure she felt about this or of the anxiety she had about making
the move to the Miller farm, which we did in June after the Millers
moved out and we had some renovations done on the house.

We converted the Miller barn from a 2nd floor wooden stable
where the cows were tied in stanchions and milked with machines
that were carried from cow-to-cow, to a modern, ground-floor free-
stall with a milking parlor. I got the parlor at an auction in Berlin,
Vermont. It was a major step forward, and the cost was as follows:

250 yards concrete	12,260
Labor for Dennis, Bob, Cary	4,662
Labor and materials for Buddy McLam	2,250
Parlor	2,000
Dividers	600
Bulk tank	1,200
Barn yard and feed bunk	1,400
Total (does not include farm help)	**$24,345**

Buddy McLam, an exceptionally capable person from West Barnet that we got to know soon after we moved to Peacham, was an invaluable help in this project. He was an electrician, plumber, and everything in between. I wouldn't have bid on the parlor at the auction in Berlin if Buddy hadn't told me he would take the technical part of the parlor down and put it back up when we were ready. Buddy died young from cancer, he was one-of-a-kind, irreplaceable. It would have been very difficult to have done everything we did without his help.

Dennis Kauppila, Bobby Blanchard, and Cary Marcotte worked exclusively on the barn renovation so their wages were figured in to the cost. The rest of us worked on the project when we weren't doing regular farm work. Ben Berwick should get special mention for his ability to maneuver the John Deere Crawler-loader in the cellar of that big old barn as he carried the cement in for the curbs for the stalls and the walkway. Ron Cochran's job was made more challenging with having to teach the cows to come into the parlor as well as to learn how to milk in it himself. Patty and all the kids worked hard and did their part except Matty, who wished he could take part. It was a learning experience for all of us. With this new free stall barn to replace the old stanchions we'd had in the village, the farm stepped into the 20th century.

We also needed to make some renovations to the farmhouse. There was no fireplace in the house, and the old system for heating water off a kerosene stove was inadequate. We added a chimney between the dining room and the kitchen, with a wood cookstove on the kitchen side and a fireplace in the dining room. We installed a hot water heater in the basement.

House Renovation:

Fireplace and replacing chimney, Armstrong	1,105
Kitchen, Quimby labor and materials	760
Bathroom shower (built in)	1,048
Hot water heater	300
Total	**$3,213**

History of the Miller Farm

1776
General William Chamberlain having retired from the Revolutionary War had become a surveyor, and while surveying Peacham had selected the site that had now become our home to build his house on. The combination of the quality of the land and the view makes it easy to understand why he chose this site.

1780
Chamberlain cleared land and built a house and moved his family up from Connecticut. He held many offices, including Congressman, and he was noted as a farmer for his design of a very efficient whiskey still. We learned that the pasture below the farm was called the Still Lot. He also is famous for introducing Witch Grass, and farmers curse the persistence of Witch Grass in their corn fields to this day.

1857
William Chamberlain's son Ezra sold the farm to Ashbel Martin. Ashbel had just returned from California and the Gold Rush and bought the farm with his earnings. In the same year he married Hannah Wesson of Danville. Soon after they moved on to the farm they remodeled the existing house and built an addition in the Greek Revival style.

Their main barn burned in 1897, and they rebuilt a grand big barn which they were able to finish in two years using lumber sawn at the Martin's Pond sawmill at a cost of $12.50 per 1000 board feet. The lumber was all sawed to their dimensions, and they paid for no waste. This is the barn that we remodeled, and it was the extra large dimensions that made it possible for us to use the free-stall design. The most uncommon dimension was the 20-foot-wide hay mow that allowed for a 7-foot stall on the back wall plus adequate room for an alleyway, and a 14-foot-wide middle section allowing for a double row of stalls, and then the section next to the front wall for the second alleyway. Barns are still being built with this same free-stall design.

Ashbel Martin died at age 69, a year after this barn was built in 1899, and his youngest son William took over the farm. William married Agnes May Shaw in 1905 and they had one child, Caroline. William was killed in a horse-related accident in June 1937.

1937
This area was still struggling from the Great Depression, and there was little market for a farm when William died. Richard Miller was appointed executor of the estate, and not being able to find another buyer, he bought the farm himself. He worked this farm for 37 years, he and his wife Eloise raised five children, she taught at the Academy and he was a trustee of the Academy as well as a Selectman. Richard was a graduate engineer, but because of the Depression hadn't been able to find a job in his field. He was a good farmer but would perhaps have been happier in the occupation he had trained for. He and Eloise were very pleased that we were buying the farm (1975).

Our lives, the children's lives were expanding beyond the farm and family, and Patty's journal reflects that. She writes about more people, more incidents, in more detail. From here on I am going to leave out the more mundane parts.

Jan 14, 1975

Here it is again with more than a month gone by. Our Christmas was nice, we had a lovely time getting the tree with horses and some on skis. It was a lovely big tree which we really enjoyed. I felt bad taking it down since it would be the last Christmas for us in this house.

Christmas Eve on the way home from Burke Mtn. with a bus load of kids, Jen lost the brakes on the Volkswagen and had a slight collision. It was actually very lucky since it could have happened in a much worse place. No one was hurt and it turned out that the damage was estimated at $1000. We have already received the insurance check and are waiting for the work to be finished.

Sam was home for about a month, it was nice. He worked quite a bit for George and got in some skiing and partying with his friends. The work on the Miller barn is coming along well. They have poured cement several times, are putting in the dividers in the free stall room, there are a lot of expenses. On January 3rd we sold the fire pond property to Anne and Sydney Wanzer, the land they had wanted.

About a month ago I talked to Diane O'Boyle on the phone and she told me that she and Pete had separated and she is living with Chris Marcotte. I was really shocked. Last Friday Craig [Marcotte] came to Peacham to stay a few days. We didn't allow Annie to go to a party at O'Boyle's, partly because of Craig, and partly because she had to get up at 4:00 AM to go to Boston. She was upset and Jenny more so. Yesterday George spoke to Craig about Annie and Craig's relationship. I guess he still feels he loves her. I don't think Annie does anymore.

Jan 16

George and I borrowed $35,000 from the Danville bank and gave Richard and Eloise $36,000 down payment on the farm. There were *many papers to be signed and it took quite a while to do everything. It's exciting and scary and it does feel different now we actually have a deed. We will be paying the Millers about $6,000 twice a year for 15 years. This will be hard, we will have to sell more land to accomplish this.*

Jan 20
We had a pleasant weekend on. We went to a dinner party at Hamilton Slaight's (Susan O'Brien's father) which was lovely. I went x-c skiing yesterday with Lori [Laird]. We've had some below zero weather lately, it is the first real cold we've had. There is very little snow this winter so far, the ski tow hasn't even opened and George and I haven't had our downhill skis on yet.

Jan 23
20˚ below zero, yesterday I took care of Bob and Belinda Blanchard's baby all day, I do that every Monday. (Bob brings him when he comes to work.) George is in the woods now getting some logs out for work on the barn, he is enjoying being in our new woods.

Feb 5
10 degrees snowing, yesterday 20˚ below, very busy days. The kids have been having at least two basketball games a week which makes them very tired. They are playing a lot better and they are really enjoying it. Last week were try outs for "Godspell." Jenny and David tried out and both got parts, but yesterday Jenny decided not to do it. It will involve lots of time and energy and she felt she didn't want to be that involved.

Feb 19
It warmed up and was lovely over the weekend. The ski tow was open, 2nd week, and everyone had fun.

Last Wednesday a French Canadian girl came to stay with us through Sunday AM. This was an exchange program that Danville High School initiated and Peacham French students hosted some of the guests. Our guest was Clair and we enjoyed having her. She worked hard at

English and did well but we had to put effort into communicating. Annie and David weren't able to speak French to her very effectively.

Bob Blanchard stopped working for us several weeks ago, we were a little disappointed but George says that it will work out okay and also cut down on the wages to be paid out. I've been worrying a little about Jenny the last few months because she's very moody and has rather violent emotional outbreaks. Also, just in the past few weeks, David seems less stable than he has been for a while. He has had some of the symptoms that he had last spring, loss of weight, restlessness, emotional ups and downs, I hope he feels better, it's hard to know what to do to help.

Mar 4
Yesterday was our 19th wedding anniversary, it really doesn't seem possible. This time of year always seems low to me, I feel depressed and without much energy or ambition. We have so much work to get done this spring.

Mar 12
Last weekend all of us, except Sammy who came home to take care of the house, drove to Boston to get the kids started on their concentration weeks. Becky [Boardman] guided us downtown to Boston Garden where Larry [Skoller] and Matty tried to make contact with the manager of the Celtics. They were unsuccessful but planned to do it the next day.

In the morning we drove to Loey's [Ringquist], picked up Loey and the girls and with Loey directing, drove to Logan Airport. We watched Annie embark on the big Jet to Bermuda, it was exciting and made us feel funny to watch her off like that.

We left at 5:30, got to Phil's Drive in at 8:45, had dinner and got home at 10:00. There was a very nice note from Sammy... Monday David went off on his x-c trip, I watched them all go off across the yard. I hope all the kids have a wonderful concentration week.

Monday–I worked here trying to get caught up. Jeff Skoller is spending concentration working here which helps a lot with the farm since all the kids are gone.

Tuesday–I drove to Northfield and picked up Gretchen and her girls and we came back to Peacham. The day was fun, I really enjoyed it. It did have a surprise ending however, as I backed out of Gretchen's driveway the clutch cable snapped. I couldn't believe something else had happened to the car, so we left it there and have all had supper here.

Wednesday – George took the VW down to Bill Cook. I worked in the house all day, baking, cleaning, had dinner at the Hummon's.

Thursday – The house was beginning to seem a bit sad without the kids.

Friday – Ben took me to McIndoe [Falls] to get the VW. David came home in PM. He had a good week skiing and being with his group.

Mar 15
Last night it snowed 8 inches and it is very deep all around. Jen, Matty, Larry, arrived in Barnet by bus around 2PM and I went down for them. They were very excited about their week. The boys had made good communication with the Celtics and had attended games and practice and had traveled from Boston to Hartford to one game on the bus with the players. They got to know some of the men and had a great time. Also they saw eight movies. Jenny had a good time too but not so spectacular. She enjoyed Loey and Nathan's [Grey] home and friends and got around Boston some, shopping, going to museums, 2 movies and one Celtics game.

I drove to UVM and picked up Sammy and we went to the airport. We watched the plane that Annie was on land from the beautiful evening sky and we watched her get off and wave to us. I was very happy to see her safe home again.

I think this week was a marvelous experience for everyone. We started the week out all being together and then gradually all went in different directions, having completely different experiences. Then we gradually all got back together and all of us are here again, the kids seem very happy to be home, but they had a change from one another and have a lot to share. I think we are very fortunate.

Mar 16
4°-45° This morning Tiggs produced three kittens. It's almost as if she waited for the kids to come home. She seemed so ready all last week. Today was a work day, but it was nice to have everyone home. It was beautiful and sunny, I went x-c skiing with Dave Dawson and his Matthew, it was lovely but hard to wax for. We had a kind of special dinner because we were all back together again. Sam stayed overnight.

Mar 17
18°-25° Beautiful day. Sewage problems, Yuk. George started tapping today, Dennis [Kauppila] is working now part-time for us. Most of the kids helped tap after school.

Mar 18
18°-45° Lovely day, George tapping, Dave, Matt, and I went to St J to the dentist, to shop, and to get David new glasses, we were all cavity free.

Mar 19
27°-45° We only got a slight peek at the sun today, it was mostly cloudy. The wind came up in the afternoon and the rain began in the evening. Annie talked to Craig today and told him her feeling for him had changed. Women's Fellowship.

Mar 20
40°-45° It poured rain all night, George found the barn quite flooded this morning. It rained much of the day and then cooled and turned windy and there were snow flurries. The crew gathered and George boiled the first sap, made 7 or 8 gallons of beautiful fancy syrup.

Mar 21
12°-20° Windy, cold, sunny, Package Day, Matty and Jen went on an all-day trek, snowshoes and skis, Annie on Vt. Wisdom, David Gospel

[?]. George went to the Peacham schools trust meeting, it was long and tedious. They read all the suggestions that had been sent in by parents and students. They then voted whether or not they'd approve the school continuing another year. It was an affirmative vote 9 to 4.

Package Day was a school event where the kids chose an activity to participate in.

Mar 22
15°-30° The day started out really beautifully but turned cloudy and then rained. We had a picnic together at the woodlot, cooked venison and fried potatoes, it was fun. I skied all around on the crust, with a little snow on top, Annie and Jenny snowshoed. George and I visited Richard and Eloise at their new house.

Richard and Eloise Miller built on land behind the big barn that they reserved from the sale of their property to us.

Mar 23
29°-32° George and I went to church. George had to file my wedding ring off because my finger was so swollen, it really bothered me. It was sad to see it cut but it felt so much better.

Mar 25
31°-48° Part of the afternoon was beautiful then it rained hard, cleared and we had a lovely rainbow. Men gathered sap, George boiled, made about 40 gals. Robert [Bartell] and Nancy [Wason] came to dinner, they will marry May 31st.

Mar 26
The weather got colder and windy all day, some snow flurries and some sun. Sam and George gathered, George boiled and canned.

Mar 27
3-8 degrees below zero. Stayed cold and windy all day. Last night was awful, evidently the temperature at Mtn. Washington was 80° below. I

washed syrup cans that George had filled and distributed some. George
and the men cut wood up at Keeney's.

Mar 28
8°-30° Men cut wood; I took Matty to look at a motorcycle he
wanted to buy.

Mar 29
0°-30° Nice in the morning, became cloudy, rained some. Matt and
I went to St J picked up Fran, drove to Agway picked up corn seed and
twine, back to St J where Matty bought the Honda motorcycle.

Mar 30
Easter, cool, cloudy, I went to church. Jen made pizza for supper, the
Bonds came and we watched slides.

Mar 31
18°-25° Miserable, cold, snowy day, I feel depressed on days like
this. George and Dennis [Kauppila] cut wood; Ben went to Maine
for sawdust.

April 2
18°-40° Sap ran some. There was a joint meeting of the trustees of the
school and the parents and students following a pot luck supper. People
brought out their feelings about the school and there was a lot of conflict
and emotion regarding various things.

I was a trustee of the Peacham School.

Apr 3
25°-30° Snowed during the night and all day, 8 to 10 inches, driving
was slippery and bad.

Apr 4
Snowed more, blew, kids are out of school because of the storm.

Apr 9
Men working on big barn with sugaring at a standstill. I drove to
Burlington with Corinne Lederer, had lunch and then went to her
hairdresser and had my hair cut. He did a quite good job and it looks
pretty good, very short. I still didn't have enough hair for a hair piece.

Apr 10
When I got home the family were so cute. They were all shocked because
I looked so different, such reactions. They thought I looked younger and
"cute." Georgie was very complimentary.

Apr 11 and 12
Great sap weather, Sam came home with Andrea Stover, she gathered
with all the kids, Sam helped George boil and can.

Apr 16
Lots of good sap weather, have made over 200 gals. of fancy and A.

Apr 21
Matt went with George to an Auction near Newport, they were looking
at the bulk tank but it sold with the real estate. They bought a few
small things.

Apr 23
27°-60° Another lovely day, snow going, although there are still big
piles around this house and in the fields in back. The girls and I went
to Miller's to check out the garden this morning and then went back
in the afternoon and raked much of the yard. It was fun to be there
working around, the girls worked in bare feet. The boys gathered sap,
George boiled; Molly Dawson came.

Apr 24
35°-45° Rained in the morning stayed cloudy in the afternoon, George
boiled although he had to wait for the oil truck to come. The kids all
went out this afternoon, gathered sap and pulled buckets, they had a

great team, Ben, Dennis, Matty K, Matty Sk [Skoller], Annie, Jen, and Molly, David milked.

Apr 28
This was a different day in our lives. I had gone to Montpelier with Gretchen and while we were at Judy's visiting Jen called to say Matty had been taken to the hospital with a possible broken leg. I called the hospital and talked with Dr Rowe, he said Matty had two broken legs, one would have to be in traction, it was a rough shock. When we got home we heard more of the details although some of it was rather fuzzy. It seems that the boys had some alcohol while they were siphoning the sap into the tank.

On the way along the dirt road Ronny [Craig] was driving with Matt Skoller on the tractor with him, he hit a bump and Matty was thrown off and under the trailer, the boys knew he was badly hurt, covered him, put him on the back of the trailer. Then Lou Poggi [?] happened to come along and brought Matt Skoller to the house, got Ben and Dennis and David. Ben called the Danville Rescue Squad and then went out to the boys, they were all scared and upset of course.

George and I went in right after supper. Matty was very depressed and in some shock. At one point his color got bad and his blood pressure went way down and it scared me terribly. I decided to stay overnight, I came home for some stuff and went back. I stayed 'till noon when Jen came in and got me. Jim [Craig] had already come in. Right from the start Matty had a lot of company.

Jamie Craig had sap that he didn't want to boil and asked if I would take it. I was reluctant to take it but Jamie said his son Ronny would bring it to our sugar house with their tractor and gathering rig. Matt was riding on the trailer hitched to the tractor.

May 1
The past few days one could have made syrup, but George quit last Friday and now the buckets are all washed and the sugar house closed. We made 300 gals. There are still spots of snow, but it is almost gone.

I went to see Dr Rowe to find out how things looked for the bones healing. He said they should be okay but it would take a long time, 2 months in traction, 4 or more in body cast and whatever later. I've heard a lot of flack about Dr Rowe and have been somewhat worried. The Stetsons say he wasn't perfect but I should stick with him and have faith. Liza [Dawson] went with me to town. There were so many kids waiting to see [Matty] that we didn't stay. He seemed in better spirits.

George harrowed and stoned on the big field across the road from the Miller farm, he plowed it last November.

May 2
I went to the hospital, went down to x-ray to see Dr Neel and have him show me the x-rays of Matty's legs. The break in the right leg looks bad, it's obvious that it will take a long time to heal. I toss around in my mind asking for an orthopedic consultation, I'd like it but it is tricky in a small hospital like this.

May 3
Lovely day, George and I went to the Livingston's auction, we bought the bulk tank for $1200. Then we went over to the Hill farm and we girls planted seeds, and George and Sam went fishing. After dinner Julie [Clark] and David cleaned up and the rest of us went to the hospital. Matt was in the best spirits that I've seen him.

The Livingston farm was in East Peacham next to Moore's farm. It had gone out of business. The Hill farm is what we called our new farm that we bought from the Millers.

May 4
We decided that Jenny would move over to the Hill farm because the Millers are sleeping in their new house and their antiques are setting in the old one. It seemed a bit risky, anyway Jen wanted to do it. It turned out that Kyle's [Lewis] mother has to go to California, so Kyle will stay there with Jenny; they moved and slept there tonight. Lois Post asked how Matty seemed to me because she was suspicious that

the kids had brought him something, that would be bad in every way, if Dr Rowe found out he'd not allow Matt any friends in; I must find out what's what.

May 10

This whole week has been warm and springy, although we really need rain. George is plowing at the Hill farm, the cows went out yesterday. A lot has happened with our "new" house. The Quimbys [Jim and Gary] put the new big window in the kitchen and started the other renovations, the window is great, you can see the lovely view from everywhere in the kitchen. Roger Armstrong came, and in looking at the old chimney recommended that it come down, so yesterday they took it down and put in cement for the base of the fireplace. The wood stove in the kitchen will back up to the exposed bricks of the chimney.

It would be nice if one could store up memories to be brought accurately back to mind at will. There are so many things that happen that I wish would never go out of my mind, small episodes with the children, things they said or did, or just how they looked at a certain time. This morning Annie came out of the barn to feed the horses. It is a beautiful spring morning, blue sky, sun shining on everything and she looks so pretty with her long hair pulled up out of the way of her work, red shirt and dungarees. She just waved at me out there, perhaps she can see me through the window, or she just saw I'm in here watching her. Now she has jumped on to Orlando's back for a few minutes.

May 13

Saturday was a fund raising day [Peacham Alternative School] and it was great fun. There were some booths, used clothing, handmade items, food, games, an auction, the band played a few songs from Godspell, beautiful helium balloons, lunch, I think they made money and it should have created good spirits.

George plowed in-between chores. Sunday Jenny went to church with me for Mother's Day, she came rushing down from the Hill farm and it sure made me feel good. David, Annie, George, and I played tennis, Jen went to see Matty, brought Aunt Fran home for the afternoon. Monday

I worked around then took Annie in to help Matty with Algebra. He had a lot of company after that, Jim [Kenary], kids, the Hummons. Bernadine's [Churchill] baby was born, boy.

Bernadine Churchill was 13 years old when her son Jonathan was born, he was raised by his grandparents on a farm that is down the hill from the Miller farm we had just purchased, and he has worked for us since he was a teenager, which is now about 25 years.

May 14
Beautiful day, leaves are beginning to come out, some things up in the garden, daffodils at their peak. George preparing corn land, Sam working full time now as Ron's [Craig] partner, milking, Dennis [Kauppila] is still with us. Fireplace is all finished except trim, and it is beautiful.

May 15
I worked all morning then Doris [Hummon] and I went to town did some errands and visited Matty. He seems so quiet and serious, it is natural that he would but we miss our happier Matty.

May 20
60°-90° It was hot last night like summer, the weekend was sunny and warm. George plowed Saturday, we went to see Matty Saturday night. Sunday we played tennis, fishing, picnicking, etc. George and I were tense with each other. I feel really depressed because there is so much to do because of Matty, and I sometimes wonder why we got into this whole thing. Financially we are getting really bad off and this transition is hard for me to make now that I've come face to face with it. I look at all the neat things we have done to this [village] house to suit our family and I feel badly to leave. There is no question that the other house offers some special things, but there is so much to do. Tea at Helen Wallace's for Nancy [Wason].

May 21

62°-92° Hot, apple blossoms coming out, asparagus coming up, all small garden stuff up, even corn. The Millers are getting back into moving now. The kids have been swimming in our brook on the hill farm, they bathe there because there is no hot water anywhere in the house. We've never owned land with a brook before.

May 22

It finally rained some last night and cooled a bit. I'm sure it was not nearly enough rain.

May 23

I spent all day in town shopping and visiting Matty, and he did some reading tests that Lori asked him to do. He had so many different people come in, it is a rather amazing experience for him to converse with everyone. Young and older people tell him interesting anecdotes about their hospitalizations and other things, Bob Fuehrer has been in and shown him pictures of his round the world trip and of some new thing they are working on at his plant. It is giving Matty a whole new world of things to think about. Also Matt finished his first complete book on his own, Wild Trek *by Jim Kilgard which Sam gave him to read.*

May 25

I visited with the Boardmans in the morning and took them over to see the hill farm. The Dawsons stopped when I was mowing the lawn in the afternoon and I took them over. George harrowed the 20 acre piece.

June 3

We've been busy since I last wrote, George finished planting corn May 30. Godspell was given Thursday and Friday nights, I saw it both times, it was fantastic. Everyone loved it. Saturday we all went to Nancy's wedding at 2:30. It was a nice simple ceremony and a pleasant reception. We all then went to the hospital to visit Matty and have a birthday celebration for Georgie. We all went in together and got him a good camera which Serge [Hummon] picked out for me in New York.

Sunday George and I painted in our new kitchen, Jenny worked in the garden and both girls got ready for their trek. In the evening they had a little hootenanny at the new house. Monday the girls went off on their treks, David went with the drama group to get ready for the performance at the Star Theatre [Godspell]. It was a great success, the theatre was quite full and the audience responded well.

June 5
Yesterday George finished spraying the corn. We've been eating asparagus for over a week. Today George finished seeding the two pieces below the corn on the Bay farm.

The name of our new farm seems to have changed from Hill farm to Bay farm.

June 6
The weather has been cool and rainy most of the week. I feel so sorry for the trekkers, when we had such great weather for so long. The weather has been great for agriculture however, the spraying of the corn is finished.

June 7
Rained all day yesterday, most of the night, still raining. Evidently Jenny's trek group was picked up by the Skollers and taken to see Godspell in North Strafford.

June 9
Jenny did get home Friday night, Annie got home Saturday, they all had a good time despite the weather. Sunday the family moved over some of the big things and did a little more settling. Jen, Sam and I went to a house warming party for the Millers, it was a surprise, it was very nice.

July 7
It's too bad I haven't written in all this time, but it's been so busy and I've been very tired. Here are some special dates:

June 10
Moved major things, worked all week cleaning and moving odds and ends, it was very hard and tiring, Lori helped.

June 12
Jenny's Graduation, very nice evening, gave Jen a small camera, Jean and Don [Clark] stayed overnight.

June 29
We brought Matty home in the pickup. We all went in to get him. The nurses gave him a big send off, with a blue ribbon etc. They thought he was a fantastic patient. It was so great to have him home. We have to move him around on a stretcher. We got a hospital bed, bedside table, and stretcher from the American Legion.

June 26
Forgot! We went to Jim's (Kenary) for Jim and my joint birthday dinner, fun.

Patty had arranged with the kids for Serge Hummon to buy a camera for me on my birthday, if I did anything for hers, it couldn't have been much. Once again I dropped the ball, Patty obviously needed my love and support, we would each have been 44 years old.

June 29
Bonds and Magnuses for dinner.

July 1
Said goodbye to the Bonds, they are off to Vienna again, seems strange and sad.

Dec 18
Here has been a huge gap in my writing. The last months have been extremely busy and difficult. First I should begin with the best things. George has gotten most of the work done on the barn. In mid July he started using the parlor. The first week was wild, but it calmed down

and has been satisfactory. The barn yard is cemented, as well as the inside of the barn, the free stalls are in, the gutter cleaner chain from the Village barn has been put in the new feed bunk as a feed conveyer. I think George has done fantastically well to get this all figured out and put together.

The whole family worked all summer on farm stuff and house and spent time with Matty. Annie pretty much did Matty's work, she enjoyed raking. Jenny completely took charge of the garden and did it very well. Sam and David worked full time for George, David seemed to strengthen through the summer. Then all went off to school.

Jenny had decided to apply to Johnson State in May and was accepted. It was kind of exciting to get her off to college. She had a nice big room to herself which she decorated very well. She did well in her courses but didn't seem to hit it off with people very well, hated the atmosphere and she got very sick with flu in October, got discouraged and came home. She was very emotionally upset because she felt she couldn't stick it out and hated to quit and waste money etc. Jenny felt I needed help which was certainly true. So from mid-October on she has been home. She has helped me lots but has not been very happy. She was trying to think of a job she could get preferably in Burlington where she could also get an apartment and live over there. Nothing worked out for her. There are so many things I should have written.

1976

"I can begin to feel that this is really home."

DESPITE SOME PHYSICAL AND EMOTIONAL LOSSES this year, there was some needed relief from last year's drama. Matty's recovery and attitude were a joy to all of us, and Patty was accepting the new farmhouse as home and finding it possible to relax occasionally. Jim Quimby and his son Gary were doing much-needed renovations on the house. They made a butcher block table from hardwood scraps that the Martins (previous owners of this farm) and Richard Miller had saved over the years. It is still in our kitchen and we love it. It has many scars where Patty and I cut up quarters of beef on it. We had and still do have a book called *The Meat We Eat*, Patty and I would consult it for instructions and discuss how different pieces might be cooked.

We sold more land, easing our financial burden. However, one of the pieces we sold was the Sugar House Hill to Anne and Gordon Mills; apparently Patty couldn't bring herself to write about it. We all loved that hill and its spectacular view, it was a very special place for all of us, we had egg hunts there at Easter, camped, hunted, flew kites, picnicked, tapped the maples and boiled sap in the sugar house. Forty years later we still suffer seller's remorse.

At the Miller farm auction in 1974 we bought nine of Richard's Holstein heifers, we put hay in the barn and wintered them there in what was still the Miller's barn. This summer we bought from a cattle dealer ten Holstein heifers and eight calves. We bred the Miller heifers last winter and they entered the herd as milk cows this fall. When we left the village July 1975 we had about 80 milk cows, this year we had about 100.

We bought a 1969 F 600 Ford truck for $1,200; the Chisel Plows for $1,450; and $1,400 for a new chain for the gutter cleaner that we moved from the Village barn and were now using in our new feed bunk. We also poured a cement floor in the sugar house on the Miller farm in anticipation of moving our evaporator from Sugar House Hill.

Jan 28, 1976
The last five or six days have been hectic and a little traumatic for me in various ways.

Thursday [Jan 22]: Matty has had the body cast finally removed after 6 months and is having Physical Therapy, his leg seems to be okay though it will always be a little shorter. I took the boys out to lunch, when we got home at about 3:00 the temp. had dropped to 10 below and the wind was blowing causing lots of drifting snow. We almost didn't make it up the hill, at 6:00 Jen, Annie, and Bunny, a teacher, rushed in the door, all three with frost bitten noses. The school van had gotten stuck in a drift on a flat before Churchill's and they had walked up. Bunny stayed overnight, the temp when they got home was -18.

Friday [Jan 23]: 30 below zero, the school group finally walked to school, the wind had died down. At breakfast Jenny told us of a plan she had made with Sam[antha] Green to drive with Liz Esser to New Orleans via Ann Arbor Michigan and then to part with Liz and go West by bus and hitchhiking. She was pretty excited.

After lunch and much hassle with things frozen, getting the school van unstuck, starting Becky's [?] car, etc., Sam and Jenny went to town to shop for Jen's trip and David left with Becky on the first leg of his hitching trip to Skidmore to spend the weekend with Sharon [?]. He dressed well for it, but I was worried about the cold.

Saturday [Jan 24]: David called to say he'd gotten a ride from Burlington straight through to Saratoga Springs with some guy going to Albany, he got there around 7:00. This day we took down the hospital bed and table from Annie's room where Matty has spent the last 6 months and put it in the pickup, George and I returned it to the American Legion in Danville. Matty finally moved into his room after all this time. He fixed it really cozy and neat, he really loves it. I had butterflies I was so excited for him. He has been fantastic through all the months of unnormalcy. Each disappointment he took philosophically and each step up he enjoyed and appreciated. He was cheerful, thoughtful, and humorous, he buoyed up our spirits.

Sunday [Jan 25] was a nicer day, George and the girls took a horseback ride in the afternoon and Sammy and I went for a lovely ski hike around the farm through Miller's woods and around our fields, it was so nice. George said he would make supper for us. It was really hectic because Jenny was washing clothes to get ready for her trip, washing hair, baking cookies, finally they left and we had some quiet, but we were very tired.

Monday [Jan 26]: The temp got warm and it rained like mad making the roads very slippery, school was called off. Sam got his stuff all ready to go back to college and then the Volkswagen wouldn't start. Sam worked on it for two hours and then decided to wait 'til Tuesday.

Tuesday [Jan 27]: Bad weather, cold, blowing, freezing, however about 3 PM Sam and Georgie loaded the pickup with Jen's pack and Sam's things. We said good bye to Jen and Sammy and off they went.

Wednesday [Jan 28]: The weather was not too good today but school was back in session. We had word that Jenny and the girls had left Jay's [Craven] place about 9:30.

Jan 29
Annie and David left about 4:00 with the basketball teams and Jim [Kenary] and Bill Marshall for a game in Rochester, it seemed so far to go.

Jan 30
When Annie got up she said she had sprained her ankle early in the game, when she showed it to me it looked bad, as if it could be broken.

I called Dr. Rowe and set up an appointment. We rushed around, ate, Jim was to drive us down to get the pickup and the school van wouldn't start, so we had to call Ron [Cochran] to come over and get us.

It was quite a scene in the hospital, first Annie fell right down on the ice as she got out of the truck, she thought it was very funny. Then when we got there everyone who knew us made comments about another Kempton coming in. Dr. Rowe looked at it, had it x-rayed and found a crack. He then told Annie she would have to stay in the hospital until the swelling went down. So up we went to the 3rd floor.

Jan 31
David and Georgie had to do all the chores. I went in, picked up Fran and visited Annie and took her some things.

Feb 2
It rained hard during the night then became colder, turned to snow and was extremely hazardous driving, no school again. Couldn't visit Annie again today but we talked on the phone, Dr. Rowe put on a walking cast.

Feb 3
Matt and I went in for his appt. and Annie was able to be discharged. It was nice to have her come home.

Feb 4
Annie went to school, her leg feels pretty good, XC with Eloise Miller.

Feb 5
I went to visit Judy [Herbert], we had a good visit, she is still struggling along, it is rough on her in all ways.

Judy and Peter Herbert had separated.

Feb 6
Annie made Pizza for a little party Matty had with Larry, Matt Skoller, Carl [Powden], Casey [Marcotte], Shane [O'Brien], and Jim [Kenary]. They enjoyed the good pizza and then played poker, and Jim played his guitar giving Annie some help with her playing. Everyone had fun, we joined in the party too, also watched the Olympics.

Feb 8
Annie has been sewing on a suit for me, also for school credit. In the afternoon I went on my skis all around the farm and into the Miller woods, it was lovely. George made supper! We watched Olympics, a Vermont boy from Guilford won a silver medal in the 30k XC race. Sheila Young won a gold, a silver, and a bronze in speed skating, she was great, I love watching these great athletes.

Feb 9
I finally caught up to this journal and I shall try to keep it up. The weather, which I have neglected to mention much has been extreme this winter, very cold, quite a lot of snow, wind, ice, everything.

Feb 10
Jim and Gary [Quimby] were here all day. The Kitchen Butcher Block table is made, a neat little corner cupboard, and a new covering on the counter, Formica. They are working on the bookcases now. I went on a skiing nature walk with Thelma [White] and a group in the after-noon. Annie got a long letter from Jenny mailed in St Louis. They are having a great time. They have been hitchhiking mostly with truckers who have been taking good care of them.

Feb 11
Not a bad day, Jim and Gary almost finished.

Feb 16
The Boardmans were here and we had a heavy discussion about the land Sunday night. Howard is looking for a job in Vermont.

We sold the field below the town roller barn to Jean and Howard Boardman.

March 5
In the past few weeks Matt has been doing a little more each day. Dave and Matt worked on the play during their concentration week. Annie painted her room with Marilyn Petrie who instructed her as they worked. Annie got her cast off Monday, seems okay. George loaned our truck to Jim Kenary to haul wood for us to sell to us and the engine went. It is really sad because the men were feeling so good about that truck. It never should have been loaned to anyone. George did decide to buy the chisel plows from Stahler [equipment dealer], now he must find a truck. It's kind of bad because we are pretty low on money. George is a little worried about his late start to sugaring, well we'll see, we're going to start tapping next week.

March 7
Friday night the School put on a Coffee House. We had a Potluck supper first and then the kids served dessert, coffee, and tea. After and during this we were entertained by songs, poems, readings, skits.

March 8
Cool, windy, Sam came home, I talked to Dick [Gulick] about coming down to visit, they also may come up here.

March 9
Quiet morning, walked with Lori and John [Laird]. George and Sammy started tapping the Keeney sugar woods. Matt, George and I had supper at Stetson's, it was fun, we played ping-pong, which is a treat for us.

Patty was an excellent ping-pong player.

March 10
Lovely day, George and all tapped again, Matty milked with Ron. Annie has about finished her room, it looks beautiful, we moved around

a lot of furniture, I will be glad to feel more settled. I walked over for the mail and came back the long way, around the Hooker road. It was refreshing, but I was really tired, I must be badly out of shape.

March 12
Lovely day, I left about 10:30, stopped for coffee at the Library then went to town, asked the A&P manager if they would like to buy syrup.

March 13
Snowed and drifted during the night, not a very pleasant day. I stayed home and worked, George combined Annie, Matty, and David into his chores team.

March 14
This is a beautiful day, George and I went out on skis and checked the pipeline, the sap was running a little.

Mar 15
Mom didn't call this morning like she usually does so I got worried and called myself. Dick answered and said she had been feeling poorly for several days. George, men, and later kids put up buckets.

Mar 17
St Patrick's Day, 5°-15°, it started snowing yesterday noon and continued all night to give us about 8 inches. It has been blowing so there are pretty good drifts. Annie told me a rumor that Jenny's truck that she just bought threw a rod and was all done. We haven't heard from Jen ourselves yet, this came through the Greens. Poor kid, if that's true she's not having a very good year. I talked to mother again today and she still feels awful. I wish I could go down but I really can't unless Jenny should come home soon and take over.

There was a Peacham School open trustee's meeting, Bill Rough wanted ideas from trustees and parents on defining the school again to help him in recruitment, also just to see where we're at anyway. It was a good meeting, Frank Randall mentioned that she had heard that

Burns Page was influencing kids away from the Peacham School, also making things hard for those who planned to come. The group voted to write him a letter asking him why he wasn't in favor of the school and inviting him to come to a trustee meeting and discuss it.

March 18
Beautiful, cold, clear morning but I never really got out. I stayed in preparing a turkey dinner for the Hummons and Shane O'Brien. Jenny and Samantha [Green] arrived home at 9 AM. Jen called from school where they had hitched to. They hitched straight home from California in about 4 days, took Amtrak up from New York and hitch over from Montpelier. They were very excited, but very tired. It was so good to have them back safely even though Jen's poor old truck had to be left behind.

March 22
Saturday was really warm and springy, temps. up to 65°, water running, George and the kids tapped trees behind Miller's, I skied around. We all went to the movies to see Women in Love, strange movie.

Sunday: it dawned clear but became cloudy, then rainy. George worked at the sugar house and the kids gathered.

March 25
Nice early then clouded up and showered in the evening. Sold our first syrup, we've made 25 gals fancy.

March 26
Everyone gathered, George boiled until 9 PM with Annie helping can. Made about 57 Gals Fancy.

March 27
Warm, pleasant day, the Mills had a skiing and supper party. I skied with the group, went out the Foster Pond road from Powden's, it was fun, good party.

March 28
Yesterday the kids helped me find a place to store the cans of syrup and put them away. It was fun and we found a good place to store them.

March 29
Jenny started work today, George and I went to Barre to get the truck he's been planning to buy. The truck seems good. The sap is running like mad, Sammy came home to see how things were going and help if he could for part of Tuesday.

April 9
Here it's been more than a week since I've written and it's been an interesting week. Friday Matt and I went in to town for a few errands, on the way home we picked up a hitchhiker who had started in Alaska and hitched around the country starting last fall. I thought it might be interesting for him to see how Vermont farmers lived so we brought him home with us. Sam was here when we got here so he took C. A. Bowman and showed him around. He stayed 'til Monday.

Saturday people did various things, in the afternoon George and I went up on the Sugar House Hill to talk to Gordon [Mills] about fence lines. Gordon was marking trees for his road [driveway]. I feel very strange about that land still. Then we went to the dump and came back to Mill's to deliver the syrup they wanted. We stayed for a drink and to figure out syrup rent barter. We never got that settled and I came home feeling rotten because of the alcohol. The kids all left and went various places before dinner and I felt bad getting home at 6 pm and everyone leaving when I had a good corned beef dinner ready. I was depressed and cross, George asked me if I would like to go to a movie, so I did, but I felt rotten into Sunday, even had a headache. It made me think it wasn't worth it for me to drink. It never makes me feel good. I think I'll pretty much stay away from it from now on.

Sunday: In the morning the girls and I walked up on Richard's hill and laid in the sun and looked at the view, it was lovely. They gathered sap in the afternoon.

Monday-Thursday: All week the sap has been flowing, Sam, Frank [Miller], Dennis [Kauppila], have been gathering, George boiling, Ron, Jen, Ben have started springs work, picking stone, spreading fertilizer, etc. They have got the new truck on the road but the dump isn't working yet.

We signed deeds to the land sold to the Boardmans and received a check, also Sam was interviewed for a job with the Ext[ension] service. One night we had an excellent discussion about TV and made a schedule so it wouldn't be on so much and we use discretion and all family decisions. It has worked well this week. Also Buddy [McLam] put in my dishwasher and it's fantastic.

Today was rather strange, little things kept going wrong, or at least not well, cows got out, lime truck got stuck, David came home sick, we were late with everything.

April 10
The family did chores and worked on sugaring, George boiled, kids and Dennis gathered. We had a nice picnic on the Sugar House Hill. I went to see Oklahoma at Blue Mtn. High School, they did a good job, Paul Chandler had the male lead.

April 11
It rained a little during the night then turned to snow flurries in the day, very raw. George boiled, has made about 485 gallons. The rest of us did things around the house. Sam left about 4:00 to go back to college.

April 13
Gorgeous full Moon!

April 14
George harrowing the field beside the house, then he started seeding it late in the afternoon. I went to the Easter Cantata, the men gathered.

April 15
Some gathered, George boiled, Ben finished seeding the land next to the house.

April 17
We got up and finished our preparations for our trips. Kids all got up, Jenny washed the car for us, Annie finished the suit she had been making for me, we had a quick breakfast together and took off. The kids were awfully nice and beautiful wishing us a good trip and good byes. Everything looked beautiful too, it was hard to leave such a nice place. We stopped in Dummerston for gas and decided to swing in by the Willard's, Ginny Brown was out raking, and within 5 minutes we were in Lavisa's living room talking to her, Judy, Judy's kids, Ginny and Stuart, we talked for 20 minutes or so. It was really wonderful they always seem so glad to see us. It really makes us feel good.

Our next stop was in New Britain, Ct. where we found a small Italian restaurant and had delicious grinders and beer. Then we drove on following Doris's [Hummon] directions, and finally got there [Jean & Howard Boardman's in New Jersey] at around seven.

Patty and I are on our way to Summit, N.J. From there, she would go to Norfolk, Va. to visit her brother Dick and his family as well as her mother. I would fly to Denver, Co. with Howard Boardman and Serge Hummon to the Annual Meeting of the United Church of Christ (UCC) Board of Homeland Ministries. Howard and Serge were members of the national board and I was a lay member serving a six-year term. We returned home May 7.

May 7
The bus trip north wasn't bad and went quickly, I was so glad to be going home. It rained some and as we got North there were snow flakes, after the hot week. Georgie met me and it was so good to see him, we rode home in the truck. The kids were happy and it was so great to see them, the house looked nice, there were some daffys blooming outside, supper was all made, it was a real treat for me.

Sept 21

Today is Annie's 16th birthday, she took her road test this afternoon in
Birthe's [Filby] Super Beetle and, nervous though she was, she passed
it, that was quite a record. Saturday David and Matthew surprised
her with a nice pair of high leather boots for her birthday. I have left
so much out of our life story by not writing for several months, but I
won't try to go back over it, I may refer back once in a while.

Right now Sam is in Oberlin, Ohio, on his way to Washington State to
find a job there; Jenny is in Arizona on her way to California with Jim
[Kenary] and Samantha [Green]. David is at Lyndon State, Annie
is out for Birthday dinner with Craig [Marcotte], and Matty is on a
trek in the Adirondacks. It's so wonderful that Matty is able to go on
this trek, I feel so thankful.

Sept 27

The past few days were unexpected and sad. Friday evening about 6:00
Eloise Miller called on the phone saying "Richard has been killed up
in the woods, Roland Aiken found him, but she would like George to
come over." It was a shock to me and I reacted, after telling Eloise that
George would be right over, very emotionally. David and George went
over, and in a few minutes later Annie and I followed. I spoke with
Eloise and then when Frank Randall arrived I went back up in the
woods with George. Jim Keeney was up there.

Richard's body was pinned underneath a big beech tree. It appeared
that when he cut the tree it had gotten hung up but rather precariously.
George thinks that Richard decided to leave the tree and come home,
picked up his axe and chain-saw and walked underneath the hung
tree on his way to the tractor and the tree dropped suddenly. It looked
as if the tree hit him on the head and knocked him down pinning and
crushing his body underneath. Dr Rowe said later that he probably
suffocated due to his lungs being compressed under the weight.

George stayed to help bring Richard's body down from the woods. Naturally he felt awful about this, he would miss Richard. Also this kind of accident comes pretty close when you work in the woods yourself. Ron, Ben, and George had been cutting beeches in our wood lot a few weeks ago. He studied the accident closely to learn from it.

Matty arrived from his Trek about 10:30 having had a wonderful time. We didn't tell him about the accident until morning. Saturday was kind of a heavy weekend on. George took David to chop corn and David didn't do very well and George yelled at him, and then took Matty. I feel awful when George does this sort of humiliation to the kids, especially David. It took the fun out of the weekend for Dave. We did play some tennis and do some nice things, but with a heavy heart, hearts were heavy anyway. David seems happy with college, enjoying subjects and social life. He went back to school this morning.

Richard Miller's death was unbelievably tragic; he and Eloise had barely gotten settled in their new house. He had had no chance to reap the rewards of retirement. I wish I could have spent more time with him and learned more about the water lines, the wiring and the history of the farm we bought from him and the people who lived on it. Instead we had a learning experience about safety in the woods.

Sept 29
Monday afternoon at 2 PM was Richard's funeral at the church. George was a pallbearer. There were a lot of people there, very difficult. We have spent so much time thinking about this situation because it affects us in so many ways. We find ourselves talking about the accident, death, and Richard much of the time.

Yesterday Matty told me that he and some of the kids had smoked Pot, and that now they were all on probation. I was very disappointed; I don't understand him getting involved in these things. It seems like he would have learned it wasn't worth it or something.

October 6
Yesterday there was a beautiful sunrise. Matthew and I went out and watched it and during that time a pair of ducks flew over. Later George ran in saying there was a coy-dog out behind the barn working a dead calf. Annie, Matty, and I ran out and watched it for a few minutes before it took off. Benny said that it came back with a second one later on.

The weather has been beautiful for almost a week, the foliage is at a peak. The weekend was very busy, Peter came with his children which I expected but unexpectedly arrived George's cousin Jo [Josephine Bigelow] and her husband [Steve Krupsky]. We hadn't seen her in years, never met him. We invited them to stay over until Sunday. Sunday afternoon was the school auction, some people from New York sought me out at the auction because they wanted to get syrup. They had gotten syrup from us two other years and remembered us so well.

Frankie was here last week and said he might have a job for Sam, so there have been several calls back and forth, nothing settled yet. Jenny is in Morro Bay California doing part time work.

This was the first of our seeing coyotes (coy-dog, as Patty wrote), some said they had migrated over the Great Lakes from the West and while doing it had crossed genetically with dogs, that's why they were bigger. Others thought they were bigger because they found more to eat here.

Oct 7
Yesterday was cloudy and mild, just a sprinkle or two of rain. George is cutting the big corn field across the road, there is so much corn it takes a long time to cut it. Sammy called last night to tell us that he talked to the Edcon office in Denver [oil exploration company Frank Miller works for] and got himself a job. He will take a bus to Denver Sunday or Monday and meet Frankie there. Then they will travel together down to Texas where the next job is. Sam was excited about it.

Oct 12

This morning I went for a walk at about 6:30, it was beautiful. The moon was full and still high in the sky, the eastern sky was pink with the White Mountains etched clearly against it. There was mist coming up in between the hills and the ground was white with frost. I loved being out then.

We were on this weekend so worked mostly but David and the kids did do a bit of bow hunting. Saturday evening the Hummons came for dinner, Sunday the Dawsons came for dessert, it was fun. Monday was a beautiful day and George turned the cows out into the lush clover at the East side of the house. During milking Ron discovered a cow nearly dead in the holding area. George came down from the field and looked at her, she was very bloated, dead. George talked to John [Stetson] about it, and he thinks it might have been due to lush, frosted clover.

Bloat is not fatal in cows if you can puncture the rumen before they suffocate.

Nov 12

The weather this last month has been unusually cold. It's been mostly cloudy with snow flurries most days and a cover of about 6 inches here, 10 inches in the wood lot. Georgie just barely got his plowing done before all this. I received my bulbs late and have only planted half of them.

It seems it has been a month since I wrote and a lot has happened of course. After losing that cow from bloat, we lost three more, one was electrocuted, one was sick, one had a strange cyst on her ovary. The cow that was electrocuted we butchered, the meat was fine, but the rest went to Maxine's fur farm [to feed mink], pretty bad run of luck. Also in the bad luck line has been a ruined tire on the John Deere and the crawler having many troubles. The Volkswagen can't be inspected so we are using it only around the farm. We don't want to invest in another vehicle right now.

Sam is in Texas and is enjoying his job, it is tedious though. He might come home for Thanksgiving, but he does plan to continue working for

Edcon. Jenny met up with Jim and Sam in Portland where they got an apartment for a while, the girls are working. She wants to make enough money to get home for Christmas. David is getting along fine at college. He's out for the ski team so he practices every afternoon. He's going with a girl, Janet, who is a junior.

Annie and Matty are working hard on school work, especially Annie, she also has the lead part in the play they will give in December, The Crucible. They work every afternoon for Georgie during corn cutting and of course weekends. This weekend the boys all plan to go to the Mack's Mtn. woodlot and camp for opening weekend of Deer Season. It's so cold though. I am beginning to feel finally that I am getting caught up and not so rushed about everything. I can begin to feel that this is really home. I can relax for a few minutes occasionally without being pressed about doing something all the time.

1977

"The whole apparatus had blown apart, a real disaster ..."

OUR WONDERFUL OLD CASE 800 TRACTOR DIED in the field across the road from the house doing springs work. Jamie Craig had bought it new in 1960 while his parents Jim and Clara were away. I think Jim was angry about it and may have decided to sell it with the Village Farm rather than hand it down to Jamie. For whatever reason, the Case 800 came with the Village Farm, and I grew to love it. It had live hydraulics and a live power takeoff (PTO), this meant you could engage them without stopping the tractor, which neither John Deere nor Farmall had at that time. It also had a better transmission with faster working gears for raking or pulling loads over the road. I loved that tractor like I would have loved a horse and rode it many long days. I traded it and $3,500 for a Case 730, also bought a hay tedder at auction for $982.

We built the first of the lean-to sheds on the big barn. This was done by spiking a 2 x 6 high up on the side of the barn and using it to rest one end of the rafters. Then you built a wall to support the plate for the other end of the rafter. The plate was lower so the roof would slant, enabling the snow to slide; a much less expensive building than one that's free standing. The cost of this shed was $5,594, it was 20 feet wide and 160 feet long.

The kids take trips and buy motorcycles and cars like they were working adults rather than teenagers. This is in part because they got paid for farm work the same as I would pay anyone else. The payroll for the kids this year was $4,622. They, admittedly, missed out on some things they would like to have done, but for the most part they became hard working, contributing citizens and they are all unbelievably good parents. As I read and transcribe Patty's diary I begin to see that I was the loser, the kids made out alright with Patty's help, but I built a farm instead of parenting; and now I don't know how to be a good grandfather.

Patty's Journal starts in February this year with a visit to Duncan and Gretchen Bond in Vienna. Duncan was teaching at the American International School and Gretchen was busy keeping house and taking care of their daughters. They had decided that Duncan would teach one more year in Vienna and then come back and teach at the new Peacham School. We had a wonderful time visiting them, but they were very busy and we felt we were imposing on them. We mostly depended on them for guidance, although we did make a trip to Venice and were thrilled by the uniqueness of the floating city. We went by train down through the mountains; the trip reminded me of a time 25 years earlier when I was in the Army and made a similar train journey through the mountains from Leghorn on the other side of Austria up to Salzburg. Patty and I went to Salzburg with Gretchen, where Patty and Gretchen both bought Loden coats. I didn't buy anything, but I marveled at Salzburg's transformation. It had gone from a very poor city with funny old trucks, many bicycles and boarded-up shops to a chic place with shiny cars, well-dressed people and very expensive shops.

We got back from Austria February 25, and Patty restarted her farm journal March 7.

March 7, 1977
George and the boys, Sam, Dave, Ben, Ron, are actually tapping out today. While we were gone they set out the pipeline and since we've been home, they have worked on the sugar house and they have also broken out the sugar roads in the woods.

I haven't been good about writing, it is great to be home and back to work again. It's good having the whole family here, even though some of them are a bit itchy. Last Thursday Jenny went over to Burlington to look for work, apartment, etc. She has her application in for Nursing

School and has an interview coming up this week. Annie was accepted at UVM for next fall, had a very nice letter from the Dean of Admissions.

Sam and David may go back to college, they aren't sure, no one is sure yet. I think they all hate to leave and yet need something specific to do. Sam seems very irritable and restless, not very motivated about doing things here. I've been thinking a lot about him and I think he ought to go back to college and finish. It would make him feel as if he's accomplished something and give him some much needed social life.

In the Miller sugar house that was part of the farmyard complex, we were putting the finishing touches on the evaporator, etc. that we had moved there from Sugar House Hill.

March 8
Lovely day, the men are tapping and hanging buckets. I am getting some things done inside that have needed being done a long time. I want to get sorting and spring cleaning done before outdoor weather arrives.

March 9
We have 630 buckets up in the Miller woods and 54 in our little "hot corner". They went back to pipeline in the afternoon. The sap was running pretty well. Buddy still hasn't wired the Sugarhouse. George and I went to a meeting in St Jay about partnerships and corporations.

The Millers referred to an area in the western part of their sugar woods as the "hot corner," because in the afternoon the sun warmed the trees, and the sap would run freely. Today, we own those woods, and we still call it the Hot Corner.

March 10
Lovely, more tapping, Redwing Blackbirds. Jenny went back to Burlington for at least a week, job and apartment hunting, she has her nursing school appointment today. Bill Marshall came for a lunch meeting with George. There are problems and he's wondering how to deal with them and wondering if it's worth continuing the school.

March 11
The boys gathered, Buddy finally came and worked all day on wiring the sugar house, George and Ron did other things to prepare to boil. I am shoveling snow away from my back stoop, hanging out clothes and it's great.

March 12
Buddy came and finished his work on the sugar house, by noon George was able to start boiling. The three boys did chores and gathered sap from the Sugar House hill. By three thirty George had some syrup. Eloise, Anne, Lois, Jean Miller came down to see the operation. We all watched for a while and had some syrup.

I went back to making beds with the new sheets I had washed and hung outside to dry. I heard a noise like a bang and came down to see if someone had come in but no one was around. In about five minutes Georgie came in and told me that he had gone into the milking parlor for a few minutes and when he went back over to the sugar house there was steam coming out the door which was strange and when he stepped in he was shocked to find that there had been an explosion and the whole apparatus had been blown apart, front pans on the floor all banged up, bricks all over, a real disaster, but miraculously no one had been inside when it happened. We were so frightened to think about this, and so thankful.

We had poured the cement for the sugar house floor in July, eight months before, and yet there was still moisture enough to explode despite two layers of big yellow fire brick covering the cement. I told many people about it, so as to warn them. The solution was to remove any cement in the fire box that hadn't blown and replace it with sand.

March 13
Rained all day today, messy, muddy. I went over to the Millers to tell them about the accident, I walked over in the rain. We felt so fortunate that the accident hadn't happened with them inside. We decided

tonight that we wanted to have Judy [Bruno] and the kids so she could do the job at St J, it will not be easy but would help her a lot and be a good experience for us. I'm so thankful Georgie was out of the sugar house when that explosion happened, he could have been so badly hurt, it's really scary, you never know what can happen next.

March 14
40°-46° Mostly cool and windy, cloudy day. Men worked in the sugar house fixing up the destruction. George drove around trying to find someone who would attempt to fix the front pans for the sugar rig. Gene Nunn agreed to try, so he came up and they pounded out the dents, tomorrow Gene will come and solder the small holes.

Gene Nunn was the road commissioner, and he and his brother Jake and a person called "little George" were the road crew. They were extremely clever and could fix anything. At that time the town barn was where the fire house is now, and in the early years when we were first farming in the village, those three guys were very helpful keeping my old equipment running. I was very fond of them and respected their talents, I don't think the Selectmen appreciated the quality of the help they had.

March 15
32°-48° David and George had a nice discussion this morning. Dave is going to work full time from now until the corn is in. Then he would like to go west and have some fun and adventure before going back to college. This is good for all. Gene Nunn came and worked on our flue pan where the drain pipe had been ripped out of the bottom of the flues, it was difficult, tedious work. Benny is spreading manure. Boys put up more pipeline when Matty came home from school, Annie worked for me.

March 17
Gene Nunn worked on the pans.

March 20
20°-50° George and I went to church. The sermon was pretty rough. There was a meeting afterward to vote on what method to use in repairing the floor beams in the down stairs of the church. We voted to use a plate and post construction. Played baseball with the kids for several hours, it was so nice to run around outside. Nice to have Jen home.

March 21
22°-45° Nice day, I went to Montpelier to be a witness to Peter and Judy's divorce hearing, Judy stayed calm and answered questions well, Peter was difficult. Boys gathered, George fired up the rig to see how it was, there are a few minor leaks.

March 22
20°-40° Lovely in the morning then it clouded up and became windy. We are supposed to have a major snow storm. Georgie boiled all day, he was a little nervous but it went okay. Sam worked for Nelson [farm in Barnet Center] and then came back and worked here. Someone was gathering all day.

Saturday Merrill McLaren shot himself in his barn, he was Paul Hooker's cousin.

Sadie got in the way during gathering and was run over by the sap trailer. Everyone was upset naturally, she didn't seem to be in pain but she was breathing strangely. Matty and I took her into John's [Stetson] and he checked her all over and medicated her for shock. She stayed there to be observed.

March 23
Snowed a little and blew a lot, we didn't get the big storm that they thought we might. George is boiling, boys are gathering, Sam at Nelson's, the kids didn't have school so Annie has been sewing, etc. inside, Matty has been gathering. John said Sadie seemed okay and that we can pick her up this afternoon.

March 24
*Very windy, George boiled all day and David canned syrup in the sugar
house and cleaned and marked the cans. They worked very hard all
day. It is really a great thing to be able to wash and mark cans there
without all the moving back and forth, and doing it in the house. Sam
doesn't feel well, he worked here part of the day, he had trouble with the
pickup but it was just a loose ground cable or some such simple thing.*

When we bought an evaporator for our sugar house from
Kitchel in 1970 it had three big oil burners, one in front, one on
the side, and one in back. We decided to change the design when we
moved it to the Miller farm. We put two burners in front and added
a preheater under a hood over the flue pan, this heated up the cold
sap with the steam from the flue pan and increased the efficiency.
We hoped it would replace the third oil burner. A side benefit was
that we caught the condensed steam in a pail, and that gave us a hot
water source for washing syrup cans and strainers.

March 25
15°-30° cold, windy, Men were going to butcher, but it was too cold.

March 26
*The day was very pleasant, the sap ran a little. Everyone worked
at barn chores, house chores. Dave and Sam went up in the woods
hunting squirrels and checking pipeline. I was a little cross with the
boys because it seems they could help me more with household things.
There is so much work for me to keep up with, I hardly ever stop from
early morning and I'm always behind. Dave, Sam, Georgie and I went
to a Marx Brothers film in St Jay.*

A young teacher at the Peacham School, Jay Craven, showed
great old movies in various public buildings on Saturday nights, it
was informational and entertaining. Jay has stayed in the area and
become a very important part of the community.

March 27
21°-51° beautiful morning, nice day, Jenny came home last night and this morning she packed things to put in the little apartment she has rented. She and I drove over in the pickup, picked up Judy on the way. [We] had Supper at Carruth's and the whole trip was fun.

March 28
20°-50° nice day, the sap ran all night evidently because when Ben went up at 7:30 to gather the tub from the pipe line it was running over and there was a pool of sap underneath it. They found buckets running over all day. Matt took half a day off and came home to help gather.

March 29
Rained last night, cleared off around mid-day, sap ran again over-night. It gradually cleared and became sunny in the afternoon. Judy called to say she had sold her house, also had the job at the Academy so she will be coming here to stay with her two children the first two weeks in April. We are looking forward to it. The men gathered full buckets everywhere, it's quite a run, and Georgie can't keep up with it. He shut down at supper time and then changed the pans around and fired up again and boiled 'til 2:00 AM. Snowdrop, Crocus in bloom and Daffys through the ground.

March 30
Beautiful day, sap still flowing, finally slowed up in the afternoon. George started boiling this morning at 5:30, boiled 'til 4:30 this afternoon, came in and rested and ate, then back out and boiled 'til midnight. I went to a potluck supper at school and evaluations meeting.

March 31
Cool, breezy, Sam and I took his motorcycle to Tink's to be repaired and the pickup to the WBG [West Barnet Garage] for some work. The kids all seem to be thinking about selling or buying some type of vehicle. Jen called yesterday to say she got her phone, likes her apartment and has more job options. George boiled all day again, he's made about 400 gallons. The boys got all gathered in, washed tubs, etc.

April 3
George and I went to church, he took the day off, went riding with the girls, etc. Judy came with the children for a week. This week I have been taking care of Beth and Amy [Judy's daughters] while Judy teaches in the morning. She gets home around 12:30 or so.

April 6
The day stayed windy and cold. After lunch George and Matt went for sawdust, Ben spread manure.

April 10
It's been cold and very windy, I find this depressing right now when I'm hoping to go outside, be in the sun. Last week really tired me a lot, I don't know exactly why except I guess I really concentrate on the three extras and then try and deal with everyone else too. It is not so much the physical exertion that does it.

In the afternoon Jen, Dave, Matt, and I took a nice walk down into the woods to see if we could locate the deer I heard, if that's what it was. We did find it all chewed, anyway the walk was fun, the weather was bright but cool.

April 11
15°-50° Beautiful morning, nice day, mostly cool, breezy. Terry and little Omri Parsons came to visit. George, Dave, Benny, butchered three cows.

April 13
Lovely day, mostly sunny, good spring showers, some thunder. George boil all day, Dave gathered alone, Sam worked for Nelson. Frank Miller is home for a few weeks. Annie and I went to a P S [Peacham School] Trustee Meeting, George went to a Deacon's Meeting.

April 14
34°-50° Beautiful morning, poured rain last night, windy and cool. Men gathered, sap still good, George boiled. He has made over 600

gallons, with no very dark syrup. Jean and Howard [Boardman] came for dinner and we all went to the Peacham School Coffee House. It was good, Annie played with quite a few combinations, she played well and looked so pretty.

April 15
Judy and the kids left this afternoon.

April 22
Starting last weekend the weather has been fantastic, sunny and warm every day, quite a lot of wind also, and we really need the rain. These are some of the things that we've done in the last week.

Cut up beef and packaged
Finished boiling
Cleaned up Sugar House
Washed all buckets
Planted all peas, some other things
Put pea fence up
Raked most of the yard
Washed some wood work
Taken down most of the pipeline

We have all been very busy and it's been fun. This week is spring vacation for the kids so they have worked a lot. Sam got a call from Edcon and they want him to go to Norway! He may have to leave with Frank as soon as next Tuesday so he had to hurry around and get his passport.

April 27
It has been cool and rainy for several days, we needed the rain, but we're ready for sun again now. Sam got word that he definitely would be going to Norway with Frank. He is pretty excited, he and Frank both went shopping and got haircuts. Jenny has decided to come home and find work around here, but first to go down and visit mom in Norfolk for a while. Yesterday Annie and I went to a staff meeting for her to present to them her reasons for wanting to graduate early.

Annie had accumulated enough credits at the Peacham School to graduate early, and I wanted her to transfer to St. Johnsbury Academy for one more year before going to college.

May 3
Last week it rained a lot and greened things up, over the weekend the weather was beautiful. Sunday was busy, Sammy left with Frankie at 10:00 to catch their flights to Norway. We took pictures and said good bye. The boys looked so handsome all dressed up. Then we got ready for our party, Georgie and I hid the eggs.

People came at 1:00 or so and we had a great party until 9:00 or later. Hunted eggs, played horseshoes, had a good softball game, then cookout and talk and music. It was a lovely day. We were even able to sit outside in the evening. The peas, spinach, radishes are all up. Today George put the herd out. They've been fencing, stone picking, harrowing, doing springs work.

May 5
We turned the cows out to pasture last night and when we got up this morning they were all lying down out front and the sky was pink and clear and beautiful. Yesterday we drove to Walden to look at a car that was advertised. It is a blue VW Square Back, 1972, 68000 miles, in good condition. Planted some more, some asparagus up in the little patch out back here.

May 16
It has been mostly cool the last two weeks, not much rain, windy. George has gotten a lot of springs work done, spreading land for corn, etc. He planted one small corn piece and seeded several. We have our VW now and everyone loves it.

Jenny flew to Norfolk Saturday to spend two weeks. We took her to the airport and then went to an auction in Greensboro and bought a hay tedder. Sunday George [planted] 100 asparagus roots, then we played tennis, later George and Matt went fishing, I worked in the garden, and the others went to a dance.

May 25
It has continued to be unusually hot and dry, the hay crop needs some cool wet weather. George has almost all his corn crop planted and sprayed and some of it is up. We've eaten asparagus, rhubarb, and radishes. Sunday Georgie and I drove to Connecticut for the funeral of Gary Steadman. Gary was one of George's sister Shirley and Eddie's sons. It was an unusual funeral because Gary had been murdered and the authorities thought it had been a Mob shooting. There were people at the funeral that neither Shirley nor Eddie knew. We could only guess if they were Policeman or Gangsters. It was a very sad and strange funeral.

June 22
So many things again, it finally rained and things are growing good, we've gotten in some hay. Gardens are pretty good, eating spinach, peas are starting to pod.

Annie's graduation was exceptionally nice, more formal than others have been, Nathaniel Tripp spoke. Now Matt is playing Babe Ruth ball and is doing very well. He has pitched two games out of four and has won them both. Matty really looks good pitching, we've been to every game so far. Annie and Jenny are playing softball on a team. Annie is working full time on the farm and Jenny has quite a business going taking care of people's yards and flower gardens.

July 21
Here it is again a month without writing. Last night was one of the hottest we've ever had, we all had trouble sleeping, all week has been extremely hot. Matt is on the District All Star Team along with Rick White and John Larrabee, they practiced all last week and this week have started the tournament. They have handsome uniforms so they really look nice. We all have been going to the games in between haying, etc.

I am sitting in the yard writing, this is where it's cool, I think we all should have slept outside last night, there is quite a breeze now. Jen has been getting plenty of work, she works for Tory Parker, Anne Mills, and new people in Peacham, Seiden and now Ham Slaight. I'd like to have her more myself. Sammy's letters indicate some homesickness and he'll be glad to get back. David and Matty have been cutting fire wood in our Mack's Mtn. lot when they could in between practice and games and haying. Dave went to Maine for a week with Larry Skoller.

July 22
Yesterday it rained finally with some thunder and lightning, it cooled off to 50°, quite a drop.

August 7
Matty's 16th Birthday! I've missed a lot again, we've been very busy. Matt's all-star team won the district championship without a loss. We watched all the games. Then the boys played in the State Tourney, that didn't come out so well, they lost two straight and were eliminated. We were a little relieved to have baseball over for awhile, we have put much time and energy into it. Matty played very well, he is an excellent member of a team, keeps up his spirit and the teams, doesn't get mad and plays as hard as he can. Steve White paid him a very big compliment saying he was the outstanding player on the team.

George has gotten started on the addition to the big barn, the logs are all cut and were sawed at White's mill in Barnet. The drought has caused us to cease using our pastures and bring the cattle into the barn to eat. The hay crop is down but the field corn looks good. David has sweet corn ready.

1978

"I had a rough summer and am still depressed and nervous."

THE FARM DID OKAY BUT DAVE, JEN, AND ANNIE had serious problems. Dave had a bad flare-up of what turned out to be a lifelong mental health problem. Over time he found a medication that helped keep him on an even keel, but he always had to work on it; he didn't go back to college this fall. Patty suffered when Dave got sick, and she had trouble not carrying the whole burden herself.

Jenny was a passenger in a ¾-ton pickup, driving from a wedding reception to another party, when the pickup left the road and flipped three times end-over-end; fortunately Nancy and Robert Bartell were following and got the passengers quickly to the hospital.

This accident, coming during a stressful period with David, did Patty in, she didn't write in the journal for eight months. She never mentions Annie's concussion. Annie was skiing at Burke during the Christmas break and flew into a tree, hitting her head hard. She was a long time recovering; she, along with the rest of us, suffered from her unpredictable, irritable behavior. It did not seem reasonable for her to return to school that winter, so she didn't. I like to think I was a loving, caring husband, but I was unaware that Patty was suffering depression.

In the midst of all of our own family's health problems, Patty showed her leadership on the board of the new Danville Health Center, she was very dedicated to it. Later, she would go on the board of Umbrella, a women's support organization in St. Johnsbury. Both groups are still going strong.

This year we began building a cabin in place of the lean-to we had built in 1970 on Mack's Mountain Road. It was two years putting it up; Sam and John Ninninger, a young man who built cabins on the Appalachian Trail, did most of the construction, they lived in a teepee on the site. The whole family pitched in to help, cutting trees and de-barking them, making roof shingles by hand using a froe, hanging the doors. I designed and built a stone fireplace and made all the hardware for the cabin in our forge. The whole project was a labor of love and the result was a real gem, just beautiful. It had two rooms, a kitchen and a living room divided by the fireplace/chimney. Over the kitchen was a sleeping loft. We moved our old wood cook stove in. That cabin provided a lot of pleasure for our family for many years. We had parties, played poker, hunted, and the kids camped overnight with friends. We were sick at heart when it burned in the early 1990s – the fire marshall said there was no doubt the fire had been set by vandals, intentionally or unintentionally, we never knew. We never did find the heart to rebuild it, and we finally sold the land with the burnt remains in the mid-1990s.

On the farm we bought a new manure spreader for $4,500 and traded our old mower for a new John Deere mower-conditioner and $3,200. We finished up the lean-to shed on the back of the big barn for an additional $500, making the total cost of the shed $6,094.

March 19, 1978
This will be a new start because I haven't written since last summer. I will review briefly what has happened in the meantime.

The Farm: Basically our herd is growing slowly, about 110 milkers now. The shed addition to the big barn is finished enough to use. It looks nice and is serving a good purpose. It is just housing heifers and dry cows now all together but later it will be divided into two parts – high producing cows on the end toward the parlor and a dry cow bred heifer group. The milk checks have been good. Our income was up this year and our real-estate taxes were high, but we seem to be managing. The kids got very good help from financial aid which was nice. Annie's year [UVM] was almost completely covered by aids and grants.

The Family: Georgie and I have had a good year. We miss having everyone here but they are back and forth enough to make it nice. Georgie has been working very hard but feels he's accomplished a lot. I've had more time for myself to knit, ski, visit people and help Georgie. I'm always trying to keep weight down and stay trim, that's hard.

March 20

6°-40° Lovely day, Jen worked for me this morning and for George this afternoon. They tapped most of the roadside trees. David left early to go to UVM and visit Annie and Matt Western, he's thinking of going west with Matt this summer to find a job on a fishing boat. Jen and Dave are on vacation this week [from Lyndon State College], Annie will be next week.

March 21

22°-50° Snow, sleet, and rain today. When Ben and Ron went home for breakfast they had a harrowing ride down the hill sideways, the road was all ice, thank goodness they didn't crash. Later this afternoon the sun came out. They finished tapping.

March 22

30°-35° Stayed cool with flurries today. George and crew butchered three cows. I went to town, tried to find something new for my Norfolk trip, but had no luck. We went to Easter Cantata at the Peacham Church in the evening.

March 23

24°-50° 4 inches snow at 6 AM. Boys gathered for first time, nice spring day.

March 24

22° Dawned a beautiful day. I am planning to fly today at 1 PM from Burlington to Norfolk [to visit mom and Dick]. Jenny and I drove to Burlington, had a bite to eat and I then flew off. The flight to New York was excellent and I talked to an interesting person all the way, a former boxer, now business-man, view of Manhattan, fabulous.

1978

April 1

I intended to write everyday however, I am in route home now waiting in Allegheny for a flight to Albany and Burlington. I had a very good week, but it always makes me so happy to live where I do and the kind of life we live, it seems so much more natural. The city closes in on me after a while.

April 6

25°-50° When I arrived in Burlington Saturday it was raining and cold-windy. It had been mild nice weather in Norfolk. I took a taxi to town [Burlington], had lunch and took the bus to Danville where Georgie met me. It was good to see him and be home. The kids all came out and greeted me, then we had such a good evening. The kids made and served a yummy dinner and we spent a lot of time talking and catching up. I love them all so much.

I've been catching up on household things this week. Nancy [Bartell] came and helped yesterday, she did windows and I washed and ironed curtains. The sap hasn't done much, George boiled once last week. Yesterday they gathered, but it's been cold, windy, snowy, rainy. We are low on hay so we will have to buy some, many farmers have been buying hay for quite some time. George boiled today, has made about 65 gallons and the men got hay and then gathered.

Matthew has been practicing for a big gym show that Danville will be putting on next week. He is enjoying it. Peacham School Trustees Meeting, George felt at odds with some of the thinking and came home a little discouraged.

Matty transferred from Peacham School to Danville School at mid-year.

April 7

20°-34° It dawned a beautiful morning but didn't last very long. Jen and Dave came home in the afternoon, the men gathered.

April 8
29°-40° Cool, very windy, sun shone occasionally and sap ran a bit, kids gathered. I went to the funeral of Vivian Churchill [Bernard Churchill's mother], there were a lot of people there. Bonds came for dinner, but everyone was tired and kind of tense.

Our good friends Gretchen and Duncan Bond had returned from Vienna. Duncan was teaching at the Peacham School, and we had transferred Matty from that school to Danville High.

April 9
Last night at 2:30 I got up to let a dog out and John Frye's woman, Janie, came up the driveway, she was crying, she had gone to see John and he had beat her up and put her out. She slept here on the sofa and went down to his camp again in the morning. She didn't come back so I guess things were better.

April 10
18°-40° Beautiful day, even so not much sap. Matty is having baseball practice afternoons and Gym practice nights, this seems a bit too much.

April 11
30°-36° Rained some during the day. Nancy worked in the morning and we got more windows and curtains done. Robert [Bartell] saw snow geese.

April 12
31°-48° Nice day, sunny, cloudy, windy. Sammy got home at 3 PM in his new car, it was so good to see him. He plans to stay here for a couple of months and get logs ready to build a small cabin at the wood lot. John Ninninger is coming over to work with him and we'll all help some.

April 13
It was a beautiful day, cloudy in the morning but the sun came out around noon and the warmth was wonderful. George boiled, Sam

helped gather and then canned syrup in the sugar house. We have made around 150 gallons and canned around 40. Nancy worked for me in the morning. Sharon Fuehrer and Anne Mills came for coffee and to discuss the fellowship.

April 14
Jean Berwick went to town with me and we delivered clothes for church world service and did some errands. Sam and Matty went up to Danville and met Annie from the bus, Annie didn't know Sam was home.

April 15
I cleaned up round the sheds. Georgie and the kids took the team [horses] for a trip up into the woods. The sap has been running, George and the kids gathered most of the day, I worked around the house. We saw some of Sam's slides of Wyoming, Colorado, and Texas.

While in the village we had bought a young mare named Penny for Jenny, she had a filly named Schilling, which was Annie's. When Schilling was old enough to ride, she was too difficult for Annie so we bought a horse from Randy Keeney named Orlando. When I rode with the girls, Jen rode Penny, Annie rode Orlando, and I rode Schilling. I worked Schilling in a light sleigh that she pulled very well, we also hitched her and Orlando up as a team.

April 23
We planted two rows of peas, 2 ½ lbs onions, some lettuce, spinach, radishes, the boys went woodchuck hunting.

April 24
Sam had a physical at Danville, gathered sap in the afternoon by himself. Ben and George spread some fertilizer on pastures, I planted some flower seeds.

April 25
George and Ben spread fertilizer and in the afternoon pulled buckets.

April 26
30°-70° Beautiful but dry on the surface, there still is snow in spots.
Men pulled buckets, Ben spread manure with the new tank spreader.
Danville Health Center Meeting, Hantman's salary discussed and
future of the clinic.

April 27
It has been cold and dry and windy much of this period with occa-
sional snow flurries being the only precipitation. Monday I went to
Burlington to a book sale, shopped, took Annie out to lunch. Saw a flock
of geese flying over Annie's dorm. George has planted oats in the Miller
piece. Sam and Ron have fenced to get ready to put animals out even
though the grass isn't growing much. We are about out of hay.

May 4
The men put three groups of heifers out to pasture, George rode Schilling
and it worked out nicely.

May 5
George, Annie, and I went up to Lyndonville to meet the boys and see
"Pippin" the musical that Jen has been working on so long. When we got
there Matty came climbing through the [auditorium] seats to tell us he
had pitched again and they had beat Blue Mtn. He was very excited.

May 6
Annie and I had lots of good conversations and she tried to get some
studying in. The boys fished in between chores. Matt spent the day at
a woodchuck hunt.

May 18
18°-48° The weather has been great lately, fairly warm, rain off and
on, some nice sunshine. George has planted corn in the 20 acre piece
and almost finished two others, Benny is spraying. The cows are going
out days. The daffodils are in full bloom, tulips coming, and lots of wild
flowers. The leaves are slowly unfolding, asparagus up well in the old
garden, one stalk in the new garden so far. Ninny [John Ninninger]

finally came and he and Sam have started cutting trees in the woodlot for the cabin. Sam, Annie, and I moved Aunt Fran [into St. Johnsbury House] Monday and Tuesday, quite a project. She is pretty bitchy in some ways, I hope she gets along okay.

July 2
I'm in Boston Logan Airport on a two hour stop over here on my way to Minneapolis to meet David and bring him home. He called Thursday and told me that he had had "a very traumatic two days" something to do with the Greyhound bus. He sounded very upset. I called Randy [Keeney] in case he could get there and stay until he felt better and then come home. Randy suggested calling Patsy Paterson in Minneapolis, we did.

Since David seemed weaker rather than stronger Patsy drove to Brainerd and picked him up at a Police Station there in the very early morning and took him back home with her. He was exhausted and upset when they arrived and looking at all angles. I decided to fly out (if possible) and bring him back. Susan at Highland Travels was able to arrange flights so I'm on my way.

Looking back at things, Sam has been in England nearly a month now. We've had letters, postcards, and slides, he seems to be happy. David wrote some excellent letters from his trip and numerous slides.

Annie is in Washington now. Georgie and I put her on the Amtrak train in Montpelier Thursday night. She has been working for me since she got out of school and it has been so wonderful for me to have her home. I love having one of my daughters at home with me. Jen has been working out mowing lawns etc., she has been very busy, also milking weekends and helping hay. Matthew finally finished school and did okay. He also did well on the baseball team. Now he is working full time for Georgie and playing Senior Babe Ruth.

Summary of 1978
I shall again try to catch up here and continue fairly frequent entries. Here are some entries of the past six months.

Sammy went to Europe in June for three months, he had a great time. David went off on a hitchhiking trip to visit some people and then head west for work. The first part of the trip was good and then a number of unpleasant things happened and he could no longer cope. I went to Minneapolis and brought him home, he was in bad shape and the balance of the summer was very difficult for him and for the rest of us.

Annie worked at home through the summer, had a trip to Washington to visit Iness [Balerin] and to Norfolk to visit mom, her summer was upset by Dave's problems, Jen's accident, my distress over all.

Jen started out working for people doing lawns, etc. It started out well for her, she was renting David's car and living at home, then about two weeks after Dave came home she was in a bad *Auto Accident*, she had several injuries the worst being a separated shoulder which kept her from doing work for any of the families she had been doing yard work for.

The farm went along well despite incidental problems. I had a rough summer and am still somewhat depressed and nervous. The fall went fairly well, Annie had a good semester. Jen and Dave shared an apartment and it was hard for a while but improved, Jen did well in school, Dave not so well. John Ninninger was here and he and Sam worked on the cabin. They thoroughly enjoyed it and we loved having them here and watching their progress and helping a little. By Thanksgiving the basic structure was finished. We had a nice Christmas.

1979

"We took out the team with the big sled and went around the Bay."

W HEN PATTY AND I WENT TO AUSTRIA IN 1977
to visit Gretchen and Duncan Bond, I played poker one
night with Duncan and his group of teachers. Duncan and I decided
that when he came back to Peacham we would start a poker group.
We did, and some 40 years later the group is still playing regularly.
Besides Duncan and me, among the early members were Alan
Greenleaf, Dennis Kauppila, Bob Morgan, Jim Keeney, Frank
Green, and Ken Danielson. (I apologize if I've forgotten anyone in
that original group, it was a long time ago, members have come and
gone since.) At one time, Dave Willard, Duncan and I were all on
the Selectboard together. People would grumble that we were running the town from the poker table. There was a little truth in that,
but it didn't do any harm, and we were popular as a board.

My sons and grandsons joined the group as soon as they were
old enough – they are great poker players. If I can remember
everyone, today's regulars include Ken Danielson and his son Chris
and grandson Jesse; Frank Miller; Matt, David, Sam, William, and
Dylan Kempton; and Mike Bussiere. My daughters Annie and Jenny
have been known to play; and Darby Bradley, Julian Kempton,
Dave Freshette, Duncan Bond, Jim Keeney, and David Willard
come when they're in town.

We play every two weeks on Thursday nights. We used to go
from 7:30 to 11:00, but we've gotten older, we need to accommodate players who do farm chores, now we play from 7-10. It's BYOB,
most bring beer. The maximum bet is 25 cents. We play the common

games – High-Chicago-High, Follow the Queen, Night Baseball, Five-card Draw, Mexican Sweat – and one we call "Christiansen's Game," after a place we used to hunt in South Dakota. Poker, like hunting, is one of those institutions in my family's life that has brought a lot of joy and camaraderie.

I have the farm account books from 1962 'til when the farm incorporated in 2000, and I looked at what had happened to the herd in the four years since the cows had been housed and milked in the new free-stall system. Herd size increased from 80 cows in 1975 to 120 cows in 1979, and at the same time the amount of milk each cow produced increased about 10%. I think it is most unusual to increase individual cow production and at the same time increase the herd size by 50%. I think a significant reason for the increase was the greater comfort of the free stalls, where the cows could lie down or walk around, eat, drink, hang out, rather than being tied by the neck through the long winter.

Equipment purchases: we traded the Volkswagen Squareback for a new VW Rabbit and $5,700, traded a John Deere 2520 for a new Massy Ferguson 265 and $6,600, an old chopper for a New Holland chopper and $4,700. Built a bunk silo for $3,600, made improvements in our home – Jim Quimby $5,737 to renovate the chamber over the kitchen into a bedroom, and Duncan Bond $1,147 for interior painting and wall papering. Matty and I bought two six-month-old work horse colts for $1,100. Matt named his Buddy and mine I named Mickey.

Jenny and Steve visited Steve's parents Joy and Grahame [nicknamed "Wink"] Harris in Sydney this summer, then went back to Lyndon State College that fall. Annie returned to University of Vermont in the fall, Matty graduated from Danville in June, as did his new girlfriend Dawn Richards. Matty started full-time on the farm, I think Dawn started college. David continued working on the farm.

Feb 22, 1979
Ben and George getting out manure, David working on pipeline; yesterday and the day before in the afternoon I skied with Gretchen, the

days were lovely, mild, and sunny. I worked at the Health Center this PM helping.

Dave, George and I went up to see Jenny in a one-act play "Tea and Sympathy" at the college, it was good, and then we had refreshments at Jen and Steve's [Harris] apartment. They have the apartment fixed up very attractively.

Feb 23
I took the Rabbit for the 1,000-mile checkup and spent the rest of the day doing errands. The men worked on the truck body they are building. Matty competed in Danville's Winter Carnival activities and then went to the Carnival Ball.

Feb 24
28° Very slippery this morning, it rained and drizzled all night at about freezing temps. The boys couldn't get the truck over to the Village this morning to do chores, they had to pull the truck back and go over on a tractor. Later in the day the sand truck went over and it thawed some. The Bonds all came to dinner and we had a good time.

Feb 26
20°-30° It snowed, rained, snowed again, we got about 6 inches of wet snow. Matty went up to Burke to ski and stay at Danny G's house, hopefully he'll bring Annie back with him tomorrow. Well, he didn't because Annie worked at the Wooden Horse at the last minute.

Danny G was a new boyfriend of Annie's that we weren't too pleased about. The Wooden Horse was a restaurant in St. J where Annie was a waitress.

March 5
I missed some days writing and I'm looking back now. Matty had a great vacation week skiing about every day. He entered some races and was second in two and 2nd overall.

Saturday we picked up Jenny and all went skiing at Burke. Sunday Jenny came out here, also Annie's friend Barbara [Hansberry], we took out the team with the big sled and went around the Bay. We walked where the road was getting bare and that was fun too.

March 5
40°-45° It rained practically all day, the snow is really disappearing. The truck body is all finished, the men put it on the truck today. Annie and I worked around here, I did a lot of baking.

March 6
40°-43° It rained again, nearly all day. Jen, Steve, Dave, George, and I all went to TOWN MEETING, it was fairly quiet. Maurice Chandler got voted out as selectman, Les Post voted in, Lorna Quimby retired from the School Board, her term was up, Marilyn Magnus was voted in. Letter from Sam: They have been having some trouble with equipment but otherwise okay. He is enjoying himself off shore in Angola.

March 7
30°-36° Pretty nice day, but the sun only peeked through a few times. Benny went up to the Health Center because his arthritis is bothering him so much.

March 8
I went to town this AM, brief errands, work continues on pipeline, manure, truck body. Annie worked 5:30 to 2, went to Danny's.

March 9
I hung clothes out on the line, first time in months, men working on pipeline. Annie worked double shift at the Wooden Horse.

March 10
Rain, snow, not very nice, worked around inside, Annie potted plants.

March 11
Rained and snowed during the night, I skied over to visit the Miller girls in the afternoon. I went to church in the morning, Dick Phillips preached and I thought his sermon was excellent. I am on the Search Committee to find a pastor for our church and we have had five resumes to read over from prospective people. I have only read two so far, they are very interesting.

March 12
10°-20° Annie started working today with George and David tapping pipeline.

March 13
5°-30° A, D, and G continued tapping on pipeline.

March 14
32°-40° Temperature gradually went up overnight, rained pretty hard during the day and a spot of sun in the afternoon with a full moon. Sap ran some but the pipeline isn't in the tub yet. They finished tapping and putting up the pipeline. I had a meeting of the Health Center board, and pot luck supper at the Currier's in Danville.

March 15
We had another Lynfield Hearing proposing a 36-unit low income housing project for the elderly on the Peacham Academy property. People were still mostly opposed to the project and many expressed their views very well.

March 17
Boys went with George to check the whole pipeline over, and put the pipe into the tank.

We didn't have an adequate way to clean the sap pipeline so we let sap do the cleaning by letting it run through the pipeline and onto the ground in the beginning.

March 18
11°-35° Again, nice out but windy, sap ran a little in the afternoon.
Jenny and Steve came out for pancake brunch, Jen, Steve, and Georgie
went horseback riding, I went running, it was a pleasant day.

March 21
FIRST DAY OF SPRING! HOORAY, beautiful day, sill a bit windy.
I had a meeting at the Health Center. Annie came home from Danny's
around 10 A M. Ben got a load of sawdust, George and Dave tapped
in the morning and GATHERED in the afternoon. I went running.
I'm trying to get my jogging endurance back and lose 10 pounds, from
150 to 140.

March 22
It didn't freeze last night and the sap kept running and there was a
lot to gather all day. The men had to unload sawdust in the morning,
George and Annie gathered. George boiled for the first time, everything
seemed to go okay and he made several gallons of beautiful syrup. I
found snow drops blooming and Daffys up. There was a poker game,
with David, Matt, George, Annie, Ken Danielson, and Duncan. I
went to Women's Fellowship.

March 23
30°-50° After lunch George, Annie and I had a difficult time com-
municating and spent quite some time talking, all of us quite upset. It
had to do with Annie and Danny's relationship and it's a bit compli-
cated. We hate having her spending so much time with him, living at
his house, and it seems like she was pushing the relationship. We didn't
make any perfect conclusion but we did communicate.

Georgie boiled all day and has made 50 gallons of fancy syrup. The
boys gathered all day. Jen and Steve came out in the afternoon, helped
gather and watched the boiling. Danny came out and had more of a
tour of the farm than he'd had before. We had a nice dinner all together
except Matty who had to go to Gym Show practice at 6. Annie went
home with Danny.

March 24
Matty went to baseball clinic in Burlington so George and David were on alone, first all the chores and then boiling and canning. We have somewhat over 100 gallons. Georgie and I went to Reeve and Richard Brown's home with Bonds, [Nathaniel] Tripps, Frisly Fultons. We had a lovely evening. I was glad to see how they had fixed up the house.

We had visited the Ralph Graves family at their dairy farm before Reeve and Richard Brown bought it. Ralph hadn't wasted money on home improvements.

March 25
34°-50° Pleasant day, mostly cloudy, it was supposed to rain but didn't. George and the boys went riding between chores and had time to relax too. We had various visitors during the afternoon. Matty has been dating a Danville girl, Dawn Richards, quite steadily lately.

March 26
30°-35° Cloudy, windy and snow flurries, George and David gathered. Ben and Ron went up to the woodlot and brought down two loads of wood. I took the pickup truck to Sheffield to get four syrup drums that Jim Perkins had borrowed.

March 27
I had to go back into town this morning to get batteries and do some other errands. The men went up to the woodlot and cut and loaded wood and brought it down to Ron's yard. Annie took a picnic up to them. Annie and I did odds and ends, worked on plants, went running in PM.

March 28
Men tapped and hung buckets, sap didn't run much. Annie visited school with Matty, I got lots of things done here.

March 29
25°-36° Raining and freezing when we got up, sap did not run much at all. George boiled what was left from the weekend and David canned grade B.

March 30
Sap ran overnight, George boiled, men gathered. Matt brought Dawn home for dinner.

March 31
Sap ran overnight again, George boiled, Matt, Dave, Annie gathered, also Ben, Ron, and Andy [Cochran] later. Georgie and I had dinner in Newbury with Jim and Dinah Keeney.

April 1
Georgie boiled, syrup has come back up to fancy, unusual. We had a sugar on snow party this afternoon with Danny, Steve, Dawn, our family, Cathy and Bruce Roy and their family. Steve and Danny canned syrup for George, which was a big help and good for communication.

April 2
29°-30° Snowed about 2 inches, then rained and blew, nasty, George boiled men gathered. Annie and I worked on the attic to make it possible for Jim and Gerry to work up there.

April 3
Annie gathered with the men in the morning, George boiled.

April 4
Annie, Danny, and I went to Woodstock to visit Pinky [Sinclair] and her children, and did some shopping. We got home a little after 5 and I had several phone calls, the last one was SAM calling from N.J. He and Frank plan to fly to Burlington tomorrow. The men brought the rest of the wood down from the woodlot and then gathered, the sap was running quite a lot.

April 5
30°-40° There were 4 inches of snow in the AM. Eloise and I drove to Burlington to pick up the boys, Georgie boiled, men gathered. It was super to see Sam and Frank home safely again. Eloise and Frank came to dinner and it was fun to hear about some of their adventures.

April 6
Great to have Sam home. George boiled, men gathered.

April 7
Jen and I did odds and ends around the house, men did chores.

April 8
Quite a nice day, Steve came out for breakfast and then later he, George, and Jenny went horseback riding.

April 9
Sam and I went to town to take clothing boxes for the church and to do some other errands.

April 10
We took a last ride on the big sled [for the winter], it was fun.

April 13
Jen, Annie and I went to Burlington to shop. We found Jenny a lovely wool suit which will be good for her Australia trip.

April 15
Easter Sunday, Dave, Matty, George, and I went to church, and then George boiled. J, S, & A went horseback riding. We had a good dinner all together.

April 16
Annie and Sam took Frankie to the plane in Burlington to fly to Denver. Men started Springs work.

April 19
30°-50° Nice day, but a cool wind, sap does not seem to flow. Men have been getting out manure, spreading fertilizer on pastures, Dave put up pea fence after George harrowed all the gardens.

April 20
Beautiful day, I have a bad sore throat, Sammy and I went to watch Matty's first baseball game. The game was at Blue Mtn. and Matty pitched, they won 6 to 0.

April 23
I took Sam to Burlington to catch a flight to Puerto Rico [for his job at Edcon]. I felt pretty empty after he took off. I hurried home, did some work, lunch, then went to Hovey's to pick out some clothes for the Fashion Show. Then back home to make lasagna for the pastoral candidate meeting. The man was young and seemed very interested in working in Peacham, we had a very good exchange of ideas and everyone was enthused about him.

April 24
Boys gathered last of sap, I planted all the early seeds that I could, also some onions. Rehearsal for Fashion Show, I'm so busy this week that I'm tired and not getting rid of this cold.

April 25
George boiled in last of sap, made 550 gallons, Fashion Show went really well.

April 26
I went to town and returned all Fashion Show things. I met Jenny and Steve and went to Littleton to watch Matt's game. He pitched; it was a super game to watch and Danville won 5 to 4.

April 27
Men washing buckets, fencing, spreading manure, chisel plowing.

April 28
Great day, we did odds and ends, fished, raked, and played horseshoes. Daffodils are blooming, a few asparagus poking through, and some wild flowers. We went to Grandpa's Cigar for dinner, met Jenny and Steve there, the six of us dined together. The food was fair and the atmosphere poor.

April 29
I slept late because of the time change, the boys went up to put tar paper on the cabin. I went up later with lunch and I cleaned up some of the boards etc. lying around.

April 30
Annie came home to work for me, but we ended up moving some of her stuff to Danny's and bring back a large load of seed from Agway. Georgie bought me Hepatica. Men washed buckets, started to seed a piece on Packard's and the Carruth piece. COWS OUT!

I don't think the cows had been turned out to pasture yet, I think Patty means the cows got out of the barn, if this is the case then they would have been wild and happy. They would have been running around on the lawn and garden, punching great holes and raising hell in general.

May 3
Stayed home and got some work done. Dave is working on taking pipeline down. Matt brought Dawn home for dinner, which was nice and relaxed and fun. Then we all went in Matty's car to Lyndonville to see "West Side Story" which Jen had a small part in, the show was excellent.

May 5
After chores the boys went up to the cabin with some stones including a huge one for the hearthstone. Then I took up a lunch and we cooked over the teepee fireplace.

May 6
Picnicked at the wood lot, Annie came home, the boys got the hearth-stone in place and the roof finished. Sam called from Puerto Rico, he talked to Dave and Matt, and he is fine.

May 7
I mowed the lawn, planted sweet peas, David taking down pipeline, Ron fencing, Benny taking out manure, and George chiseling, etc.

May 8
Georgie and I went to see "The Great Train Robbery" it was excellent.

May 9
Another nice day, I planted some more seeds. We have eaten rhubarb and the asparagus is coming up fast and my herb garden looks good. Frankie Miller came over and played poker with the boys.

As I write this in September 2017 Frank has reduced his role with Edcon and plans to retire at the end of the year. He plays poker regularly with us and is very much like a son to me.

1980

"After lunch we all did a hunt from the cabin ...
now we have two deer hanging."

HUNTING ALWAYS PLAYED A BIG ROLE IN OUR
family life. I got my first shotgun when I was at the Newton
School, it was a 20-gauge bolt-action shotgun with a clip. It was
there that I shot my first legal buck, a 7-pointer. Patty loved being
in the woods with me, and I bought her a 20-gauge side-by-side gun.
She got her first and only buck in 1981, 5-points. None of our girls
showed any interest in hunting, but the boys did, and we bought
them all guns as they got old enough. I taught them how to dress
out a deer, we hunted deer and birds, and Matt and Sam still do – I
gave up deer hunting when I got bird dogs. We would say that in the
winter our house was a ski lodge, in the fall it was a hunting lodge.

We developed a spring below and east of the farm buildings, on
the boundary with Bernard and Joan Churchill. We put a pump in
and buried a pipe from it to the cistern in our cellar. This gave us
a second water supply for use during dry times at a cost of $2,450.
We bought a wood splitter that mounted on a tractor for $600, a
loader for the Case 430 tractor for $1,500; and we traded the Case
730 and $14,500 for a new Italian tractor made by Same. It was our
first 4-wheel-drive tractor, and the added traction let us get on the
fields earlier in the spring, as well as work them later in the fall, it
also was very handy in the woods for logging. Matty and I started
harness-breaking our yearling colts, Mickey and Buddy, and bought
two more baby work horses, both fillies this time, named Daisy and
Maggie. This gave us seven horses with Penny, Shilling, and Orlando.

We switched the sap evaporator back to wood from oil. I thought 64 cents a gallon for oil was too much. I bought some doors and grates off an old arch that Jim Quimby had, re-cemented the floor of what was now an ash pit under the grates, and somehow made it work.

In November Patty and I went to Windham to visit the Newtons. Since the Newtons played such a key role in my life and also were responsible for Patty and me meeting, I will fill you in a little more with what happened to the Newton School and the Newtons after the school closed in 1950. Pappy and Mom Newton continued to live in the original farmhouse, the former school building, which is where Patty and I stayed when we visited. Son John and his families also lived in the farmhouse in rooms over the kitchen. They shared the kitchen with Mom and Pappy and looked after them. When daughter Mary Newton married Dave Western, they lived in the Music House, built for a former music teacher, which was situated across a field from the main buildings. Mary and Dave had five children, Sam, Matt, Margie, Joanna, and Tony. John Newton and his first wife Jane Spross had five children, Mike, Sallie, Becky, Pete, and Jimmy. John and his second wife Jane Greenwood – "Jane Two" – had one son, Amos. John and his third wife Jill had no children, their passion was performing music at square dances. John was an excellent caller and Jill was a renowned fiddle player. When John married his fourth wife Anna they moved out of the big farmhouse to her home. Pappy Newton died in the spring of 1982, Mom died some years later. John's sons Pete and Amos and their families continue to live on the Newton property – Amos in the big farmhouse and Pete in a new house that he built up the road.

March 15, 1980
I can't seem to keep this journal going but I will try again. I will only give a very brief picture of what everyone is doing.

Sam in September went to John [and Maureen "Mo"] Ninninger's wedding, and then to Denver for a while, had a week's school in Texas and from there to Denver en route to Shanghai for a job offshore there

[Edcon]. He was in Shanghai until just before Christmas, during his three weeks' vacation he went to Sydney to visit Steve's [Harris] family. Then he went to the Congo, via Paris for another job. We have had a rough time getting his mail to him and he feels out of touch, also tired of sea jobs! He may be home pretty soon and we will know more about everything.

March 16
This was a very lovely Sunday and George, David, Matty, Dawn and I went to Burke for the day. It was the best skiing Burke has had this year and the only day Georgie and I have skied this year. We all had a super time and got very tired.

March 17
22°-40° A mild mostly cloudy day, some sun, the men tapped and hung buckets in the Miller Sugar woods.

March 18
Jen and Steve arrived last night after we had gone to bed, we had some visiting time this morning, then they had to spend the day in Lyndonville. The men tapped the rest of the Miller Sugarbush. Jen and Steve were back for dinner. After much discussion we finally made some definite plans for the wedding that seemed agreeable to everyone. 1 PM May 17ᵗʰ at the church, reception at home, Howard Boardman and Richard Hough-Ross doing the ceremony.

March 20
20°-65° Lovely day, boys finished hanging buckets and gathered a load. Some of our roads are getting really bad, snow is going fast. The Carruths and Bonds came for dinner and we looked at the Bond's slides of their summer in England, Scotland, and Wales.

March 21
31°-40° Cool and cloudy, it was predicted to rain a lot today but it never did. I went to town and accomplished many things including wedding invitations and talking about wedding cake and sandwiches.

I had my usual lunch at the Wooden Horse, Bloody Mary, Spinach salad, and coffee, very relaxing. George did a little boiling, first time in the sugarhouse with wood, not enough sap to make syrup.

March 22

I took a good walk, Dawn and I had a good conversation. Then Georgie broke through the horse barn floor with a tractor. The tractor was hung up there and it was frightening to think what might have happened. I was pleasantly surprised when Georgie, Matt, and Dave were able to get it out by pulling with the big Case and laying planks across the hole in the floor.

March 23

This early morning was wonderful and I jogged, really the first time this year. I loved it. I went to church, the boys, George and Dawn gathered one load.

March 24

28°-50° Nice day, men gathered most of the day, I helped a while. Jean and Howard [Boardman] are in town so they came to dinner, Jim Keeney stopped by so he stayed for dinner too, it was fun.

March 25

28°-40° Georgie boiled all day and it went very well with the reconstructed wood rig. He made about 25 gallons of A. Sandra Craig and Jean Berwick visited. David got a letter from Sam saying that his job should be done by the end of the month and then he was going to France for a while to visit Larry Skoller and travel.

March 26

27°-37° A little snow again this morning, a nice day but not too much sun, sap not running particularly. Matt, George and Ron worked on tapping pipeline, Ben was piling manure.

March 27
27°-60° Lovely day, rather unexpectedly, finished tapping pipeline, sap not running too wildly.

March 29
Georgie boiled all day, I made raised doughnuts to have with hot syrup at the sugarhouse. Georgie and I went to see "Going in Style," which I had seen before, and then we stopped at the Wooden Horse and talked 'til almost closing.

March 30
Palm Sunday, we all went to church, and then George boiled.

April 1
22°-50° Men split wood, and then gathered sap. It was warm enough to sunbathe. The Wedding invitations are ready.

April 4
While we were getting dinner who should arrive but SAM! Wow, what a surprise! He'd spent the night in Burlington at Dennis's [Kauppila] then taken a bus to Danville where Mary Jo Quimby picked him up and gave him a ride home.

April 5 & 6
Easter weekend, fairly good weather, Jen left by bus Saturday PM, Dawn went to church with me on Sunday. It was a good sermon and very well attended.

April 7
George and Matty split wood all day, Ben spread manure, Ron and Dave moved hay from the village to here. Sam helped split wood and worked at his desk.

April 8, 9, & 10
George boiled and has made about 200 gallons of A and B. A few crocuses and daffys are poking through, and snowdrops blooming. Boys

had a special poker game for Sam down at Duncan's, and I had a Church Council Meeting.

April 11
Warm day, nice sunshine, George washed sap holders, the others moved hay and split wood. Jen had a fitting of the wedding gown with Eloise. She is doing a super job altering [my wedding dress] for Jen. At eight, we all attended Vera Power's wedding at the church. It was a lovely candlelight ceremony.

April 12
Georgie and I went to Woodsville to look at the large mirror I had thought we might get for the hall. We bought it and went to lunch at the Happy Hour. Some of the kids spent time at the cabin in the afternoon. John Ninninger came and had with him a fellow from England he had picked up hitchhiking. The boys stayed overnight at the cabin.

April 13
George and I went to church, Richard's [Hough-Ross] sermon was about Peace and why it's so hard to obtain. Some of his thoughts were pretty controversial, we thought the sermon was excellent. Jen and I finished the wedding invitations.

April 14
Buddy McLam finally came to put in our wood furnace which has been sitting in the cellar with wood next to it since October. We had been very upset with him, called several times and George wrote him a firm letter. He has a lot of electrical work to do also to comply with standards for an insurance company. The men chisel plowed, picked stone, and did some harrowing on the Hardy lot.

April 15
40°-50° Rained during the night and some in the morning, then it cleared somewhat and the sun shone for a while. Ben went to Maine after sawdust. Matt, Dave, and Ron split wood. George helped Buddy on the furnace. SENT INVITATIONS!

April 22
27°-55° Cool, breezy, sap has run some in the past week. George has boiled several times, he had a lot of company in the sugar house on Saturday. Jen and Steve came Saturday to spend the week and most of the time now until the wedding. We have begun doing clean up chores outside and in. I had a bug yesterday and today and Jenny has taken over for me which is so nice. I have rested and gotten a few things done in the way of desk work and sewing.

Patty didn't write from April to November, she was very busy with a number of things and one of them was Jenny's wedding. I will describe the wedding briefly. Howard Boardman and Richard Hough-Ross did the ceremony at the Peacham church, and the reception was in our front yard. I remember Ann Mills saying how much she enjoyed it, she thought it was a perfect wedding. Steve had many family and friends here from Australia. His parents Joy and Grahame (Wink) Harris stayed with Eloise Miller. We had a little drama, my father passed out and we had the ambulance come, they treated him and he was fine. It was a wonderfully simple wedding and reception on a glorious day.

Soon after Jenny and Steve's wedding we got a call that Sam was in the hospital in Cody, Wyoming. Patty flew out to be with him. Instead of a sea job Sam was doing a land job for Edcon from a helicopter, and the helicopter crashed, killing the pilot and navigator and leaving Sam alive but injured and alone on a mountainside. The helicopter company got worried and flew over the crash site before dark, but figuring that everyone was dead they left and came back in the morning. Sam, with several broken bones, crawled around and gathered some bits of insulation from the crash site to keep warm and managed to survive the night. I like to think it was nothing exceptional for a farm boy. Annie and David flew out to get him when he was well enough to come home. He went back to UVM that fall. Annie decided that since she had missed a semester with her skiing injury in 1978, she would go to UVM that summer so she could make up work and graduate with her class.

November 2
I have missed so much time writing and many things have hap-
pened. I may take time and write a catch up sheet, but here I'll just
start with now.

Friday evening, Halloween, Georgie and I had a party, costumes, jack-
o-lanterns, and all, it was great fun, very relaxed. Fuehrers with very
good Indian costumes; Mills 1940s collegiate, also good, both had on
wigs; Duncan, the "hanging judge," super; Crismans, Jo a Gipsy and
Ron a cowboy; George a troll and me a witch; Powdens came without
costumes. Jo told fortunes with little cards she and Ron had drawn.

Saturday we did chores and then the men and Dawn went to the cabin
with a load of wood and stacked it in the wood shed. I went up later
with food and we cooked lunch. They went for a hunt and I started
dinner. Jen and Steve came all the way up to have dinner with us and
it was fun. Just before dinner the Berwicks drove in to show us a black
bear that Benny had shot up in Craigs' land near Randall's.

Nov 3
I cleaned the pantry.

Nov 4
George and I put up some storm windows, VOTED, put hay on
George's strawberries and walked home, visited the Boardmans and
then our new neighbors the Mercadantes. We went down to the Bond's
to watch the returns. Very early it was obvious that Reagan was win-
ning big. As a matter of fact, Carter came on TV by 10 PM and gave
his concession speech, it was very sad.

Nov 5
Fairly pleasant morning, I brought in my beets, carrots, and turnips.
In the afternoon it got cooler so I worked inside in the work room. The
men are rebuilding the stone wall across the road from the house, it
looks wonderful. Dr Griffin came to castrate the colts but could only
do Mickey because Buddy has one undescended testicle, he will have to
do it with another technique.

Nov 6
George and I had a nice day, we left at 10:30 and drove to Woodsville to pick up a shot gun that George had bought for me last week, did some farm errands and had lunch at the Chimes in Bradford. Then drove to Topsham to Freddy Miller's store and got a few things, then across to Northfield to see Tony Giroux [Gretchen Bond's father] and draw up plans for a desk he is going to build for me. I think it is going to be lovely.

Freddie Miller's store in Topsham was a trip into the past, with horse harnesses hanging from the ceiling, axes and hardware, groceries and wool shirts, an old fashioned general store.

Nov 7
Nance [Wason Bartell] came to help me clean this morning. Our new 4 row corn planter was delivered this noon. Yesterday while we were gone our new 4 wheel drive Same tractor was delivered, it looks pretty new and powerful. This evening the Bonds and the Mercadantes came for dinner and we had a very good evening.

Nov 8
We had a little hunting this morning, I shot my new shotgun which shoots very nicely. Matt and Dawn are moving in. We left about 3:30 for Windham, stopped in Hanover to buy Mary [Newton] some flowers as a birthday gift, she was turning 50 as we would soon be. David ["Pappy" Newton] put on a lovely dinner with about forty people, followed by a dance which John and Jill [Newton] and Jill's band played for, a very nice party. We spent the night at the Newton seniors'.

Nov 9
We had a good sleep got up late 9:15, had breakfast with Mom and Pop Newton and really had a good visit.

Nov 10
Cold, snow flurries, the men butchered 3 cows.

Nov 11
Very cold and snowy, one to two inches, mostly blowing around, we brought home the dry cows and heifers because of the wintery weather and seemingly more of the same to come. Sam called and said he hasn't been feeling well, went to the infirmary and had some test which indicated MONO, so he'll have to slow down again for a while.

Nov 12
I spent the morning outdoors which was nice, first walking the colts with George and Matt, and then trying to get the bull and two heifers out of the pasture. It was exciting, used the saddle horses and all of us finally got them out and home. George and I started cutting meat.

Nov 13
Still cool, but the sun did come out for a while this morning. We sighted in rifles and I shot my shotgun, we cut meat from 11 to 4:30, I had a church council meeting after supper.

Nov 14
Packaged hamburg, did household stuff. Matt and Dawn went to Barre and got the engagement ring, so now it's official, they plan to be married in May!

Nov 15
Opening weekend of Deer Season, but it was a weekend on for us. Jen and I went out for an early hunt; we enjoyed the sunrise and the tracks, but no deer. After breakfast and chores Georgie, Dave, Matt, and I did a hunt down across the road and it worked perfectly, David shot a small buck, he had a doe tag, perfectly through the neck.

Nov 16
Jen, Dawn and I went to church, which I enjoyed very much, they too I believe. The men did a hunt after breakfast and chores. After lunch we all, including Dawn and her brother Chuckie, did a hunt from the cabin. Steve, Dave, Chuck, and I pushed down from the cabin toward George and Matt and Dawn, We had only walked ten or fifteen

minutes when we heard two shots. Matty got a fairly small doe that Dawn had caught sight of first, now we have two deer hanging. We had a nice dinner, quite noisy and fun, and Matty played his guitar and we all sang a little.

Nov 18

Snowing at 6AM, about 5 inches, it was a beautiful snow storm, we ended up with 8 to 10 inches. George and Matt skinned David's deer and cut up some of it and took it with them up to the cabin. Dawn, Dave, and I went up for supper. The cabin was very warm and cozy.

Nov 19

I did things around the house and then skied over to Eloise's to visit. It was a lovely ski. I did more things around the house and then took the doggies up to the cabin and had supper. It was a beautiful moonlit night.

Nov 21

I made mincemeat today and Jenny made cranberry bread, Sam got home about 2PM, visited with us and then he and Jen went up to the cabin. Dawn, Dave, and I went up later and had supper.

Nov 22

Jen, Annie and I made pies.

Nov 23

A lot of fog in the early morning which froze on everything and it was a beautiful sight. Jen, Dawn and I went to church, I love having the girls go with me. After we got home we all worked on getting our Thanksgiving dinner ready. The men came down from the cabin and we sat down around 1:00. The table looked very pretty with my new table cloth. We toasted champagne and gave a little gift to Dawn and Matt in celebration of their engagement. The dinner was delicious and relaxed, one of the nicest. The men hunted, Jen, Annie and David went riding, Dawn and I took a walk.

Nov 24

I worked here in the morning then Matt came down and picked me up to the cabin. We had lunch with Georgie and then Matt went back home and worked with the colts and Georgie and I stayed at the cabin. We had a very good time talking, loving, eating, and sleeping.

Nov 25

Georgie and I slept rather late, had breakfast, then went for a hunt down by the beaver ponds. We saw two Partridges; Bear tracks, Coyote tracks, Deer tracks, but no fresh ones until we were almost back. We split up then and Georgie jumped two deer which ran toward me but I missed seeing them, I saw the tracks and followed them a while. We came back down around 3:00, the boys hunted, I bathed.

Nov 26

Mother's 83rd birthday. Sam arrived about noon and went up to the cabin to meet George and Matt. I cleaned etc., I also have a cold, sore throat and don't feel too well. Dawn and Matty went to the cabin for overnight. The older boys played poker here with Duncan and Bob Morgan.

Nov 29

Dawn and I did some Christmas baking.

Dec 15

20° below zero – George and I drove over to Northfield to the Giroux's and got my desk which Tony had finished. It is really a superb desk, beautiful to look at, spacious and organized, just what I've been wanting. We paid $700 for it, but it is certainly worth much more. While we were gone the kids took the new tractor up in the woods and cut a tree to light outside. We were amazed when we got home because of its huge size and beautiful shape. Sunday Dawn and I went to church and enjoyed the youth program very much. After church and chores the boys put my desk through one of the front windows because the desk was too big to go through an inside door, then they put lights on the outside Christmas tree.

Dec 25
30° below zero – we had a lovely celebration Christmas Eve. Jen and Steve arrived in the afternoon, Dawn came home from work, and we had drinks and pork pie for dinner. Then we sat in the parlor and looked at the lovely tree and sang carols before opening gifts. It was such fun. Christmas morning we had a super breakfast and opened our stockings. George and the boys had to do chores and it was dreadfully cold, a wind along with 30° below.

Dec 26
We spent time over the weekend with the horses. They rigged up the horses to the single bob sled and we rode around the field, the colts were very good.

1981

"Dinner was very special with champagne,
the good silver...very special for us."

AFTER MISSING A SEMESTER BECAUSE OF HER
skiing accident, Annie had been able to catch up to her class
at UVM and graduate with them this spring, quite a feat considering she had also skipped her 12th year in high school. Sam continued at UVM and was recovering from his helicopter accident. He
received some money from the insurance company because of the
poor way the rescue was handled, and he invested some of it with
the farm. At the time, interest rates were quite high and we paid
him 14% interest. David went back to college this fall at Lyndon
State, and met a girl that he fell for named Cindy Ladue. Jen and
Steve moved to Killington, Vermont; Jen was working at Marble
Bank in Rutland. Matt and Dawn were married in the Peacham
Congregational Church May 23rd and the reception was held at the
Creamery Restaurant in Danville. It was very nice, and I believe they
paid for it all themselves.

On the farm this year we bought a new John Deere corn planter
for $4,700, we extended our manure pit for $1,141, bought a spray
rig at auction for $500 and bought a second New Holland hay rake
for $2,130. This rake had dolly wheels in front so it wasn't carried
by the 3-point hitch of a tractor, this allowed the rake to follow
the terrain better and do a cleaner raking job. While it was true
that it raked cleaner, it also had two other advantages for us. One
was we could hitch it behind our old rake and rake two windrows
at the same time, and the other was we could put a seat on it and

replace the short pole used for pulling by a tractor with a long pole designed to be used by horses. The horses did very well, but with the big mower we covered a lot of ground and the rake had to go faster than a horse's walk in order to keep up.

Jan 1, 1981
Last night George, Annie, David, and I spent a nice evening at the Bond's and saw in the New Year. Yesterday Sam returned to Burlington, today Annie took a bus to Burlington in preparation for both Sam and Annie to fly to Florida for the week.

Jan 2
28° below

Jan 3
30° below – George and Matt worked the horses and hitched them to the Pung sleigh. We went to Crisman's, XC skied and had supper and party there. The kids had a pizza party here.

Jan 4
35° below – not even church today. It didn't go above 15° below today and by 5:00 it was already 30° below.

Jan 11
22° below, windy – Friday Sam and Annie came back from a week in Florida with the McCakes, Sam's roommate's family. Last weekend Michael Claghorn arrived and spent three days here. He was a good guest, but a very mixed up person. We think it was good for him spending time here cutting pulp, talking, playing pool, but I think he will never lead a normal life. George and I went to a dinner party at Ed and Beppy Brown's with the Toby Balivets from Danville and the Danielsons, it was a very nice party except George drank quite a lot and flirted and hugged Claudi Balivet and Karin [Danielson]. I am embarrassed and upset about it. Today we just hung around did chores etc., it was too cold for much outdoor fun.

Jan 13
18° below – David, George, and I drove down to Killington to see Steve and Jenny's home. We had coffee there and then went to Pico and skied together with complimentary tickets.

Jan 26
Last Wednesday I went to Bretton Woods and skied with Marilyn Lent and Pat Dodge. We had fun and the view was beautiful of Mt. Washington and the hotel at the foot. But when I got home George had bad news for me, that Don Clark had killed himself. It was a shock. I called Betsy [Arnold] and told her and then called Jean and told her I would come down for a few days if she wanted me to. She did.

Thursday I prepared for the trip and left Friday at 9:30 AM. I was able to talk to Jean alone right away and she gave me all the details of the past weeks and days. Don had been discharged from the hospital Friday and he had had a bad weekend, but still back to work on Monday. Wednesday he came home from work, found his deer rifle, went outside the house and shot himself. The neighbor found him, called the police and then Jean arrived, it was a terrible shock but she was very aware that he wanted to die.

Much of the weekend was spent talking with [Jean's] family and friends, general talk but a lot about Don and his problems and why he did this and how people were feeling about it. The Memorial service was very lovely, a number of good scripture readings, hymns, a compassionate homily by a friend and a down to earth prayer by the presiding minister. It was real and loving and even uplifting somehow. I left Monday morning and I'm sure she'll be terribly lonely, but she has superb friends who will stand by her, I know.

Jan 28
A very beautiful day, Richard Hough-Ross had lunch with us and then I went back with him to do some reports. When I finished I walked home, it was lovely.

Feb 1
Slept 'till 8:00, then went to church, had a great party in the afternoon.
Bonds, Browns, Danielsons, George and Matty took the children and
Karin for a sled ride behind the horses. The rest of us went for a nice
little ski trip, plenty of supper and everyone had fun.

Feb 2
It is pouring rain and windy, and creosote is coming down the chimney
again with rain water. It rained all day then flurried a little snow in
the evening. Roads hazardous, Ron and Ben walked over.

Feb 3
George had an all day meeting on pesticides in Morrisville. I walked
to the Village and back, boys started cutting firewood.

Feb 4
We are over-drawn again, milk check hasn't come, and we're just
hanging in there lately and face income taxes soon. George and I had
our pictures taken at Jenks. I hope they come out okay, we had to get
all made up.

Feb 10
George and I left home at about 6:30 AM. It was a lovely morning
and sunrise. We stopped in Brattleboro for breakfast and then drove
to Southington [Conn.] where we arrived at 11:20 at the Meixell's
[Jean Clark's parents]. We had a very good visit with them, lunch,
and a little walk. We left at 2:20 and I drove to Alpine, New Jersey to
Nancy and David Andrews.

Feb 11
We got up at seven, we had breakfast with Nancy and she left for work
and we left on our way. The wind was blowing very hard and soon
it began to pour rain. The driving was very difficult out of the city
area and on to Hackettstown. We found the cemetery and drove in
and found the Ayers-Gulick plot just where I remembered. It seemed
strange to see IVAN EMORY GULICK on a gravestone. We stayed

a while thinking about Daddy and also thinking ahead about burial ground for our family.

We drove on then toward Eastern Allentown. By three we were in Amish farmland and quickly came across Smucker's Harness shop that Pete O'Boyle had told us about. We went in to see, about 10 people working. We talked to the owner, looked at some harness and then ordered a double workhorse harness for our colts for $700. One of the boys working there said his father had an old combine he would sell so we got directions. It turned out we found the wrong farm, but we talked to the young Amish farmer for quite a long time. He showed us the eight mules he owned and how he hitched seven of them up with four across and three in front, George was intrigued.

Feb 20
It was fun to get home safely and to be home. Everything was just fine here, everyone got along well. The weather here had been mild most of the time we've been gone and since we've been home it's been like Spring, with MUD. The night we got back we couldn't get through the mud by Allen Thresher's it was too deep for our VW so we went around through the village.

Sunday we had a nice ride in the old express wagon with the colts pulling and the fillies hitched with their halters behind. Boys have been tapping the Danielson sugar woods for the pipe line.

Feb 25
It started snowing in the early AM, the power went out with the heavy wet snow. We got about a foot. Steve left for Pico at about 9:30. Jen and I worked around, talked, walked, and started our weight loss program. We are hoping each to lose 15 pounds by diet, exercise, and reminding each other every three or four days.

Feb 26
Jen and I had my favorite lunch at the Wooden Horse, spinach salad, and she took the bus to Pico to go back to work tomorrow.

Feb 27
20°-33° Tapping continues on the pipeline. I talked to Jean Clark last night and she's really having difficulties, working out her financial situation, dealing with Don's violent death, and Julie plans to be married early in April to someone Jean isn't happy about.

March 3
Our 25th WEDDING ANNIVERSARY! Sam, Jen and Annie came home last night, we all had breakfast together and then all went to Town Meeting. We didn't stay for lunch. The girls got lunch here and we sat around and visited a long time. Afterward we took out all the horses, colts pulling the wagon, fillies hitched behind, and three people riding Penny, Shilling and Orlando. Sam and the girls got dinner. Dinner was very special with champagne, the good silver and a lovely dinner, it was really fun and very special for us.

Mar 5
18°-50° It is a Beautiful day, sap is flowing, buckets are up in the Miller woods and on Mill's hill. We received many anniversary cards and I want to thank people.

Mar 6
It snowed an inch or so. Then it was just cloudy with occasional streaks of sun. Georgie and the boys finished tapping today, about 2300 taps. I went to coffee hour to visit and thank people, also got books for everyone to read. Dawn and Matty are planning to go to Bermuda for their honeymoon.

March 7
George and the boys set up the sugarhouse. Gretchen and Duncan [Bond] came for dinner and we went to see The Marriage of Maria Braun.

March 8
Dawn and I went to church, then we all gathered sap including Danny White. Danny and Matty went Rabbit hunting and the rest

of us did odds and ends. I worked at my desk and Dawn cleaned and washed clothes.

Mar 9
The boys gathered and George boiled, he made some lovely fancy syrup.

Mar 10
Eloise and Lois came to visit, the boys gathered and George boiled. He made more fancy. Nancy came to help me and we started spring cleaning.

Mar 11
George boiled, men split wood, gathered some, I went to lunch at the Danville church which was followed by a Lenten talk by Father Ward.

Mar 12
Ben went to Maine to get sawdust, the others worked on jacking up the barn, they finished by unloading the sawdust. Nancy came and we did more cleaning and curtains.

Mar 13
The sap ran unexpectedly, the boys gathered and George boiled.

Mar 14
George boiled in the morning, it was cold and blustery, in the afternoon we drove over to Burlington to visit Annie. We visited the UVM Dairy Farm, visited at Sam's apt. with his roommate, and then went to dinner at Deja Vous which was lovely.

Mar 16
The sap ran some overnight and the boys gathered as the weather turned colder. George boiled it all in, he has made 120 gallons of fancy. I talked to Jen and she had a bad week. Someone came into her apartment and stole her best jewelry including mother's ring. Then Steve got a letter from the immigration office saying he had to leave the country in order to change his visa so they decided they probably should go to

Australia. Steve may leave as soon as April 1ˢᵗ and Jenny will go in June. It's too bad and rather a shock.

Mar 17
It stayed cold and breezy today, the boys are jacking up the barn, and Ben is taking out manure in the truck. I'm having a difficult time with Annie's sweater.

Mar 18
Most of the week it was cold and no sap. The boys cut some more fire wood, some pulp and split fire wood. Nancy helped me one day, the other day I worked on the work room, sorting and cleaning, I moved the big drawers by myself and I like the room ever so much better. Jen called to say they have got their plane tickets for Australia, Steve April 3ʳᵈ and Jen June 3ʳᵈ. She will spend most of these two months with us which will be very nice.

Mar 23
George boiled and the men gathered. I started running today, it felt good.

Mar 24
31°-45° The sap ran all night and kept on running. The men gathered all day but were unable to get Mill's hill or the road buckets. George boiled from 6AM to 7PM, his leg hurt a lot, syrup total is 225 gallons of fancy. Jen and Steve came at noon. Jen and I made two kinds of doughnuts for dipping in warm syrup.

Mar 25
28°-45° Beautiful sunny day, sap flowing. George boiled all day and also after dinner until midnight, the syrup still grades fancy. I went to the Lenten luncheon meeting and enjoyed visiting as well as listening to the message that Richard [Hough-Ross] gave and went to a fellowship meeting that night.

Mar 26
Another beautiful day, the boys gathered and George boiled all day. Nancy helped me clean, we did pantry and kitchen. George boiled at night again, still fancy.

Mar 28
George got up the usual time and started boiling, Matt took over so George could have breakfast, then Dave joined them and they gathered, boiled and canned A syrup all day.

Mar 29
35°-70° I went running at 6:30 and it was nice and cool, but by the time I went out for church it was very warm, nearly 60°. I saw a flock of geese. It stayed very warm and then it became windy. George boiled all day, the grade has dropped to B.

Mar 30
30°-48° It is warm, and humid, boys all gathering, George boiling, making B. I am choring, bread, meals, errands, clean up, etc.

April 16
Obviously I haven't...

1982

"George has been thinking of this day for years."

W E HAVE BEEN IN PEACHAM 20 YEARS NOW, AND this year marks another big advance on the farm – making our own grain. We had been buying dairy ration – a pre-mixed feed made of a small grain like oats or barley or wheat; dry-shell corn; and a soy-mineral mix. Les Morrison, a grain dealer who built a mill on Route 5 in Barnet, had given a lot of thought to raising grain – it wasn't something that farmers were doing in this area. Les encouraged us to grow our own grain, buy corn and soy separately in bulk, and mix them ourselves. He built us a mix mill, we started growing barley, and Matt and I went to an auction near Cortland, New York and bought a used combine to harvest it. The mill ran on a 5 hp motor, and there was a dial to control the proportions. The combine was a lot of fun to watch as well as to run, with lots of bells and whistles, and people would stop to watch when we drove by on the road or had it working in the field. Because it set us up to handle commodities with the augurs and the bins we'd built for the corn and soy, mixing our own feed prepared us to transition easily to the Computerized Grain Feeding System that we installed in 1985 and then to the Total Mixed Ration (TMR) system six or seven years later.

Most of the equipment purchases this year were related to making our own grain; the exception was the 25KW generator that we purchased by trading our old generator and $1,600. Yesterday, June 4, 2017 – 35 years later – I looked at that generator on that trailer and they are the same, and we still use them, although we have a stationary 65KW generator that we run our new parlor with when the power goes out. We use the old 25KW generator to supply our old dry cow barn and home, and we can also use it at our farm up the road that has a different electric company, which means the two farms are not often out of power at the same time.

Grain related costs: combine $5,000; cement for the base for the corn and barley bins $1,035; the two bins $11,646; grain mill and related augers $7,335; auger to elevate our barley, dry shelled corn, and soy beans into their respective bins $1,800. The total cost for us to get into the grain business was $26,816; the savings by not purchasing the complete dairy grain mix was about $5,000 a year.

We lost two excellent workers on the farm – Ron Cochran and Ben Berwick. Ben, who had worked when most employees wouldn't have because of sickness, was unable to work after October. We continued to give him his full pay and housing until his wife Jean asked us to stop so she could take advantage of government benefits. But three of our kids worked fulltime on the farm during the year: David, Matt, and Sam. Sam went back to work for Edcon in November, and I started sharing the farm profits with Dave and Matt at the end of the year.

February 2, 1982
I am going to try and write again daily and perhaps occasionally ramble about things I have not written about in the past. Jean Clark was here all weekend and we all skied every day and had a sleigh ride too. The x-c skiing has been lovely, lots of snow and good weather. Last Friday Ricky White got caught in a side-unloading wagon while working at David Randall's farm. Fortunately he was not killed, but unfortunately, tragically, he lost part of his right leg. Yesterday we had quite a snow storm, 6 to 10 inches.

Feb 3
Rain began during the night and continued all day and into this evening making terrible road conditions and school closings. I listened to Memorial services on WDEV for Rusty Parker their early morning broadcaster who died Sunday morning. He was a very well known and

popular person not only for his many years at WVEV but for his other civic work. We loved listening to him in the morning before Georgie went back to the barn after breakfast. They will play poker tonight at Danielson's.

Feb 4

It was supposed to snow but so far at 1:30 PM it hasn't, the men went back to the wood lot. We heard this morning that Steven Smith, a friend of the Schoolcrafts who rents Phil Dawson's house, had suffered an aneurysm to the brain last night at 11:30, he was ultimately rushed to Hanover. I am setting up a collection of food and money for the family. This little town seems to have too many crises and as Reeve Brown commented, mostly affecting our men, our young men. In the past year accidents or illnesses have affected Glen Marceau, Richard Brown, Fred Thresher, Bill Eastman, Ted Farrow, Bill Marsh, Ricky White, and now Steve Smith, not to forget Sammy's accident a year and a half ago.

Feb 5

It is mostly sunny and pleasant, but the back roads are very icy. The men worked in the woodlot. We got a call saying a cow we had sold had tested for Brucellosis so we have to have our whole herd blood tested next week. It's surprising and scary. I spent all day cleaning and preparing for dinner party. Ken and Karin Danielson and Pete and Jan O'Boyle came and we had a very nice time.

Feb 6

George and Matty are doing chores without David this weekend because he and Cindy are on a weekend for engaged couples put on by the Catholic Church. Jamie is doing chores in the village barn. We went to the complete dispersal auction of David Randall's cattle and equipment. He decided after Ricky's accident to get right out of farming. He had planned to do so in the spring. We didn't buy anything and stayed only through the equipment, not for any of the cattle. We went to the Library's lasagna supper with Matt and Dawn.

Feb 7
George and Matt did chores and I went to church. After lunch Georgie and I took a nice x-c ski trip up over the Miller hill, down across Danielson's sugar woods, into the Bean pasture and down the long downhill in the Danielson's big field, then across in front of Eloise's and home.

Feb 8
Men at the woodlot, I took up lunch and the dogs. I visited the Carruths and handed the church clerk job over to her with much relief. In a way I didn't mind doing it but it always seemed to hang over my head.

Feb 9
The dept. of Ag sent technicians here today to blood test our herd for brucellosis. Matt and George went to the woods for the afternoon. Matty is training Jesse and Milly to heel. I have worked on Milly some, but he is a better trainer. I'm anxious for her to be good at heeling so I can take her places where she might have to be confined.

Feb 10
It was very sunny this afternoon. I skied up to Eloise's with the dogs and had a nice visit and then we took another trip for half an hour or so. It was velvety new snow on top of a crust and warm sunshine. I had a Church Council meeting this evening. Our fellowship and the community have been raising money for Ricky and Janet White and we've been gathering groceries and money for the Smiths, both families are in financial distress.

Feb 13
A little work with both teams hitching them in tandem. Jean Clark arrived at noon and she, Georgie and I went skiing in the afternoon, it was lovely. We went to dinner at the Mill's with about 24 people from St J, Littleton, Peacham. It was fun, we made valentines after dinner, some people had clever ideas.

Feb 14
Jean came for breakfast, then she skied, I cleaned etc. getting ready for the Dawsons to come. The Dawsons came about 1:30 and then we all took a very pleasant ski trip around the six mile loop, with some variations. Jean and Eloise had baked bean supper with us, I was tired.

Feb 15
After breakfast we all skied again, this time down our big field, over to John Thresher's hill, around and back on the snowmobile trail to the woodshed. The Dawsons left about 11:30, we enjoyed their visit very much. Jean, George and I skied again in the afternoon, this time we went up on Snow's beautiful hill and around. It was quite warm now and the snow conditions were difficult, but it was beautiful.

Feb 17
Joan and Todd [Snively] came about 10:00 and son Todd went to work with the men in the woods. Joan and I visited and then went up and had lunch with them and looked at the cabin too. Joan and I had a lovely X-C trip in the PM. Before she left Joan asked if it would be possible for Todd to work here for a while for his board and room. We had anticipated this somewhat due to knowing Todd's problems and lack of a job. Nothing was decided until Todd called 2 days later and asked about the possibility. George agreed to take him on.

Feb 18
Annie came over and took me to Burlington to catch a 12:25 flight on my way to visit mother. We flew to La Guardia Airport and as always I enjoyed the view coming in to New York. This flight was exceptional, we flew low all the way so there were great views of the mountains in the North and the gradual diminishing of snow, I think I saw the Tapanzee Bridge, and when we came down over Manhattan the pilot gave us a special flight down the East River, across the end of the Island with a great view of the Statue of Liberty and back up the Hudson so we could see absolutely everything, it was beautiful.

Feb 23
Georgie met me [in Burlington] and we went out to eat and visit with Sam. It was nice and so good to get home.

On Monday, while I was still in Norfolk, Annie called to tell me that she and Michael wanted to get married May 1ˢᵗ and that she was 2 1/2 months pregnant, quite the news. So ever since then this turn of events has been on my mind, so many plans have to be made. Poor Jenny has to decide what to do about coming home.

This week has been cold, windy and bright, I have skied every day except one and it is wonderful. Saturday Georgie and I made a parts trip to Derby Line and stopped on the way back in Lyndonville at the Colonnade to check out the reception possibilities there. It's a very nice layout for a wedding reception, only it will be very expensive to provide food, drink, and music.

Sunday George, David, Matty, Annie and Michael went downhill skiing at Burke. I stayed home, walked to and from church and later I took Milly with me X-C skiing. I enjoyed the skiing but I learned when I got home that Eloise's mother Anna Bayley had died.

March 1
15° below-20° The men all went to the woods including David who has a weeks vacation. Nancy came to work for the day, it was such great help to have her because I have so many things to do. Eloise's mother's funeral service will be Wednesday so I am trying to plan the fellowship's help in doing the luncheon after the service. Met with Annie for lunch at the Wooden Horse. We then went to Mrs. Dussault the dressmaker to see about making Annie's wedding dress out of the Chinese silk Sam brought back, also to make me a dress from another piece of the silk. We then went on to Troll's press to order invitations.

Mar 2 through 5
This week got hectic; it started with a very nice X-C skiing party at Powden's Town Meeting day night, I didn't go to Town Meeting. On Wednesday Thelma, Karin and I served a lunch after the Memorial

Service for Mrs. Bayley. Jenny called on the 3rd to wish us Happy Anniversary and to say she plans to come home for Annie's wedding on April 17th. Today the temp went up to 40° and the men Butchered 3 hogs.

Mar 6
We cut up one of the pigs, David and Todd [Snively] drove up to Kirby to get our big crock which Dave had up there for beer.

We needed the crock for curing the hams and slabs of bacon.

Mar 7
27°-32° It was raining and freezing on to everything, we had planned to drive to Windham today with the Keeneys to David [Pappy] Newton's Memorial Service but due to the weather we stayed home. The rain later in the morning turned to snow and it snowed the rest of the day. I skied up to Miller's to say good bye to Frank and his sister Mary. Frank went out with me and it was a winter wonderland, 8 to 10 inches of new wet snow sticking to everything, we had fun and got drenched.

Mar 8
It cleared off and showed a beautiful white world with blue sky and sunshine. Ben took three cows to Lyndonville for beef; one was condemned due to Brucellosis titer but okay to go for beef. George and I rode in the Pung sleigh behind Mickey and Buddy over to the village for the mail, it was lovely.

Mar 10
We got up at 4:30 to get ready for the boy's trip. When Matt came he told me that Jesse was sick and had been vomiting all night and was starting to bring up blood. He was very worried and it wasn't a good start for the trip. After they left I couldn't go back to sleep because I was worried about Jesse and I felt really sad and worried about them leaving. Then after Todd and I had breakfast, I spent most of the morning and evening on the phone organizing a lunch for the Smiths after [Steve Smith's] funeral and food to be brought in these next few days.

The "boy's trip" was for Matt and me to go over into northern New York State and buy a combine.

Mar 12
The men worked on the sugar roads and started tapping, Nancy came to help me. I worked with several others to serve refreshment after the funeral service of Steven Smith. It was a very sad occasion, a very hard time for the young wife and family.

Mar 13
At one time or another all the kids were here today. Cindy and David are here for the weekend, Matt and Dawn stopped by, and Annie and Mike stopped on the way to Burlington. Dave and George tapped some more.

Mar 14
It is very windy and snowed an inch or so this early morning. George and I went to church, later George Wilson stopped to visit. The kids went up to the cabin and shot the pistol at cans, then we all had left over spaghetti for dinner.

Mar 15
20°-40° We planned on the combine arriving in the AM, but the trucker called and said he was leaving about 10 AM. Todd is sick with stomach pains. Georgie and I went to the bank and borrowed $8,000 to cover the combine and Jen's trip etc, then did errands in town including the dentist and the dress maker for a fitting for my dress. The trucker Ralph Stole called at about 7:30 from West Barnet and George went down to get him. He got stuck coming up the hill and Matt pulled him with the Same 4wd tractor and they got ashes etc and finally got it up here. Then it took an hour and a half to unload it, quite a job. Ralph had a little supper and then went on his way; he's a very nice person.

Mar 16
Men tapping Miller sugar woods, we are not going to tap the pipe line this year due to lack of time and a glut of syrup in this country and

in Canada. Todd still sick, I took him to the Health Center, they gave him medication. He thought it was a rip off, and didn't think the tiny pills would do him any good.

Mar 17
25°-50° Snowed about 2 inches, the roads are slippery. The sap is running and the men are gathering except for Ben who's gone for sawdust.

Mar 18
24°-50° A beautiful sunrise and a lovely day, men gathered and I helped for a short while in the afternoon. It was so nice and sunny that it was hard to do anything inside. George started boiling and Todd worked a short time and then said he felt bad again.

Mar 19
25°-40° Another lovely day, the men gathered and George boiled; he has made 25 gals of fancy. I did some errands and kept meeting people I knew and having pleasant conversations. We had a sick cow, septicemia, John and Doris both came and we had a visit after John had treated the cow.

Mar 20
24°-40° This is first day of spring, the men gathered, George boiled all day. Dawn and I skied in the afternoon and it was beautiful granular snow.

Mar 21
22°-34° It started out sunny and then became cloudy and snowy, there was even some thunder and lightning. I went to church, rode down with Dave and then walked home. Matt and George worked with the horses. Todd is feeling okay now but seems really bored. I guess he will be glad when this whole episode is over. It is kind of a drag having someone around who is not really into it.

Mar 22
George canned syrup all day, the others tapped. I left at 11:00 and met Annie and Leona Guyer at the Town and Country for lunch. We went back to Annie's apt. and worked on invitations 'til 5:00, it was fun being together.

Mar 24
Annie came out and we finished writing invitations. Joan came for Todd and had lunch with us and we had a good visit. I think Todd was glad to leave. I hope the stay here was positive, I really feel relieved to have him gone, it was oppressive.

Mar 25
It's a beautiful day the sap is flowing; yesterday George lost a large amount of sap due to a valve being stuck open on the holding tank. I sent the wedding invitations out, it is a little unnerving knowing that we are really committed now to this huge reception.

Mar 26
Nancy came and cleaned and did lunch.

Mar 27
It is cold, windy and miserable; I went to the Bonds to see their lambs. I made donuts while David, Cindy, Matt, Dawn and George played Monopoly. We went with the Bonds to a Democratic Pot-luck and dance. We talked to Madeleine Kunin and Mark Kaplan who are running for Governor and Senator.

Mar 28
I went to church with the Danielsons and when I got home Sam was here with his new car. He told us about his excursion by bus down to Washington to participate in a rally against US involvement in El Salvador. In the afternoon Michael's family [Guyer] and ours had sugar on snow with doughnuts, etc. it was a nice gathering. Georgie and I had a quiet evening at home.

Mar 29
Men gathered a little and replaced buckets that had frozen and split in the very cold weather. I went skiing in the afternoon, it was beautiful, I saw a white rabbit so did Milly and she barked. The new harnesses came.

Mar 30
15°-50° A lovely day, I took Milly out for her practice heeling and it was so beautiful out that I came back and got my skis. We went down into the Still Lot and into the big field and I skied all over up and down on granular crust. It was really fun and so beautiful and warm in the sun. I SAW A COYOTE.

Men tapped and gathered, Milly's leg was run over by the sap trailer but she seems all right.

Mar 31
The men gathered and boiled, John came and vaccinated calves and gave the dogs rabies shots. I worked inside, the boys have poker here tonight.

April 1
George boiled in all the sap on hand, made grade A.

April 2
George and Matt worked on the combine and then they hitched up both teams this afternoon using the brand new harnesses. The snow is disappearing and there are Tulips and Daffys up in the front gardens. We are getting some answers to the wedding invitations now. Today I talked to the Gilmores and they seemed pleased about the invitation, they also noticed how pretty they were and the LOVE stamp. I appreciated their mentioning that because I think the invitations are exceptionally lovely looking. I'm rather intrigued by nice stationery anyway.

April 3
20°-32° We are having unpleasant weather with snow, sleet, rain and wind. This is a weekend on, there is no sap, George and Matt worked with the horses some but George has a bad cold.

April 4
I went to church, Palm Sunday, then Matt and Dawn had lunch with us after they had worked some with the horses. David is home for a week. This weather is depressing and I have no energy. I need to stir myself up and lose some weight too.

April 5
Men started taking down a small structure behind the milk room to make a place for a barley storage bin.

April 6
Ben is spreading manure, the others are finishing taking down the building.

April 7
0°-5° The wind blew dreadfully last night, evidently this has been a terrible storm. From NYC North and from Chicago etc. some places got two to three feet of snow. All airports serving NYC were closed down, Yankee Stadium cancelled a ball game. The worst storm in April in NYC in a 100 years.

The men have just done chores today. Everyone had trouble getting here this morning due to drifts and there really is no job that can be done.

April 8
10°-20° It is still windy but the weather is clearer and some better. George and I drove down to Windsor today to visit [George's] dad and Mata in their new apartment in the old Windsor Prison.

April 9
Sam and I took a nice ski trip in the morning, enjoying the skiing, the sun and good conversation.

April 11
Easter Sunday, I got up at six and went out skiing with Milly. It was gorgeous. The granular crust was just right for my yellow Klister and it was fun, I even sat in the snow in the sun on the back hill. Annie, Mike, Matty, Dawn, Sam, Georgie and I all went down to the church for breakfast and then the service. It was wonderful to have that many of the family all together. We came home all went out to gather sap.

April 12
25°-40° We have more snow and it is slippery, the men had to walk up the hill again.

April 13
George bought a 10 gauge shotgun from Michael [Guyer] for duck and goose hunting.

April 14
The men are gathering and boiling, all grade A, haven't made any B yet. The boys have poker tonight, I have Church Council.

April 15
22°-60° I found one Daffodil from the new group in front of the wall, the ones in front of the house are popping up all over the place, even through the packed snow.

May 9
I have been so busy I haven't been writing, this is a brief recreating.

April 16 – Samantha [Green] and I drove to Montreal to meet Jenny. It was wonderful and exciting to see Jen again. We spent the night in a Best Western Motel, pretty grubby but okay. We had breakfast and hoped to be in Burlington by noon. Alas, I neglected to remember any route numbers and we got lost completely for three hours!!! Got to Burlington about three and met Sam, Annie, Michael and roommates and had a nice visit.

April 18 – We had a wonderful party for Jenny, dad and Mata and all the family with a big dinner and festivities.

April 19 thru 22 – Bachelor party and Bachelorette party were held.

Patty didn't write through the summer, during which time two weddings took place. Annie and Mike were married May 1 in the Peacham church, and the reception was in Lyndonville at the Colonnade. The Guyers, Mike's family, were a large, well-known, popular Lyndonville family, and the wedding and reception were well attended. David and Cindy's wedding and reception on August 7 were in West Lebanon, New Hampshire, since Cindy's family, the Ladues, lived in Wilder, Vermont. The reception was in a conference center, and it included mostly family.

Later in May, after Annie's wedding, Sam graduated from UVM. As you recall he had left UVM, gone to work for Edcon, and while working for them was involved in a helicopter accident. While recovering from the accident he went back to UVM. He lived at home through the summer and worked on the farm.

In June Ronny Cochran said he thought that with David getting married he should find another job to make room for David on the farm. We were disappointed, we were very fond of Ronny and his family. Two of his sons had worked on the farm, Andy and Jamie, but he thought it would be best, and he left and went to Vernon, Vermont to work for a farmer there. Matt and Dawn moved to the Village farmhouse where the Cochrans had been.

Aug 18
I am going to try to discipline myself to write again. I've missed so much, but perhaps I'll go back over it. Monday this week we started combining Barley. This was the real start of a dream come true because George has been thinking of this day for years.

Picked blueberries again yesterday, Annie came over and we picked with Gretchen and her kids. Today there weren't many berries left. This afternoon was busy with visitors, the Crismans came for syrup, several people came for [Dave's]corn and I sent them up to pick their own.

Dave was raising sweet corn to sell.

Aug 19
Matty finished the custom combining job we had agreed to do in Danville. We were glad to have it over because it was a bit far to take the combine away, and also our barley is ripening very fast now. I rode around while George did his first combining in the field behind the barn, it was interesting to watch and exciting to see it happening.

Aug 20
The farm crew raked hay, spread manure, fixed stalls and did some more combining. I went to bed very early, I have been very tired lately, my legs ache a lot and I'm drowsy and wiped out.

Aug 21
Matty and George worked all day on hay and combining along with chores.

Aug 22
I finally got to church this Sunday, I sat with the Hummons and Richard's sermon was wonderful. Sam and I took a lovely walk up in back with Milly. We found a few blackberries and flushed about 12 partridges in a group. George baled hay and straw and David and Cindy pressed apples.

Aug 23
It was supposed to rain but it turned out to be a nice day. The men got in hay and straw and Matty started combining the Village piece. Annie's fetus is in an upright position and doesn't seem to be turning. We are hoping it will change position so she can have a normal delivery.

Aug 26
This morning is beautiful following a very wild stormy night. It rained for several hours and the wind blew very hard and trees blew down all over town. The power went out at 8:30 last night and didn't come on until 2:30 this afternoon. We hitched the generator up this morning to milk but at 7:00 it quit so we built a fire in the kitchen stove and got breakfast. We called Buddy McLam to see if he could fix the generator but he couldn't, we were however able to borrow Mercadantes generator to cool the milk. Yesterday before the rain Jean Clark and I picked blackberries at George Wilson, we picked about 6 qt. or more. I made jam, a pie and froze some.

Aug 27
Becky and Dennis [Kauppila] were married at 5 PM at the Boardman's house with just the family there.

Aug 28
This morning for the first time since June and Ronnie left Georgie was able to sleep in. George, Ben and Matt tried to get the combine started but found they needed points. I did odds and ends and visited.

The Boardmans big celebration of Jean and Howard's 40th Wedding Anniversary and Becky and Dennis's wedding started at three. It was a nice day but deteriorated into a cold windy nasty evening with a few showers. We played some volleyball and horseshoes then visited and had a good pot luck supper. In the midst of this we were informed by young Ben that Ben had been overcome with stomach pain and taken to the hospital with possible kidney stones.

Ben Berwick Sr. kept working but we knew he was sick. This spring when it warmed up enough for Ben to shed some of his layers of clothing, we saw that he was very thin.

Aug 29
33°-50° There was snow on Killington, frost in East Peacham and spots of frost here.

Aug 30
Men worked on the combine but didn't get it going. They picked up straw bales and raked 2nd cutting.

Aug 31
Boys got the combine going and finished combining. I froze broccoli.

Sept 1
I made a cake and did other house chores, and then I helped Dawn get ready for [Annie's] shower. There must have been 45 people at the shower and Annie was rather late getting there so we all waited quite a long time. She was expecting something else and was totally surprised.

Sept 4
We finally have a weekend off, I worked around in the morning and George took Milly fishing and walking.

Sept 5
We slept rather late, but were up in time to have breakfast with Sam when he came in from milking. George and Milly and I took a walk, we flushed a family of Partridges again, then after lunch we played a set of tennis with Matt and Dawn, and later with Howard and Jean.

Sept 7
I cleaned and sorted old clothes in the morning. I took clothes out of the big closet in Dave's old room to make room for Sam. He has cleaned the room and is gradually moving in there. George raked and baled hay. Matt is spreading manure on the barley land after which they will chisel plow it in. I walked the dogs and found blackberries, rose-hips and Partridges.

Sept 8
The ASCS [Agricultural Stabilization and Conservation Service] Committee visited the farm to look at the barley land and the chisel plowing. George said they came, not because there was any federal funding, but because it was new and they were curious.

The ASCS Committee were local farmers elected to oversee federally funded programs.

Sept 9
It is a very nice day, I had a nice walk with the dogs and we saw one partridge. I made rose hip jam and did other odds and ends.

Sept 10
I harvested more onions and broccoli then Annie came out for lunch and we took the dogs swimming. The Barley land is almost all spread and chisel plowed.

Sept 11
George and I had a real good game of singles and then went swimming at Miller's camp. The water was cold and invigorating; it was the best swim of the summer. Then I had to rush to the dump and I just made it as Mary Shatney was about to pull the chain across. Sam had a party at the (lean to) where did that come from, I mean Cabin. He had a keg, pot luck, corn roast. We went up for a while, it was a perfect evening without bugs, you could be in and out, Sam had built a fire to roast the corn.

Sept 12
After chores Ben and Jean came up and we had a good talk with him about his situation. We had already decided that we could afford to keep him on and hope his health would improve steadily.

Sept 13
It is very warm again today, I sat out on the porch writing and watching the violet sky and the fog in the valleys, it was very beautiful. We brought the heifers up from the fire pond piece, Sam ran in front all the way, I drove the pickup and the others ran and rode. It went quite well. Ben is back to work, he is fertilizing hay fields.

Sept 14
The men are putting wood in the cellars, spreading fertilizer, and building a trailer for the new generator. They are using the running gear that was part of an old hay elevator that was part of the equipment we bought with the Craig farm. George seeded down the Lower Johnson piece.

Sept 15
It is a little cooler today, Doris Stetson said they had 1 ¼ inches on their rain gauge. POKER NIGHT.

Sept 17
I worked all day and accomplished quite a lot. The men are getting out logs, Spruce, Fir, and Hemlock from our lower woods across the road to be sawed up for various building projects we need to finish.

Sept 18
George's weekend off and he took Milly out for a short hunt before breakfast. Later we went to Tink and Ruby Goslant's auction, they aren't moving, just too much stuff, and it wasn't very interesting. George took Milly again and went fishing at the near beaver pond, they saw a small black bear, and they also brought back some fish.

Sept 19
We went to church today for a change.

Sept 20
The day became quite lovely, I did bread and laundry with Carol's [Strickler] help in the morning. George is mowing alfalfa to chop and put in the bunk silo, Matt and Ben had trouble with the blower on the chopper. Sam and Dave fenced. Carol and I picked enough blackberries for a pie. We're still anxiously waiting for Annie to deliver. Today was my daddy's birthday and I was hoping it might be today. I do worry about my little girl.

Sept 23
Men were chopping grass but they got rained out, then they started putting wood in our shed.

Sept 24
The men finished chopping grass and Ben is taking the grass head off the chopper and putting the corn head on. George and I talked to the Agway insurance man about Medical insurance as well as other types; we plan to make a change in the next few months.

Sept 25
Opening day of bird season, it was predicted to rain, but it was a beautiful warm day. Michael and Annie came early. Michael and Matty went over to the Foster Pond fishing access and hunted back this way, George, Annie and I went out back. We saw a few birds but Milly was too excited and flushed them too far away sending the birds out of range for George. Michael and Matty came back with two partridges and a woodcock. We all hunted again in the afternoon and Milly and I flushed a few birds to George, he got one. It seemed like a lot of activity for a little pregnant girl that is a week or more overdue.

Sept 26
Another lovely day except it took a while for the fog to lift. I didn't go out for the morning hunt, I had planned to go to church, but I cleaned and caught up instead.

Sept 27
Michael called at 7:15 PM to say that Annie had delivered a nine pound boy at 6:18, they named him Adrian Michael. Georgie and I went right in to see them, Michael was ecstatic, Annie tired but happy, and the baby adorable and resembling his dad.

Sept 28
George was working with Les Morrison. George was building a bin inside the barn to store soy bean meal that would be part of the dairy ration. Les and Dennis were installing a mix mill that would grind

and mix the shelled corn and barley from the outside bins and the soy bean meal.

Sept 29
Annie was discharged from the hospital this morning and Michael was going to be home all day, so I stayed here and tried to get some work done. I did make some tomato sauce, along with laundry, meals, cookies and errands. This afternoon I took a short hunt with both dogs and they flushed two partridges right in front of me but I didn't get a shot off.

Today the shelled corn arrived. Matty took the truck and went to Bradford and got a load of soy bean meal and all this was augured in to various bins. Les and Dennis got the mix mill ready and tried a little to see how it worked. There are still some adjustments to make but basically we are ready to start putting together our own complete dairy grain. The culmination of a lot of thought and work, it was very exciting.

Sept 30
Carol [Marcotte] arrived at the farm at noon and started her duties of feeding the men etc. The men cut corn all day, and Ben was back to work.

Oct 1 thru Dec 31
Here I'll jot down some of the highlights of the fall of 1982 because after Sept 30 I have not written.

We had a wonderful bird hunting season. Both dogs loved it and learned a lot. George and Matty got quite a few partridges, ducks, and woodcock. We hunted birds until the season ended, Dec 31, with the exception of the two week deer season when we hunted deer.

Just before deer season George and I took a short hunt down into the beaver ponds below the cabin. I was standing by the pond and George and Milly walked around the pond to push Partridges across the pond for me to shoot. Several things happened in the space of about 15 minutes. First of all there was a mini-blizzard and it was beautiful! Then

I heard Milly barking and was prepared for birds, but instead, looking in the other direction I saw two huge birds, geese, on the pond not too far away. I shot at them. One flew up in front of me and I shot again, it kept going, I yelled at George. The goose flew over where he was and he shot it down and Milly retrieved it. Then he came along on the other side and I told him there was another still on the water, then he saw it and was able to finish off the wounded goose. Milly swam in and brought the huge bird out.

George on the combine, 1982

Sleighing around Green Bay, ca. 1983

1983

"It was quite a blow, a real downer, and no happiness
after the meeting, even by the winners."

W HEN I THINK ABOUT THE YEAR 1983, WHAT
stands out the most to me was the fun we had with the
horses. The boys, Mickey and Buddy, were four years old that spring,
and the girls, Maggie and Daisy, were three, and we spent most of
our free time that winter doing sled rides. In the process of teaching
the horses how to stand to be hitched and to pull together, Matt
and I learned a lot about working together.

As you have noticed in this journal, the Peacham Congregational
Church was important to Patty, she attended regularly and was a
strong supporter. This year controversy broke out in the congrega-
tion over its membership in the United Church of Christ (UCC).
Some members were very angry about liberal positions that the
UCC took, starting with opposition to the Vietnam War and support for a nuclear weapons freeze. They wanted the church to pull
out of the association. The minister Richard Hough-Ross and other
church members including us wanted to stay in. The situation was
very difficult for Patty and me and for many of our friends. I was
a lay member of the UCC board, Serge Hummon and Howard
Boardman were also on the board, and I was also the Peacham
church moderator when the surprise (to us) motion was made at
the annual meeting to pull out of UCC. The best I could do was
get agreement on a 40-day wait period before a final vote was taken
in February.

On the farm we had income from a new source, sale of hay and straw. The straw was a by-product of growing barley; the combine separated it from the grain we were using for feed. Horse people wanted the straw for the horses when they foaled, it was hollow and made excellent bedding, clean and absorbent. They were willing to pay $4/bale for this first crop, we were producing 100 bales/acre, suddenly we had a whole new industry, we had no idea, just stepped into it. This year the income from selling hay and straw nearly matched syrup: hay and straw $6,146; syrup $6,451.

Milk sales were $172,230, with total income at $196,155. We traded an old manure spreader for a new one and $5,000; we bought a used 4wd pickup with plow for $2,500; and a Farmi Wench to go on the Same tractor for lifting and pulling logs for $1,700. We spent $5,082 on improvements to get Dave and Cindy into the tenant house after Jean and Benny Berwick moved out as Patty will explain.

Jan 1, 1983
It is really a very pleasant day with quite a lot of sun. There is only a dusting of snow on the ground. George and David are on this weekend. George hasn't taken any days off since Sam left in late November.

After chores today George harnessed Mickey and Daisy and with some trial and error got them hitched up to the big sled and we went up into the woods a ways. Yesterday we all went up toward the beaver ponds and cut out dead trees and branches which were blocking the way. Also yesterday we took a last bird hunt with the dogs. Matt got one partridge which Milly found for him. In the afternoon I cleaned and straightened the house. We had a nice quiet dinner with spare ribs and then watched some good TV on ETV [Vermont public television].

Jan 2
There were some very pretty snow flurries this morning which left a dusting. George hitched Mickey and Daisy again. George and I had a light supper in the parlor in front of the tree. I have enjoyed our tree so much this year. It's a beautiful, natural tree and our ornaments look exceptionally pretty on it.

Jan 3

I did laundry, patched coveralls etc. in AM, in PM I took the car down to WBG [West Barnet Garage] to get inspected and then I visited Ben and Jean. Benny is feeling terrible following the chemotherapy and they are having trouble financially. I attended my first Umbrella meeting as a new board member. It was extremely interesting to learn what the group has done and what it is doing; rape crisis work, safe house for battered women, employment help, menopause meetings, etc. etc.

Jan 4

Jean Berwick called to say they had had a chimney fire and that they were having trouble with the furnace still. They are having serious financial problems and I don't see how we can help. If we cut the rent I'm sure welfare would cut their money.

Jan 5

8°-30° Nice day, I did household odds and ends. Men cleaned and bedded the Village barn in the morning, then cut wood in the barley field in the afternoon. A big maple had blown down into the field. The cows were out all over and George and I couldn't handle it alone so we called and woke up the boys and they came up and we got the herd in without too much trouble.

Jan 8

George and Matty got finished chores early and after breakfast hitched up Mickey and Buddy. The Bonds came over and we had a nice sled ride up the woods road. Matty and Dawn had lunch with us and then hitched up Maggie and Daisy to the sled and rode around the fields.

Jan 9

Matt and George hitched the boys again and took them up the woods road. "Little John" [Mercadante] came with our eggs and announced the birth of six puppies, Jesse's progeny. Quite an evening, to bed early.

Jan 10
George had another difficult time with David – over chores today.
Marine Special Services people in the area doing a maneuver.

I gave the Green Berets permission to do military exercises
behind our farm.

Jan 11
40°-45° Poured rain last night, took all the snow away. Matt and
Dave cleaned and bedded the village barn and George started his taxes
in the afternoon. I took both dogs on a good walk out to the beaver
pond and back they flushed two partridges right by me, it was beautiful,
almost spring like muddy.

Jan 12
Nancy came and worked this morning and we got the dining room all
done including washing, mending, and ironing the curtains. George
and David, among other things, got the smoke house ready for our pork.
George had poker tonight at Duncan's and I went to Church Council
at Rosemary's. It was decided to raise money for Ben and Jean through
Fellowship, not an Official Decision. After everyone had left Richard
[Hough-Ross] and Rosemary [Miller] had a big discussion of the UCC.
Rosemary hates it and thinks it is "Pink." She wants us to go it without
the affiliation and I guess others do too.

Jan 13
George and I went to the Church Annual meeting after dinner. There
was a motion made by Phil Carruth and quickly seconded by Peg
Newburn that our church secedes from the UCC immediately. There
has been a lot of dissatisfaction about UCC and our putting so much
money, $1100 out yearly for small returns. Also the fact that the UCC
makes stands on issues that some object to, sic the Nuclear Weapons
Freeze. The meeting finally decided to wait 40 days to vote on the ques-
tion so that more people could think about it and be better informed.
Some people are not happy with Richard and it would seem our church
is "divided."

Jan 14
Very nice day, Matt spreading manure, the others are cutting up a tree that fell on David Field's land. I cleaned and got ready for company dinner. I did take a walk with the dogs, flushed FOUR partridges who were sunning themselves.

Jan 15
David seems uptight again. It's too bad and hard to figure out why and what to do since it is hard on the farm team. Early to dinner and early to bed.

Jan 16
20° Snowed most of the night and most of the day, probably 8 to 12 inches. After chores Matty, Dawn and Michael came up. We had a lovely ride on the big sled and Michael rode Orlando behind, beautiful light fluffy snow. We delivered the big semi-annual check to Eloise. This afternoon I knitted and watch a little TV, fairly early evening again.

Jan 18
-8°-5° Cold, bright day. Nance called and said she could work today, so we did a big job in the kitchen. George has been working on books figuring out taxes. Mid-morning a TV crew came with some of the Green Berets to do an interview here in regard to their exercise. I was rather shocked and didn't react very well toward them but George was nice and gave them an interview. It will evidently be on channel six tomorrow night.

Jan 19
-17° Cold day.

Jan 20
George left around eleven to go to an auction because there was a Martin manure spreader that he was interested in. He arrived home at 2 PM, having gotten there and found it already sold, however for $9000 which was much more than he wanted to pay.

Jan 21

George and I went to Hummon's for dessert and had a good visit. We talked quite a lot about our church, Richard, and the UCC.

Jan 22

17°-30° Beautiful, sunny day. After chores George and Matty harnessed up both teams and hitched both up, the boys to the big sled and the girls to the pung sleigh. We rode up through the fields by Danielson's and into the Bean piece. This afternoon Jean [Clark] and I skied out to the beaver pond. We met John Mercadante and son and cousin snowmobiling, it was the first time I had seen snow m. tracks up in those woods and pasture. I would have been annoyed if it hadn't been our neighbors. Jean had dinner with us then George and I watched "How Green was My Valley."

Jan 23

18°-33° Beautiful sun rise, George and Matty finished chores nice and early. I went to church with Jeanie. Richard gave a good sermon directing it to our conflicts regarding UCC etc. We had a council meeting afterward to plan how to go about educating ourselves to be able to vote to stay with or to leave UCC. Our meeting was shortened somewhat by the onset of freezing rain.

Jan 24

Icy all over the area, all schools closed. David slid off the road with his pickup even with chains on, when they went to get it later the body came off. I worked inside at my desk much of the day.

Jan 25

I worked inside again, boys brought Dave's pickup body up in pieces, it's going to be difficult to fix it up. We watched and listened to President Reagan's State of the Union address. He never seems quite realistic to me.

Jan 26
POKER NIGHT

Jan 28
0°-30° Very bright day, beautiful. Found out at the bank yesterday that Dave is badly overdrawn and behind on his loan payments. I hope he can work this out and get on the up and up, it's a drag. Bed early, tired.

Jan 29
After chores Matt and George took the horses out, both teams. A small mash up going over a stone wall, pung damaged a bit, had to walk the horse home and load the pung on the big sled. I worked at the Umbrella office for several hours this afternoon. We had a moonlight sled ride at 6:30 or so, Crismans joined us and then we went to their house and had a shared meal, then much talk and discussion, some about church.

Jan 30
Jean and I went to church; Richard gave an excellent sermon and service including 4 or 5 minutes of silence, a fairly long council meeting after church to decide how to go about the information writing. A committee was formed to do that; Richard, Nancy Bundgus, Rosemary, Peg Newburn, and myself.

Jan 31
I made bread and did some house chores, but I had many phone calls to make, some in regard to church and Fellowship, plus some others. I spent quite a good deal of time on the phone. This issue of whether to secede from the UCC is causing all sorts of pressures and problems in the community. Among these are the problems of the Hummons and the Boardmans. They have for years planned to retire here and belong to a UCC church, for them it is extremely important. I am trying to understand both sides but I don't have time to read endless things and I am very biased toward the UCC.

Jean and I visited Reeve Brown and her new baby this PM. It is rather special to have a chance to visit with Reeve's mother, Anne Morrow Lindbergh who in her own right and because of her husband is quite a famous lady.

Feb 2
*Jean and I went to Lebanon to meet Betsy [Covalt Arnold], Joanie
[White Snively], Anne [Rantoul Conner] for lunch. We ate at a place
called Owls Nest, we spent a long leisurely time and it was very enjoyable. That was really quite a reunion, the four of us from Summit and
then Anne.*

Feb 3
*34°-42° Raining. Last night Georgie and I both heard a weird noise
and jumped out of bed and went to the window. It sounded like coyotes
yipping very loudly, then some dogs started barking across the bay and
Milly was wild, fortunately it didn't last too long. It rained most of the
day and the snow is almost gone.*

My guess is that the noise we heard was coon hunters.

Feb 4
*After lunch I met with Rosemary, Richard, Peg Newburn, and Nancy
Bundgus to form a letter to let people know about the vote on UCC. It
was a tedious meeting because there are so many underlying emotions
involved. We finally came up with a good simple letter, I think.*

Feb 5
*-5°-10° After chores Georgie went rabbit hunting. A young man from
Monroe came looking for a job, Mark Burrill, he seemed very nice. We
talked to him quite a while. Stuart Kimball came to talk about a job.
George hired Stuart Kimball. David, Cindy, Matt, Dawn, Georgie
and I went to the Happy Hour in Wells River to the Annual meeting
of the Eastern States Breeders Ass. We saw quite a few farmers we knew,
had a good Buffet Dinner, and took part in a somewhat boring meeting.*

Feb 6
*Mark Burrill came back this morning to see about the job. We were
sorry to tell him it had gone to Stuart. George talked to him a while
and I took apart the crib and the oak table to take up to Annie and
Michael. We put them in the pickup, picked up Jean and went up*

(Milly too) to find the new place in West Burke. The apartment is wonderful; it is half a house, upstairs and downstairs, very spacious and open, lots of cupboards, counter space, very nice. We unloaded, put the furniture back together and had lunch at the oak table with some soup that Jean made.

Feb 7
10°-20° SNOWED ALL DAY, beautiful, around 10 inches by evening. I went out to the store and mail in the morning and then stayed in, made bread, washed, etc. My Umbrella meeting was postponed as was everything scheduled for last night, even Shop and Save stores closed at 6.

Feb 8
10°-15° Snowed lightly all night, we have about 12 inches.

Feb 9
Men went to the wood lot to start cutting next winter's wood. Nancy came here to clean for me. I went to Lyndonville to help Annie clean the old apartment. Poker at [Susan and Alan] Greenleaf's, the fellows had some trouble getting home through the snow drifts.

Feb 10
Minus 8°-3° Sunny, cold, the men to the woodlot. I did odds and ends, finally shoveled the porch. Doris Hummon visited in the morning. I visited the Boardmans in the afternoon. Our minds are very taken up with the UCC rift. I really hate to imagine what it would be like if we voted out.

Feb 12
WEEKEND OFF A lovely day, we took a nice trip up into the woods with Buddy and Mickey. Skied in the PM with Jean, from the village farm to Ha-Penny.

Feb 13
Church followed by meeting re UCC. There were eloquent speeches, some discussion. We came away with some hope that we'd stay in. Jean, George, and I skied out around Mud pond this PM, it was lovely. I'm terribly stiff and achy in my legs, arms, neck, back, it hardly goes away. I don't feel too good.

Feb 14
Thursday night our church voted to get out of the UCC, 32 to 16. It was quite a blow, a real downer, and no happiness after the meeting, even by the winners. It is very hard to know how to deal with this.

Feb 19
George and Matty took out both teams on the big sled. Richard Brown came and took pictures to try to get something for an Old Granddad Bourbon ad. Jean called and said she had hurt her ankle and barely made it into the house.

This may have been the first time Matty and I had hitched the two teams of horses, one in front of the other, to pull the sled as a four-horse hitch.

Feb 20
Jean called to say that Ken [Danielson] had stopped to look at her leg again and made an appointment for an X-ray. We tried to find someone to take her in since we were planning on Annie coming out and all of us going on a sleigh ride but I took Jean in at about 10:45, they did the X-ray right away and found the leg was broken just above the ankle. I left her there to have the cast put on. When I got home I found everyone had waited for me to go on the sleigh ride. The men had been rabbit hunting. We all went out both teams both sleds and babies. It was so sunny and beautiful and fun.

Feb 21
28°-50° Beautiful. I skied up to get Jean some breakfast and do some things for her. Came back for lunch then Nancy came and worked here

and I went back up to help Jean. It was warm and I didn't wear my long unders. I planned to go to the Historical meeting but was too tired. Also went back up with supper for Jean. The men started tapping the pipeline in Danielson's sugarwoods.

Feb 23
Jesse bred Milly today, they got stuck together and Milly cried and I was scared and I called Georgie, finally, 15 or 20 minutes, they came apart. I called John. John came this AM to check some cows and gave Rabies shots to all the cats and dogs and he said it was normal. Poker at Ken's.

Feb 26
George and Milly took the boys out on the sled and up to Danielson's sugarwoods. We watched them go by from Eloise's.

Feb 27
We went to a church breakfast and to church. We came home and got ready to go skiing. The Greenleafs called to see if we would like to ski with them, so the four of us went out around the back of Morse Mtn. It was quite a long trip, very enjoyable. Coming home through the back pastures we saw black smoke right over the farm and hurried the rest of the way in fear, when we came out of the sugarwoods we saw it was Gib and Frank Randall's barn that was burning. Our horses were racing around because Marceau's heifers which had been wintering in Gib's barn had been driven out and had come up to our place and gotten the horses out.

George and I went down after answering many phone calls and looked around. From the kitchen back it was destroyed, the rest of the house was saved except for smoke and water damage. We then went up to Eloise's to talk to Gib and Frank, ended up staying for dinner as Les Post had brought a lot of food in from the Church Fellowship.

Feb 28
25°-55° Wow, gorgeous, men tapping and hanging buckets. Nancy came and worked for me today. Watched the last Mash.

Mar 1

28°-40° Town Meeting Day. I spent the morning at the Town Meeting, Dave Cindy, Matt, Dawn, all sat with us. We had hoped Frank Randall would get selectman, but she missed by a few votes to Russell Powden. Doris Hummon was very close but lost to Ron Crisman for lister. Super pot luck luncheon. Post card from Sam from Oman, Africa sent Feb 15. George and the boys came back from Town meeting after luncheon and went to tapping.

Mar 2

28°-35° Rained most of the day then a little snow. I bought a small hall table for the dining room corner from John Hale, oak, carved sides for probably too much money, $125, I liked it though, it fits in there very well.

Mar 3

Men tapped, George boiled. In the evening George and I went to the creamery to have dinner and celebrate our 27 Anniversary.

Mar 4

At 9:15 I called for Verma Kinsey and we went to a world day of prayer service at South Church in St J, others from Peacham were there too.

Mar 5

I went down around 10 to help clean at Randall's, Kay Thresher had organized a work bee. There were quite a few neighbors there to help.

Mar 6

22°-50° Beautiful day. I went to church, then Matt, George, Dawn and I and the dogs went for a ride on the wagon with Mickey and Buddy, it was Wonderful. The sun warm and bright, so relaxing, even the dogs were satisfied to stay on and ride. Had dinner at Matty and Dawn's, it was an Anniversary dinner and we enjoyed it. The house looks nice and they seem very happy.

This week I didn't write for some reason, busy I guess, but I am going to try to sketch out the days; temperatures didn't vary greatly, no lower than 20°, could have gone up to 40°.

Mar 7 – Rained much of the day, men gathered all day.

Mar 8 – School Out. George boiled all day, boys did chores and tapped.

Mar 9 – George boiled, has made 57 gals of fancy syrup.

Mar 10 – It rained all day. I took Jeanie down to Joanie's [Snively] in New London, NH. Nance worked here, got lunch, etc. POKER, and church council. The Church Council Meeting was full of tensions, bitterness and anger, Very Bad.

Mar 11 – Odds and ends, men gathered. Boardmans and Nancy Bundgus came for dinner, talked a lot about the church of course.

Mar 12
I had a nice ski trip out to the beaver pond, saw John Mercadante's new sugar house and buckets out on "our" ski trail, it was lovely skiing.

Mar 13
26° About 5 inches of wet snow. We went to church, then Matt and Dawn came up and we had a real nice sleigh ride, both teams, both sleds, Jennifer Gilman came too, out the road to Martin's pond and back.

In those days the town didn't sand much and it often was good sledding on the road.

Mar 14
Nance helped in the morning, George boiled all day, the men gathered in the PM. I skied later in the afternoon, went out to the Mercadante's little sugar house and visited John and Barbara for a while, then went out to the beaver pond and back. The snow was heavy and wet and

very tiring. I checked buckets in our sugar woods and the sap was drip-ping very fast. I checked the pipeline tub and it was more than half full.

Mar 15
Somewhat nice in the morning, then it rained all afternoon, cold. Boys gathered all day and got way ahead of Georgie with sap. I went to a quilting class at 9:30 AM. It was very good, very interesting, but if I pursued it I would have to spend hours of hard work, much more than I can do, so I think I will have to call that a mistake in judgment. I am going to ask Ann Cochran to take my place. I made doughnuts in the afternoon because we expected Jean and Ben to drop by. They didn't but Bob Heishold stopped in as did Joan Churchill and had doughnuts and hot syrup and coffee. George is very tired from boiling.

Mar 17
George boiled all day, and canned more up, grade A, he has made about 200 gallons. The sap was all gathered in yesterday so the boys were able to get to the Village barn chores and other things, tractor maintenance, etc. I got sugaring supplies from Moore's and did errands in the morning, cleaned and cooked in the PM.

Richard Hough-Ross came for dinner and then we had a meeting of people concerned about our pull-out from the UCC and Richard's stands. It was done for sharing of similar ideas and ideals, and sup-port for Richard. I asked a lot of people and we had a good group even though a number could not come. It had a very positive feel, no partic-ular plans except not to be intimidated by the other group and to work through the system if we can.

Mar 18
30°-40° or so – mostly cloudy but the sun did come out for a while and it was mild. Men went to the woods but weren't able to accomplish much without chains on the tractor, etc. They canned syrup and did other odds and ends. I worked on the rummage sale in the morning.

Mar 19
38°-40° It rained nearly all day. I worked at the church rummage sale all day, 9:30 to 3:30. We did quite well and had a good time. It was amazing the number of good clothes we had there. What we didn't sell will go to Church World Service and to a church in St J that has a good will store.

Mar 20
SPRING, 40°-45° Some rain, cloud, a little sun. George and I went to church after chores. It was the first Sunday upstairs for the spring and first day of Sunday school. I presented to Reeve for Sunday school and Fellowship the gift of a lovely Story Bible in celebration of Jonathon's birth and appreciation for her work in both groups.

March 21
21°-34° Rained all day, a little sleet and freezing rain. I worked inside all day, boys did chores. Matt used the new Martin spreader all day.

Mar 22
31° and dropping all day, cold, raw, a little snow. The sap ran all night so the boys gathered everything today to prevent ice in the buckets as it kept getting colder. I worked inside again all day. I am catching up with sorting, organizing and cleaning.

Mar 23
George and Matty went to a crops meeting all day in Lyndonville, Stuart [Kimball] and David did chores.

Mar 24
0°-25° George boiled all day. Annie and I took Aunt Fran out to lunch, and then we did some errands. The axle broke on the MF [Massey-Ferguson] bucket loader during afternoon chores.

Mar 27
20°-33° Palm Sunday. We picked up Jean and went to church, Matt joined us. It was a very nice service, the choir sang The Palms which I've

always loved. Eight people joined the church including Duncan, Reeve, Dave and Marilyn Magnus, and Colleen Cochran, a great boost for Richard. We went to see "Tootsie" in St J with Dustin Hoffman, wonderful, extremely funny.

Mar 28
25°-35° Snowed 8 or 10 inches. George and Matt went to Lancaster [N.H.] and bought a pickup truck/4 wheel drive with a plow that Matt had looked at Sunday. Chris Danielson is working this week. I felt terrible all day, it actually started last Saturday night, some bug I guess. Matty and George don't feel wonderful.

Mar 29
28° at 6 AM, 20° at 8 AM, 10° at 4 PM. George found quite a lot of sap in the buckets out front but the pipeline and other taps hadn't run much, so no gathering and then it all froze up. The weather was so cold and blustery and the wind blew like mad. George and I took Jean's car over to Eloise's and packed up her stuff. It will seem a little strange without Jeanie, I will miss her. It is too bad her nice visit was interrupted by the accident. I look back and I feel guilty that I was selfish at the time and wanted to spend time with my family rather than helping Jean. It is quite a test of ones Christianity.

Mar 30
I was sick all day, diarrhea, fever, aching. George and Matty took a trip, to do some errands, to Montpelier to register the new truck, Swanton to look at a grain drill, Highgate to order some combine parts, they didn't get back until 5:00 PM.

Mar 31
10°-45° Sunny day. Jenny called and both George and I had a good talk with her. They are in the process of moving to an apartment that will be very close to where Steve works. Things are okay with them but I know Jen wants to conceive a baby and also come back here, neither one of which is happening yet. I miss her, I wish she'd come back.

April 1
Boys gathered, I got ready for Sandy and Wayne [Gulick] to come.

April 2
Sandy and Wayne arrived about 10:30, we had gone to bed. I took Zack [Gulick] out before breakfast to see Uncle George in the milking parlor, he was all excited about everything.

April 3
Snowed great big flakes this morning, then turned to sleet, then turned to rain, a very grey day. It was not grey in church. The flowers were beautiful, we all went except Wayne. The church was full and the service very good.

April 4
Boys gathered all day, George boiled. I went in to the Umbrella office and learned how to train volunteers. Had to go back in for a long board meeting at 7.

April 5
Boys gathered, finished the rounds, George boiled. We had 45 children from Adams St School where Kathy Bussiere works come to see the sugar house. George told them all about it and gave them samples. I had to go into Umbrella to interview a volunteer, she didn't show but another woman did, so I oriented her instead.

April 6
George boiled, Stuart went to Bradford for Soy Meal, Matty and David bedded the barn up here and did odds and ends including fixing the fence in the still lot for the horses. POKER

April 7
George boiled, has made about 400 gallons. I made bread, cookies, washed, etc. Tried to get caught up from being away so much.

April 8
40°-48° Rained last night, showered some today. George boiled; Stu went to Fiske's and brought back our MF that was being repaired. I gathered with the boys in the AM. I cleaned, etc in the PM, the boys gathered, sap running quite well.

April 9
30°-60° OFF WEEKEND, BEAUTIFUL DAY. George and Matt took the dogs and went to check out the fishing, I puttered around. After lunch we hitched Buddy and Mickey to the big wagon, rode to Martins pond. We had a quiet evening.

April 10
The whole family with the exception of Jen and Sam, gathered here for lunch. Mata and Dad came up, George went in for Aunt Fran. We had fun all together, we took four generation pictures and Michael set his timer and got the whole family.

April 11
32°-34° Rain turned to snow and now there's about 3 inches of very wet slush. Actually it snowed most of the day, so wet it settled a lot but there's about 5 inches. George boiled, boys gathered, then Matt and George canned B which he finally made. SAW ROBINS! I think this has been the greyest late winter early spring that I can remember.

April 12
31° Still wet and grey. Nancy worked today, men worked up some wood for the sugar house and other things. I went to the Health Center at 11 AM, I had lost two pounds and BP was 110/78! Bible study, only George and I were there with Richard, but we had a good general discussion and then we got reading and studying Acts. It was good.

April 13
27°-60° Beautiful, we had hoped to see some sap run today but there was very little. Boys did chores around including trimming cow's feet and thoroughly cleaning the milk room and parlor. George helped

a hay customer who bought 200 bales and will want 600 more. He paid us with three hundred dollar bills. I met the new owners of the S Peacham store, John and Jean [?]. We also sold a fair amount of syrup. Council Meeting included several conflicts, one was whether the church should allow Richard, on church time, to attend the Annual Meeting of the [UCC] Conference and supply someone in the pulpit. There was serious disagreement but the vote was 7 to 5 to allow and support this.

April 14
I am about ready to leave for our trip to Washington and Norfolk with Annie and Adrian. I always hate to leave Georgie and home and Milly too, but this should be fun.

While Patty was on her trip south, I kept up the farm journal:

April 15 (George)
30° Misty morning. We gathered sap yesterday didn't get much of a run from that snow, guess it didn't freeze enough. I'm going to take my lunch to the sugar house today and the boys will cut fence posts and spread.

April 16 (George)
32° Windy but no rain yet. Matt spread on the Tavern land, I cleaned up, boys cut fence posts. Milly and I fished in the afternoon, I caught two little ones, Milly got quite tired. I'm going out with Michael [Guyer] tonight.

April 17 (George)
27° Pat called and everything is fine. It snowed last night 4 to 6 inches, the sap might run today. I'm not sure what I'll do today, right now I'm waiting for John [Stetson] to come and look at the # 31 cow, and see what's wrong with her.

April 18 (George)
26° Snowy. Sap ran some on cold trees, Stu and Dave cut fence posts and Matt and I took down the old fence below Bond's, the dogs swam in the fire pond.

We had decided to take down the permanent fence along the road between Bond's and the Cemetery and put up an electric fence. The permanent fence was always getting beat up by the snow plow, the electric fence would be dropped in the fall.

April 19 (George)
28° Waterbury said 3 to 5 inches of snow due this afternoon but by breakfast we have 2 inches. We'll bed the Village barn and try to keep busy. Jim and Dinah were here last night, also the Hummons stopped by with a coffee cake and visited. I'm going to Danielson's tonight.

April 20 (George)
34° Snow, rain, and sun, we gathered today and pulled, I'm going to Greenleaf's tonight and poker at Matt's.

April 21 (George)
30° Same kind of stormy weather, I'll boil today and get Patty, WHOOPEE!

April 21 (Patty)
I made it, whoopee, Georgie met us at 4:30 or so in Burlington, we were very glad to be home.

April 22
Georgie finished boiling, made 505 gallons. Boys are picking up buckets, etc. We've been selling quite a lot of hay at $1.50/bale and some straw at $1.00.

April 23
65° Super beautiful. George went fishing with Milly in the morning. I did chores, started yard work, visited Cindy. We both worked all

afternoon on the yard. George cleaned out and mulched raspberries, and harrowed the garden. I worked on the flower gardens and lawn.

April 24
35° *Started raining by nine, rained all day. We went to church, had quite a few conversations, came home and had lunch. All afternoon we read, worked at our desks, George watched TV. Yesterday George put straw in the whelping box because Milly was "nesting." She liked rummaging around in it.*

April 25
40°-60° *Some rain, cloudy, a few rays of sun. Milly was very restless all night and kept me awake a lot. She scratched at her bed, squeaked off and on, hyperventilated, went down stairs, came back up, she wanted her bed more than the straw. She has been the same today, she didn't even want to take a walk, wanted to come right back, hasn't eaten much. Sold more hay, this PM Matt took syrup to Newport, drums.*

Milly really started labor about 6 PM making quite a fuss, she finally stayed in the whelping box and around nine gave birth to her first one. We were a little worried because at one point it looked like she was trying to eat it. Then she had three more, about 15 minutes or so apart, cleaned them up nicely and calmed down a bit. Each is differently marked, all liver and white, all strong and active and beautiful.

April 26
During the night I heard puppies crying several times, I came down the last time and she was in the process of carrying each one over to a chair in the TV room. When Georgie came down we moved everything in to the dining room and she seemed happier there. They are nursing constantly and she is resting. Later Milly moved the babies back to the chair.

April 27
George got a load of fertilizer early this AM. I didn't sleep much because I kept worrying about the puppies smothering in the chair. I

got up about every two hours to check and move one if it was too far underneath.

April 28

I didn't sleep well again. We both heard the rain in the middle of the night and George got up and put the truck under cover. Boys planted barley, picked stones, and fenced. I am really tired from not sleeping and worrying all the time about the puppies. Nancy told me I should not get so worked up and that Milly could take care of her litter without much help. I realized she is right so determined to calm down. Also Milly took her babies to her own bed which we had put down and that seems reasonable. We blocked off the chairs.

April 29

Gorgeous day, I took Mil for a short walk, and then raked for a while. George has 27 aces of barley planted. Milly has kept the babies on her bed.

May 2

Very rainy, boys worked on washing buckets. Mary and Dave Western called from Hanover and said they would like to visit. It worked out well because George was hampered by the rain anyway. They had lunch and dinner with us. Umbrella meeting at seven, I had to do the minutes which I found quite difficult.

May 3

I spent most of the morning writing up the Umbrella minutes. Matty spread manure and George and Stuart spread commercial fertilizer on fields and pasture. Annie brought Lori [Raymond] out to see the puppies and she picked No. 4 and named him Barley.

May 4

Men finished buckets and other... POKER.

May 5
Nice for part of the day, it never really rained. Stuart and Dave fenced,
Matt spread from the pile at Packard's, George worked on planting
barley and I got odds and ends done, bills, letters, sorting. Boardmans
came for dinner, THEY ARE ALL MOVED IN.

May 6
Stuart and Dave fenced, George planted about 28 acres of barley, Matt
spread from pile at Packard's, I went to town and Nancy was here to
get lunch and clean and baby sit. I went directly to Umbrella and met
with Barbra. First we talked to a woman who was seeking a TRO
[Temporary Restraining Order], we got in touch with Kathy Bergeron,
who was on for safe house and she came to talk to the woman and went
to court with her. Barbra and I had lunch and came up with a proposal
for the board concerning the office.

May 7
I had a bad night with Milly, she kept coming up every ¾ of an hour
and wanting to go out, she was panting constantly, very restless. I was
so upset, I finally called John. He really didn't know what the problem
could be except maybe udder congestion. He suggested giving her two
aspirins which I did. She calmed down and then at 4 AM I awoke with
a puppy screaming. She was upset too, that went on for a while, and
then finally I slept for a while. George took Mil with him fishing all
morning. Georgie roto-tilled for me and worked on his berry patches.

May 8
Nice day mostly, Mother's day. Yesterday Matty and Dawn brought
me a pretty floral spring arrangement, Cindy and David brought a
present which I opened at breakfast, a pretty vase. Annie sent a card,
Jenny phoned! She's okay, still wanting to get pregnant and not having
success. They are saving money to come home eventually to stay. I went
to church; George and Matt went fishing up at the cabin beaver ponds.
Barley is up and also some Asparagus.

May 9
Rained and thunderstorms over night, some snow today. Boys cleaned village barn, etc, PUT HORSES OUT. I did odds and ends; also I was nominated for Fellowship President.

May 12
Men put more cattle out to pasture, spread manure and fertilizer. Sam called from the Seychelles and he is having a wonderful time now vacationing, says the place is really like a paradise.

May 13
I went to town, got home early so I could give George the inoculants for his alfalfa seed. Barley is all in and two pieces are seeded.

Legumes like alfalfa need to have inoculants on their seed when planted to ensure their ability to fix nitrogen from the air into their roots. We had a three-year rotation with the barley, two years straight barley, and the third year we seeded it down with alfalfa and timothy, with the barley as a cover crop.

May 14
George finished seeding, Dave planted his sweet corn and I planted my pansies and then helped David. Carol and Bob Bigelow came to look at puppies and plan to take Streak for $150. They hunt and just lost a young female whom they loved. I think Streak will have a good home.

May 15
George and I went to church after chores. Matt, Dawn, George and I went to Fryes barn to Ben and Jean's 25th wedding anniversary party. Saw many people and had a good time.

May 16
Pups three weeks old and very plump and sweet. George fertilizing pastures, Matt spreading manure. I had an Umbrella meeting at one. We got the office problems partly resolved.

May 18
Tulips blooming, bleeding heart, manure out, picking stones and harrowing corn ground. George has the corn planted on the Tavern land. People by the name of Spaulding came to look at puppies. They were from Craftsbury, older people, very nice. I took a good walk with dogs. Gretchen stopped by with seeds for me. POKER AT KEN'S.

Patty stopped writing after May 18 this year, and because of that she didn't record the birth of Tiffany Kempton on July 30 to Cindy and David.

1984

"Both of us always have a hard time leaving home."

PATTY AND I HAVE BEEN ABLE TO MAKE A GOOD start farming here, and I think there is a good opportunity for the next generation. This year the farm made serious progress toward the idea of a farm partnership with our children, and the prospect is becoming clearer. I like to think that all five of our children were potential partners.

Sam was very knowledgeable in both Maple and Agronomy and he had learned to milk when he was young and had done a very good, responsible job. He had made a large financial investment in the farm and was being paid interest on it, but this was an investment decision rather than an intention to join the farm. He was pursuing other career opportunities. Jenny loved the farm and I think would have been very happy here, but her life took her to Australia, and there didn't seem to be an opportunity for her on the farm at this point. Annie was a good farm worker but now was very busy with her family and her husband's logging business and seemed to have a plan for how her life would go that didn't include the farm.

Matt and Dave were the most likely partners. It would be fair to say up front that Matt had a heads-up, as we had found while working with the horses that we worked well with each other. But there were other factors as well. I have been giving what I call in my account book "Business Gifts" to Matt and Dave to help them build up an account to be able to buy into a partnership. Matt and Dawn invested every penny they could in the farm. In addition to the business gift, they added $1,000 of their own money some months this year. They now have nearly $10,000 invested, and I pay them what I would pay the bank, 12% interest.

Dave continues to have mental problems, and his marriage with Cindy is not going well. This is doubly troubling to us; while Patty worries more about his mental health and happiness, maybe I am more concerned about his ability to join with Matt and me in a partnership. He has been unable to build up any money in his farm account and has withdrawn all of it.

We started formally working on a partnership with the help of Verle Houghabome and Dennis Kauppila. Verle taught at UVM and was the Extension tax expert, I knew him from the annual classes he gave to farmers to help them with their taxes. Verle and Dennis were very knowledgeable and helpful.

Dorcas Gill asked me to take over farming their land, Elkins Tavern, which joined David Randall's land on the upper side. David Randall sold out in the middle of the winter; there are always a number of factors that would get you to this point, and with Dave womanizing may be the obvious one.

Our equipment purchases were: we traded our old VW Squareback for a new VW Hatchback and $9,786; traded an old spreader and $6,989 for a new grain drill (it is now 34 years old and is still used every year); traded a John Deere mower for another new JD mower and $6,900; and bought a used 4X4, ½-ton pickup/plow for $4,500. This year the hay/straw sales exceeded the syrup sales, $5,116 to $3,358.

One of the big things that happened this year was our trip to Sydney, Australia in March to visit Jenny and her inlaws, the Harris's, and to meet our newest grandson, Christopher. Matty took on the farm journal and the handling of the farm while we were gone. When we returned on March 23 Patty made a few more entries in the journal, and then she left off for the rest of 1984, so she did not record another bright spot of the year, Annie giving birth to a second son on August 15, Nicholas Ivan Guyer.

John and Jane Spross Newton's daughter Becky died. She had fought a Hepatitis C complication for years.

I went in as Selectman this year; Russell Powden and Les Post were the other two on the board. Les for several years had insisted on being the road commissioner rather than hiring a road foreman. Many in town thought he did a poor job of it, and they came to the selectmen's meetings to voice their complaints. In fact it got to be a fun night for some, and they referred to the meetings as "Post Roasts." Russell and I wanted to put a stop to this party atmosphere and tried to convince Les that we should appoint a road foreman. We were unsuccessful at convincing Les, so we took a vote. The vote was split 2 to 1 to appoint a foreman; I hate split votes, particularly on a three-member board, and try hard to avoid it.

Jan 23, 1984
Here I will try again to write and perhaps backtrack somewhat. Weather-wise, this winter we have a fair amount of snow, it has been the best year, December was excellent, that the ski area has had for years. January has been cold, Saturday night it was 27 below and this month has had many mornings below zero.

This was a weekend on, Saturday we didn't do much between chores because it was so cold. Sunday I missed church but we went sleigh riding on the road with two teams hitched to separate rigs. Sam is in the Persian Gulf or the gulf of Oman for a short job. He has been there for more than a week so I expect to hear from him soon. George and I went to hear Richard [Hough-Ross] talk about Russia and show slides.

Jan 24
Quite a little blizzard this AM, I had a physical with Harriet at the Health Center and everything was in good shape, a slight anemia for which I'll add some iron to the vitamin and mineral supplement she has me take. George and boys went to the Farm Show in Barre. I skied with Marilyn Magnus in PM, rather heavy wet new snow drifted in the fields. Sam called from New York, the job was done, he was on his way back to Denver.

Jan 25
Men to the woods, George and Matt took their lunch. I cleaned and then took Milly for a training walk practicing hup, Heel, etc. I called Frank [Randall] and she had just had a call from Bob Bean. Bob had just told Frank that Frank's husband Gib had died out on the snowmobile trail where they had been grooming. She was still waiting for official word. I was shocked to have her say this when I had called for a very everyday thing. Poor Frank. Bob Bean had to leave Gib in the woods to come out and call for help. The whole episode took a long time, Bob was terribly shaken.

Now the Bailey Sisters, Eloise Bailey Miller and Frank Bailey Randall have both lost their husbands.

Jan 26
We got 25 ton of shelled corn delivered this morning. The town had to super sand the hill for him.

Jan 27
I visited Nancy Bartell at their new home, and then had lunch with George at the wood lot. We read aloud a letter from Joanie Snively asking if it might be possible for their youngest son, John, to spend some time here working. He has been badly damaged by drug use. We discussed this at great length and decided we would give it a try. George showed me where they had been cutting. It has opened up the view on the back side of the hill, lovely. Had a request to safe-house someone, I said no because it just seemed too much. Talked to Joan and they will bring John on Sunday.

Jan 28
George hitched two teams and we went up in the field. We skied in the afternoon with the Greenleafs and Bonds. We went up Galusha Hill in East Topsham; the view from the top is magnificent, almost 360 degrees, coming down was fast and exciting. We had lots of fun and stopped for bloody-marys at Greenleaf's.

Jan 29
Worked around 'til eleven or so, making bread, started beans, etc., then I went skiing. We all went to Gib Randall's funeral at church. Richard did an excellent job. Snivelys arrived and we went for a pleasant sleigh ride, had dinner and a good visit. John is here for as long as it seems reasonable.

Jan 30
John worked all day despite the medication he is on, and did okay.

Jan 31
David is upset about a number of things, mostly because we don't mea-sure up to Cindy's expectations and she bugs David about it. He talked a lot about it to me this morning. Poker tonight at Matty's instead of Alan's [Greenleaf].

Feb 1
Minus 10 degrees, cold, windy, men moved hay to Forrai's. I did odds and ends, didn't feel well enough to go skiing.

Feb 2
Minus 10, beautiful, clear. Dave worse, lashing out at George ver-bally. To add to the problems after breakfast he found the water wasn't pumping around in his heating system and the house was cooling down. Cindy was to arrive back and Dave was in a real panic about them coming and finding another problem. We looked at it, couldn't figure it out, couldn't get Buddy [McLam], called Dunbar who said he would come late afternoon. Cindy went home again to her parents even after David pleaded with her and I asked her. Finally Buddy came only to find that a switch had been inadvertently turned off.

Feb 3
David still upset, he has problems with about everyone, even expressed that having John [Snively] here bothered him. If we had thought John would be a threat in some way, we would not have taken him. However I don't think it should be a problem for Dave in itself. He has certainly

gotten out his hostilities this week. George gave him the rest of the day to go down and bring Cindy home. Sandy and Wayne [Gulick] were due to arrive between 8 and 9, but they called at 11:30 because they couldn't make it up the road because of the ice. We made arrangement, at that hour, for them to stay at the Peacham Inn.

Feb 4

The roads were slick until after ten and people were having lots of trouble. Sandy and Wayne tried to drive here before asking anyone and couldn't make it, got nervous and decided to go home. We never did see them. Omri Parsons slept in his car on the Mountain road because he couldn't go. He had coffee here after he got to our hill and couldn't make it, and then when the sander came he finally made it home. Didn't hear from Dave or Cindy all day although we tried to call several times and couldn't reach them. I wish Dave could resolve his problems, but it looks very difficult.

Feb 5

Went to church, Dave came and seemed pretty emotional, cried briefly, I felt bad. The service seemed like a great one for him, I hope it helped. He made a date with Richard and I thought maybe it was for some counseling but learned later he just wanted to join the church. Really I think he was reaching out. George called Dave just to see how he was, talked to Cindy, who was not admitting to some of the obvious problems. At that point they both said everything was fine, Richard could not come. We have tried to help but really don't know how, we just seem to make things worse. I hope Dave will be okay.

Feb 6

Nice day, snowed last night so there are 4 to 6 inches of new snow. Steve Harris' cousin [David, from Australia] called from New York to see if they [David and his friend Ian] could stop by and visit us on their way from New York to Stowe. I invited them to stay here if they wanted to. They arrived about 9:30, they had gotten a little lost. They are very pleasant boys.

Feb 7
The Australian boys [and David] went off for skiing at Stowe, left about
8:15. At the end of lunch Ian, Steve's cousin's friend, called to say that
[our son] David had collapsed and been rushed to Colby Hospital by
ambulance. Ian explained to me that David had passed out suddenly
and had irregular vital signs. They had trouble getting a pulse, it was
very frightening. When we got to the hospital David was in the waiting
room. They had given him O₂, checked him over, done a bunch of tests
including EKG, and decided he could go home, despite all. George and
I went to Bond's for Pizza and slides, and later I talked to Ken about
David. He might check him out in the morning.

Feb 8
David seems okay, but weak, he slept alright.

Feb 9
The boys left around 8:30 to go to Stowe and then back to Staten Island.
Joan picked up John to go to the psychiatrist and he will stay home for
the weekend and talk about how he is doing. There's always the ques-
tion of whether he is being helped and also how much of a drag it is on
all of us. Dennis came today with Verle Houghabome to teach us about
incorporation and partnerships. Dawn took the day off and Cindy
also came, we spent most of the day asking, discussing. There are some
interesting options.

Feb 10
Men working at the wood lot. I went to town this PM, I took Aunt
Fran's things to her but did not visit. She was so nasty to me on the
phone the other day, I didn't have the energy to see her. Then I decided
to go to Highland Travel to pay for our tickets [to Australia]. I got quite
a blow there, Linda said the rates had gone up and the time frame had
changed for when you could buy the tickets and get the reduced rate.
It would have cost $2300 instead of $1328. She was able to wrangle
a better price but the cost is still $1583. I was pretty angry, it seemed
that the travel agency could be up on changes enough to inform their
clients and avoid such disasters.

Feb 11
Jean Dedam had an 11 lb boy at around 5 AM. George and I mostly prepared for our party during the day. We had around 16 people for a sleigh ride, pot luck, and baby shower for Becky and Dennis. It almost rained but not quite. We went all the way around the bay.

Feb 13
Watch Olympics for three hours this evening. Two U.S. girls won the giant slalom, Debbie Armstrong and Kristin Cooper. They skied beautifully and it was so exciting, a gold and a Silver.

Feb 14
Vet came to check pregnancy and vaccinate calves, later the men went to the wood lot. POKER at Alan's.

Feb 15
40° Rain, the snow is disappearing and the roads are muddy. George and Matty went to an Agway crops meeting for the day. John Snively called to see if he could come back up. He said he was feeling a lot better. I really didn't know what to say so I told him I would call back.

Feb 16
Nance came and helped me clean, it was great! George and Dave went to the maple meeting, Matt was here for lunch with us. After lunch Nance, the dogs, and I walked over to see Jean and her baby, Alfred Nathan Dedam.

Feb 17
29°-40° The snow is really going and everything is messy and the roads are terrible and muddy. Mary and Dave Western arrived at about 10:15 for the weekend. I called John Snively to tell him it was best to have him not come back up right now.

Feb 18
We went out through the sugar woods with Daisy and Mickey on the
big sled and Maggie and Buddy on the dray. Annie and Dawn had a
little shower for Jenny this PM.

We had just built the dray that Mattie's horses were hitched to.
The shower for Jenny was a baby shower for Christopher Jon Harris,
who was born in Australia four days later, February 22.

Feb 19
We were going to church but instead we went to the cabin, built a fire,
took a walk, came back and sat by the fire, drank wine, talked. Mary
and Dave left about 2 pm, Dawn and I took a long walk with the
dogs. We watched the Olympics and the Marie twins won gold and
silver in slalom.

Feb 20
I did desk work and laundry, Men did barns. I called Andy Cochran
to see if he might stay here while we are away and he said he'd like to.
He stopped by at lunch and we made plans. That is a great relief to
me! And George too!

Feb 24
Nice day, men tapped and gathered some. The Hummons visited and
I packed and then went running, I flushed a partridge.

Feb 25
George boiled made syrup, I worked around then took a walk with
Milly. It was so sunny and warm, walked in short sleeves, laid on the
picnic table in the sun.

Feb 26
George couldn't finish boiling yesterday because everything was frozen.
We went to church this morning, enjoyed the sermon, visited with
many. Our family all came for lunch, it was fun. Men shot a little
skeet, played pool; we girls got lunch and watched the babies. Later we

went over to look at David Randall's farm. We were able to climb in a window and wander through the house. It all looks rather ugly and depressing the way it is.

Feb 27
8°-30° Cold but lovely, Andy Cochran arrived, and Sharon Bellevance worked in the morning cleaning. George and I went to town, and got our travelers checks.

Feb 28
14°-20° Snowing at 5 AM, snowed much of the day, sleeted some. Boys worked on tractor, George worked at desk most of the day and I finished packing and did many necessary things to get ready. Tired! Andy is all settled in and working. He likes the dogs and I'm sure he will take good care of Milly.

Feb 29
We will finish packing and try to leave at about 11 AM. We are excited about the trip but both of us always have a hard time leaving home. We love our home and our life here and always hesitate going away from it. We are very anxious to see Jenny and Steve and our new little grandson. Matty is going to keep this journal for Peacham while [we are gone].

Feb 29 (Matty)
We got the starter back in the little tractor and it works. We pretty much finished cleaning up for the inspector, now we have to keep it clean. Dawn couldn't make Dole Hill because of the tires on the Subaru and the car in front of her couldn't make it so she had to stop. Andy and I went down and drove it home after they had sanded.

March 1 (Matty)
Minus 5 to 10 – blustery, Dave went down to White River to see about buying or leasing a new car. The rest of us went to the woods.

March 2 (Matty)
Dave got his car things worked out. He is going to lease a Mercury Lynx. Stuart, Andy and I cleaned up the wood from yesterday and got a little more today which amounted to two pretty good loads. Well we'll see how Andy and I make out this weekend.

March 3 (Matty)
Frances Moore was tapping. Chores went smoothly for Andy and me. Damestee [?] cleaned in the house all day and made Andy and me breakfast and lunch.

March 4 (Matty)
Chores went well. I washed the milk tanks mainly because Donny [Moore] said we had a high count last week and he thought it could be from a build up in the bulk tanks, he said to use Clorox.

March 5 (Matty)
Stuart got most of the shit out. We got the barns bedded and Andy and I fixed six grainers, pretty good day.

March 6 (Matty)
20°-30° – then the temperature dropped off again before dark. Town Meeting day, we took the day off. Dave and I did chores in the morning and Stuart and Andy worked afternoon chores. Dad got voted in [Selectman] by a large majority over Mary Jo Quimby and Dave Willard. Larry Varnum was the main opposition to everything. He wanted as little money as possible to be available to the selectmen. He wanted to elect another road commissioner but legally we couldn't.

March 7 (Matty)
We had planned to start hanging buckets but it was pretty cold and the forecast was for it to stay cold for the rest of the week so we puttered around. We fixed another grainer, loaded buckets and covers on the sap trailer so it would be ready to go and then in the afternoon, we fixed the floor on the big truck and put the number plate bracket back on, as

*well as the number plate. We also fixed the seat bracket and replaced
the seat on the 265 tractor.*

I can't help but feel proud of what Matt calls "puttering around."

March 8 (Matty)
*I went down with the big truck to Bradford to get a load of soy. The
boys did chores and put five cows out to breed and set the auger up to
put the soy up into the bin.*

March 9 (Matty)
*Dave had a stomach bug so he took between chores off. I hauled the
shit out in hopes we could start to tap Monday, we will see. We putted
around and did some repair work in the Village.*

March 10 & 11 (Matty)
*Weekend off, Mike and Kathy [Bussiere] came for the weekend. It was
cold but we did take the boys out on the pung and Mike and Andy
rode Orlando and Shilling, we also went sliding down Cemetery hill.*

March 12 (Matty)
*Monday, cold as hell, windy, 30 to 60 mile an hour wind last night.
We cleaned and bedded the barns. The corn auger broke, Les Morrison
is coming up to fix it.*

March 13 (Matty)
*We went to the woods to tap finally but the weather didn't cooperate, it
was cold and snowing hard. We got the corn auger fixed but the snow
won't stop, we ended up with 20 to 24 inches, biggest snow storm on
record for the month of March. We spent Wednesday moving snow, first
record cold now record snow, unbelievable.*

March 16 (Matty)
*We wish there was still 6 inches of snow, we're tapping and thinking
about gathering.*

March 19 (Matty)
Monday the last week. Stuart got some shit out and we gathered a load of sap. It wasn't running much but in the afternoon the temp. went up to 45° to 50° and the sap started to flow.

March 20 (Matty)
I started boiling and the boys gathered all day.

March 21 (Matty)
I started to boil as soon as I could. The barometric pressure changed and I took off some heavy syrup, I compensated, hope I didn't mess things up. The boys finished gathering and tapped some more in the afternoon. I boiled in the last of the sap Friday morning, we have about 60 gallons now.

March 24 (Matty)
Dawn and I finished tapping Saturday. Dave, Stuart and I finished hanging the buckets.

March 26 (Patty resumes the farm journal)
14°-35° Sunny and windy, George boiled, boys gathered, Stu spread manure. Sharon [Bellevance] came for two hours in the morning and cleaned while I did dishes, sorted, went to the village, etc. Several people called to welcome us home, Ann Cochran, Jean Boardman and Eloise [Miller]. We both feel weary.

March 27
15°-40° Sunny, breezy, boys gathered, Stu spread, and George boiled. Andy working until tomorrow, tonight actually, he is moving out tomorrow. He did a great job taking care of Mil, the cats, the plants and helping the boys.

March 28
I did not sleep well, felt achy. Went back to bed until 7:15 this AM. I worked around slowly this morning. In the afternoon I walked up to Eloise's and visited, Jean [Miller Dedam] walked down to meet me and

Eloise walked me home. After I got back Jean Boardman and Becky stopped, having walked over, it was wonderful to see them. George boiled and the boys gathered some. Sap did not run very much and they quit at noon. Stu spread some and Matt and Dave checked the pipe line over. George had his first Selectman's meeting tonight. It was long but it went okay. They voted to appoint Ernie Shatney, Road Commissioner.

Dec 31
New Years Eve! We met John and Doris Stetson at the Creamery Restaurant, had a nice dinner and active discussion. We stay apart in our political thinking. We came home and watched the end of "Top Hat" with a young Fred Astaire and Ginger Rodgers.

1985

"I'm having some trouble handling all this."

PATTY CONTINUED THIS FARM JOURNAL UNTIL 1999, but this will be the last year that I will transcribe it. I think we have given a good picture of our early years in Peacham, and this is the year Matty joined with me in a 50/50 farm partnership that became effective January 1. A succession plan for any business is difficult, and probably farming is no worse than any other, but it is a very hands-on business, and the older partner has to learn to take his hands off.

Maurice Chandler and Ann Goss were our DHIA (Dairy Herd Improvement Association) testers. We had been DHIA members since we started farming; our tester when we first moved to Peacham was Ronny Cochran. The testers at that time tested each cow's milk for weight and butter fat; nowadays they also test for protein and somatic cell count. It is only with this information that we could evaluate changes in feeding and management of the cows. This was important for us to be able to evaluate the benefit of the Computerized Grain Feeding System that we installed this year. A great deal was discovered about the way a dairy cow utilizes her feed.

We learned about these new discoveries from going to classes about cow nutrition, cow comfort, and stall design that were given in St. Johnsbury by travelling veterinarians from Wisconsin. Our vets at that time were Rick Price and Steve Mills, who figured that healthy cows and successful farmers would be good for their own business. Rick and Steve offered a deal to their customers that if we would go to the classes in St. Johnsbury, they would credit the $75 cost on our vet bill.

What we learned is that feeding a concentration of grain to the cows all at once, which is what we farmers were all doing, made it hard for the cows to digest it. The Computerized Grain Feeding System monitored and controlled the amount of grain fed to each cow. The cow would wear a computer chip, the higher their milk production, the more grain they could digest. In six or seven years researchers would find that mixing grain with the cows' roughage was even better than controlling the amount of grain, and we switched to the Total Mixed Ration system. But the computerized feeding was progress.

We tried growing lupine this year, a short-season source of protein, hoping to replace some of the Soy Bean Meal that we were purchasing. We planted it in the two-acre piece below Elkins Tavern, and though it came up well it started dying out. We sent a sample to UVM and found that the field had been used for potatoes, and there was a fungus in the soil that killed the lupine. We never tried it again.

We traded our 5/14 Grime evaporator for a new 5/14 Lightning and $5,400; Case 430/loader for a new Dauze-Allis/loader and $7,000; JD 336 baler for a new JD 327 baler and $3,500; a MF 175/loader for a new JD 2350/loader and $17,010; a NH 718 chopper for a new Heston chopper and $8,500; and, finally, we installed a computerized feeding system for $16,086. Andy Cochran worked with me on my weekends "on" until February, when his younger brother Jamie came to work for us full time.

Patty's mother came to live on the farm. Patty and her brother Dick had decided this was best, but I'm sure their mother never thought so. She was never happy, and she made it difficult for others to be happy around her. A bright spot was Lisa Marceau, a neighbor girl that helped out with Mother. Mother liked her, and Lisa found she had a talent for nursing. She has made a career of it and is an excellent nurse and a lovely person.

Patty stopped writing the journal this year on May 22. Dave and Cindy had their second daughter Melissa, a lovely, bright girl, on September 17.

Jan 1, 1985
We instituted monthly meetings of the farm team to discuss manage-
ment, finances, dairy problems, working conditions, other new ideas
and incentive programs. George and Dave did chores in AM, all
three did chores in the PM. George and I took out Mickey and Daisy
pulling the big sled. Took Howard and Jean [Boardman] and Barbara
[Boardman] and Jack, it was snowing then raining, we had good fun
and good conversation.

Jan 2
Men started cutting wood in the Foster Pond woodlot.

Jan 9
[Dick and I] studied options for mom; nursing homes, companion in
larger apartment, stay here with us.

Patty went to Norfolk, Va. to discuss her mother's living situation with her brother Dick.

Jan 11
George met me at Burlington Airport around 2:30, came right home.
He finished chores with the boys. It's great to be home, we had a nice
steak dinner....

Jan 12
Matt and Dave's weekend on. George and I slept 'til 7:30, after break-
fast, went rabbit hunting. Then we took a XC ski trip with Matt and
Dawn, around Mud pond and Fosters and to the Village, lovely.

Jan 13
4°-20° Lovely day, sun, some flurries, after breakfast George and I went
for a very nice XC ski trip. At two we went for a very nice Memorial
Service at church for Jonathan (Lindberg Brown). It was a beautiful,
loving service with a full church. Reeve [Lindberg Brown] planned it
and took a large part, speaking especially to children. It was an event
people will remember for always, I'm sure.

Jan 14
Men working in the woods, I'm trying to begin to get caught up and get ready for mom.

Jan 15
Boys worked in the woods, I went to town after lunch, dentist, shopping, visited Aunt Fran. Jean Boardman told me today of a move to get a mediator for our church.

Jan 16
-18°to -2° Wind roared last night. George ASCS meeting. Matt helped some movers who couldn't get up the hill in the Village. George had Selectman's meeting tonight and I had Fellowship.

Jan 17
Elaine [Berwick] helped me clean, men cleaned the barn and then Matt and Dave went to class at the extension office. I met with the "Spinning Group." Church Annual Meeting, Richard Resigned, has job with Bridges for Peace.

The Spinning Group was started by Marilyn Magnus and Gretchen Bond, because they both had sheep.

Jan 18
Matt cleaned out the pit, George and Matt bucked up wood on the landing. In the afternoon all three went up to the woodlot landing and brought home a big load of wood. I worked in the house, went to the bank to deposit the milk check and a cow check and to pay off the loan on our new car.

Jan 19
Andy [Cochran] and George did chores. Matty and George went rabbit hunting. After lunch George and I went for a sled ride with Mickey and Daisy up in the woods, it was beautiful.

Jan 20

Pretty day, George and Andy chores, I went to church. Jim Glasser preached. Jim Glasser's sermon was on the idea that we are always able to "become" if we allow ourselves. That just because we are older doesn't mean we stop growing, learning and changing. Later in the day I went for a sled ride with Matty. He took his team across the field to Eloise's driveway then around and down to the village. It was fun to drive around in the village.

Jan 21

President Reagan sworn in for four more years as President. Not as cold here as predicted but very cold in the south. The Inaugural Parade and outside ceremonies were cancelled. The events took place in the Capitol Rotunda. It got windier here this afternoon, the boys ran 10 heifers from the Village to here, I followed in the truck.

Jan 22

The men worked in the woods. George had a long selectmen's meeting working on the budget and I worked on the living room, we moved the sofa and my big chair from the parlor.

Jan 23

11°-24° It was very windy during the night and snowed several inches today. Men spent the day doing necessary jobs around the farm rather than going to the woods. The Agway serviceman went over the milking system.

Jan 24

Men cleaned barns and Matt and Dave went to their class at the Extension office. Spinning group, Gretchen, Marilyn [Magnus] and Susan [Greenleaf] came for lunch and ski. We went up through Danielson's woods and then up on the hill behind Snow's, beautiful. It helped to talk to the girls about mom coming.

Jan 25
Matt got out manure, George got parts for the hay chopper and finished bedding the barn and Dave split wood. In the afternoon they all went up and got a good load of wood. I cleaned and made pecan pies.

Jan 26
George off, he took the horses up into the field and woods. I spent the day preparing for company. The Danielsons, Bonds and Crismans came for dinner and we went out first for an evening sleigh ride. It was a beautiful ride and a good evening.

Jan 27
We slept a little late then after breakfast we went with Matty and Dawn on the pung sleigh with his team around the bay. Later we went up to Annie and Mike's and took them the youth bed for Adrian. My daddy bought that bed for Dick and me and then we used it for our children and now for our grandchildren, I'm sure he would be pleased. Cindy and David are expecting another baby!

Jan 28
I went to town this afternoon, met Annie for coffee, bought linens, slippers, boots, etc, for mom. Maurice [Chandler] and Ann [Goss] tested this morning.

Jan 29
Men went to the woods, Matt went to Bill Cooks to get two chainsaws fixed and took a bucket to country road equipment to get a bucket adjusted, a new bucket we are buying. Elaine helped me get Moms room ready etc, and then I went skiing with the dogs.

Jan 30
George and the boys went to the farm show. Jim Quimby worked on mom's closet.

Jan 31

Boys cleaned barns and did odd jobs. I cleaned in the morning and then Reeve picked me up and we went to Susan's [Ross] for lunch with her and Marilyn [Magnus]. We skied a nice loop from their house, it started to snow heavily late in the afternoon.

Feb 1

Matt took manure out, George and Dave helped John check pregnancies, John also gave the dogs rabies shots. I went to town, had a mammogram at hospital, visited aunt Fran.

Feb 2

George and Andy on, Annie and kids came out. We took them on a sleigh ride, fun but kids got cold. Nice lunch, kids napped, George took dogs rabbit hunting, we sewed and visited. George and I went to dinner at the creamery, nice evening.

Feb 3

George and Andy chores, Andy sick with flu. I went to church, then Matt, Dawn, George and I had a nice ski trip, beautiful. Chores etc.

Feb 4

Jesse was castrated today. Last minute preparations for mom. Boys went to the woods. I asked Howard and Jean to take me to the Lyndonville airport to meet mom's plane, George had a meeting. Annie met us there with the kids, plane arrived safely, had brief visit with Dick and then rode home in the ambulance with mom. It took her a while to get adjusted but she did very well, even sat with us at dinner. Pretty, very, good night.

Feb 6

Boys worked in the woods, I worked here in AM. Elaine cleaned and Marilyn [Magnus] came to evaluate mother. At 1 PM I went to a Fellowship bylaws meeting and then to the bank. George had a selectmen's meeting.

Feb 7
George and the boys went to Agri-Mark [dairy co-op] Luncheon
Meeting, Annie and kids came out and had lunch, visited. Jean
Berwick came so Annie and I could ski but we just went out a bit with
Adrian. Mom had a bad night with itching. I'm having some trouble
handling all this. Poker.

Feb 8
-8° to -2° Very cold ALL DAY. Dave and Matt went to an all day
computer class. George worked on my plugged kitchen drain and the
big barn door that fell down, etc. Sandra [Craig] stayed with mother
while I went to town, amazingly wintery.

Feb 9
Jean Berwick came so George and I could do something. We did go
skiing for an hour, it was fun.

Feb 10
Matt and Dawn went for a sleigh ride with us, we took Buddy and
Mickey, lovely. Mom didn't mind being alone for a while. Matt and
Dawn stayed for steak and salad lunch. We skied after mom's nap,
beautiful. We seem to be getting along pretty well.

Feb 11
Gorgeous day, up above 30°. Mom had a poor day. She didn't want
the home health aide to help her bathe and was upset about the whole
thing. Hummons visited after dinner brought mom a plant.

Feb 18
This week sped by and I didn't get to writing. It was a mild week with
some rain, busy with Jean [Clark] and Wendy [Gulick] here.

Feb 20
Mother seemed very depressed much of this week.

Feb 21
Duane Dunbar called to say for various unexpected reasons he couldn't keep his pup. I am seeking possible new owner.

Feb 22
Wendy flew back, Jean and I took her, and Sandra stayed with mom. We made a quick trip to the airport in Burlington and then had time to shop in Montpelier and have coffee, it was fun.

Feb 23
George and the boys have been studying computerized grain feed systems and trying out tractors.

Feb 24
George and I had a pleasant, quiet weekend, Annie and Mike made a surprise visit on Sunday.

Feb 25
George and the boys went to Gilman with a Blue Seal Grain Rep to see one of these computer feeding systems in action. "Little bird" who is now known as "Lady Remington" was adopted by Chris and Lori [Raymond] because Duane Dunbar couldn't keep her. I'm glad.

Feb 26
22°-40° Lovely and sunny in the AM. George made a trade with twin city, new John Deere tractor and baler for MF 175 and old baler + $21,000.

Feb 27
George talked to two Computer Feeding Systems salesmen this morning. There were heavy snow squalls. Anna Wilson died yesterday.

Feb 28
George and Matt cleaned barns. In PM they tried to start tapping but tapper quit. I went walking with Jean Boardman and Tiffany [Kempton].

March 5
14°-20° It snowed all night, 10 inches or so, pretty. Lisa [Marceau]
came while we went to Town Meeting. It was a quiet Town Meeting,
Les Post was beaten by Frank Randall for Selectman. We went to Mill's
for dinner with Crismans, Powdens and Fuehrers.

March 6
Buddy [McLam] and Jim [Quimby] came and got the new bathroom
all done except toilet set in and medicine cabinet. Tiring day for mom.
George had ASCS Meeting, boys worked on pipeline.

March 8
Mom had a very bad day. Pipeline all tapped. George and I went to
hear Beethoven's Ninth in Lyndonville.

March 9
George took dogs rabbit hunting, I did things in the house with mom,
etc. Sam called and we both talked to him. He is working part time
for Edcon and taking two courses. Lisa came, I skied, George worked
on sap trailer, beautiful afternoon.

March 10
Lisa came for the day, we went to church and then skied up into the
sugar woods and into Danielson's pasture, it was lovely. After lunch
George worked on the sap trailer and I visited with mom, sorted papers
etc, we are seriously studying a partnership.

March 12
32°-40° It rained all night and most of the day. Men cleaned barns.
Jenny Guen, who works for Home Health as a consultant, came and
talked to me about our situation with mom. It gave me some insights
although mom was not at all receptive. Matt and Dawn came to
dinner and we discussed the particulars of the partnership.

March 13
Six inches of snow this AM, beautiful with everything covered. Power out about 3 hours. George went to the dentist, because he had lost three fillings. Boys tapped in Miller's sw [sugar woods]. Reeve brought Claudette Ruggles for tea, she will be working part time for me when I leave for the day.

March 14
Claudette Ruggles came to stay with mom for the day, she also made lunch for the boys. I went to Annie's and had lunch with her and the little boys, Adrian was so excited and cute.

March 15
Men tapped, more snow last night, windy, cold.

March 16
20°-40°

March 18
Jamey Cochran started working full time. Men were both tapping and starting to get ready for the new feeders. I worked around and then decided to go skiing with Mary Daly but got a call from a trucker bringing mom's stuff. Matty and Jamey went down to S. Peacham which was as far as the trucker got and loaded mom's stuff on our pickup and brought it here.

March 19
Mom preferred to skip her dental appt., so I worked on unpacking and sorting her things. She seems glad to have them. I went to town in PM, med for mom's skin, etc, boys tapped, Matt took out manure.

March 20
28°-30° It stayed cool and breezy all day, George boiled from 9 AM to 9:30 PM.

March 21
Boys poured cement for feeder stations and then tapped. Poker.

March 23
5°-20° Nice day, George and I had a sleigh ride this morning up into the woods, it was lovely. Matt and Dawn took their team out also with the dray. They lunched with us. Matt got a VCR for mother with several movies to try, she doesn't want it. After lunch everyone except me gathered, I did chores laundry etc. Jean Berwick came so we could go to the Creamery and attend Vienna Choir Boys concert which was lovely.

March 24
I went to church, George boiled all day. I got some pictures sorted and odds and ends done. Lisa stayed while we had dinner at Matt and Dawn's, very delicious, and watched Casablanca on the VCR.

March 25
Mark Breen said of the weather this week "If you've been Flustered by the Bluster, you can Ease into the Breeze." George boiled and the boys gathered, they found a lot of ice. Mom and I had some Friction and she was depressed, but felt better as the day went on.

March 26
12°-50° Matt went to get soy, they are cleaning up to get ready for the new feeder.

March 27
George boiled, has made about 100 gallons, the syrup this season started at B but he's worked it up to A, boys gathered. I cleaned, did errands, got ready for Richard [Hough-Ross] farewell party, hectic day.

March 28
40°-60° Warm, springy, it rained some in the evening, George boiled, boys gathered. Jean Berwick came at 11 AM, I walked to Gretchen's for lunch with the spinning group, we knitted etc. and talked. I walked home, saw a small flock of Geese fly up from the big field, beautiful,

I had a great day. Some lady smashed into the gas pumps at the S. Peacham store, going too fast, lost her brakes or something.

March 29
32°-40° George boiled boys gathered.

March 30
George and Jamie [Cochran] on, George boiled in between chores. I stayed around and worked on my spring sorting etc.

March 31
18°-40° George boiled after chores and finished up by noon. I went to church, Lisa came for the afternoon and evening. Roys visited in the afternoon and then I walked over to Eloise's during chores. We went out for pizza and movie "Witness", snowing hard on way home, some of our power went out.

April 1
It snowed several inches last night, George went to the dentist and the boys worked on computer room, wiring, shelves, etc. getting ready for the feeders. Maurice tested.

April 2
23°-35° More snow. Boys cleaned barns then all four gathered sap which ran VERY well. Elaine came in the AM and cleaned. Eloise visited mom and me in the afternoon.

April 3
20°-35° Mostly cloudy with flurries. George boiled, boys gathered, I worked with them in the afternoon, many full buckets. Sandra stayed with mom, Jean Boardman visited.

April 5
Matt working with Agway people setting up the computerized feeding system.

April 7
George boiled, I met Matty, Dawn and Annie's family at church for Easter service, it was Richard's last Sunday. Matt spotted 3 snow geese in Bernie's [Churchill] field so we went down to see them, got quite close then flushed them.

April 8
George boiling, boys gathering and the computerized feeding system is going in. I took mom to Dr Spaulding – Dental Surgeon for evaluation. She was unhappy with the office and him.

April 9
George boiled, Mom and I met Jean Boardman at the Creamery for lunch. Then I took mother to get her hair done. The job was well done but mother didn't like the place. I took the dogs for a walk.

April 10
Claudette came at 9 AM, I went to town to a Church Woman United Meeting, had lunch with Doris Stetson, visited Fran, and shopped.

THE CUMPUTER FEEDING SYSTEM IS COMPLETE.

April 11
The men did odds and ends, George didn't have to boil today. They let the cows eat the grain in the parlor grainers until they were empty and then the cows went on to the new system. I went to Bonny Griffin's for lunch with the spinners and George had Poker tonight.

April 13
Buddy came and worked in mom's bathroom, toilet is in but no seat, medicine cabinet in but no switch for lights. Matty, Dawn, David gathered with Jamie, George boiled. We went to a movie, "Rear Window", James Stewart and Grace Kelly.

I chuckled when I typed this, Buddy McLam the plumber was a wonderful person but he could cause most anyone to be a little frustrated.

April 14
George boiled, I cleaned in the morning, I would like to have gone to church, as Jim Glasser started his interim ministry this morning.

April 15
4 Snow geese living in Randall's corn field, crocuses blooming and some daffys and tulips are up. We have seen Killdeer, Bluebirds, Robins and Woodcock. George boiled, boys gathered, Lisa came, I went to town in PM. Buddy came at supper time with toilet seat.

April 16
George boiled, boys gathered, I worked here, I cleaned the car, etc. Storm in afternoon, hail, rain, wind.

April 18
Rained and late in the day it started to freeze on bushes etc, nasty weather. George boiled, boys gathered and pulled, Lisa stayed with mother while I went to Burlington with Doris Stetson. We shopped, lunched and looked at a super retirement place for mom. Mom had quite a fit when I said we going away overnight Friday.

April 23
We had a pair of Mallard ducks in the corn pile today. Then on a walk with Milly at 6:30 AM I saw a handsome Coyote. Boys stoned and harrowed and George started to plant barley. RAKED.

April 24
Boys prepared land, George planted barley, I took the pickup to Montpelier for oil, saw two deer and a partridge.

April 25
George planted barley, Matt harrowed, Boys fenced, I had the Spinning group here for lunch.

April 26
George boiled in last of sap, made 525 gallons for the season. Boys cleaned barns, picked stones, Matt harrowed barley land.

April 27
George and Jamie chores, George planted barley and seeded piece on Danielson's, I raked, planted peas, lettuce and spinach.

April 29
George planted Lupine on a small piece below the tavern, Matt harrowed.

April 30
Planted last of barley, about 60 acres.

May 1ˢᵗ
Matt spread manure on corn ground from a pile on David Field's. George cleaned up his grain drill and went to Old Fox for a load of fertilizer, and then chisel plowed on corn ground. I took a nature walk with Thelma [White].

May 3
Manure pile all spread and chiseled in. George finished spreading fertilizer on the pastures.

May 4
George and Milly went fishing, later we played tennis. In the evening we and the Bonds went to Newport [Vt.] through Craftsbury and Albany, a very pretty drive and then we had dinner at the Landing. We had a real good time.

May 5
George and I went to church, Annie and Mike came out later and George and Mike went fishing.

May 6
Met with Verle Houghabome and Dennis regarding partnership agreement, I missed some because I took mom to the eye doctor.

May 7
Matt spreading manure at Village farm, George ASCS Meeting, later he chiseled and harrowed. Sold 9 drums of syrup to Don Moore's cousin, then he sprayed the lupine.

May 8
Matt finished Village manure pile, George chiseled it in on the Hardy Lot. George and Jamie got the rest of the buckets out of the Miller Sugar Woods and then built a nice bar way for Eloise.

May 9
George and Matt spreading on both Packard's and Flat Iron, they had a flat tire on the newer spreader, Matt got it fixed; boys fencing down below Bonds. I had lunch with Spinners at Susan's, later took the dogs out for a walk and saw the Coyote again up in the blackberry patch, we stood and looked at each other.

May 14
Harrowing and stoning.

May 15
Boys finished stoning the big piece across the road, lots of stones; it took two days to do it. Jean [Boardman], Sonia and I met Sister Judy Fortune at the Creamery for lunch. She spoke in the afternoon at Fellowship on Spirituality, it was wonderful.

May 18
George, Matt and Andy went fishing at Levi Pond.

We dragged two canoes in on the half-mile, snow-covered access road and found Levi Pond barely free of ice. Milly and I were fishing from a borrowed, round-bottom, 15-foot canoe, and Matt and Andy were in our stable 17-foot canoe. Milly got interested in something in the water on the side of the canoe and rolled us over. While I was busy swimming around gathering up the life preserver seat, the paddle and the canoe, Milly headed for shore dragging my fish pole by the hook which had caught in her fur, and the boys nearly fell out of their canoe because they were laughing so hard.

May 19
The Bonds, including kids and Susana Brown came up to the cabin with us. We walked down around the beaver ponds, men fished, then had a lovely supper cooked over the fire place. The cabin looks so beautiful with daffys blooming, new shingled roof, rain barrel, etc.

May 20
Big maple in the village was cut down by a specialist, boys are bucking it up.

May 21
George planted corn.

May 22
George finished planting corn, he was just 3 days. Boys washing buckets, fencing, put out some heifers, got soy.

Patricia Kempton

2018
EPILOGUE

A S I WRITE THIS IT IS 2018, 30-PLUS YEARS after the farm partnership was formed between Matty & Dawn, me & Patty. I have many blessings to count. The farm continues to grow and prosper, as does our family. Sam married Julie Clark on May 30, 1987, they have two children, Julian and Miko. Annie and Mike have had a daughter Jacqueline and another son Josh. Jenny and Steve had another child, a daughter Hannah. Matt and Dawn have three boys, William, Amos, and Dylan. William and Dylan have joined the farm. All of our children live on or near the farm.

My father died on August 21, 1999, 93 years old.

Patty left this life on December 15, 2012. We had a wonderful marriage and family, and she enjoyed the blessings as well. I have tried to tell the story of our beginnings and of our starting a family and a farm. I think Patty's journal offers an unusual insight into a young farm family's life and needed to be recorded. I hope you have enjoyed reading it.

George Kempton

Directory of People Mentioned	
Andrews, Nancy & David	Nancy is Pat's friend from nursing school
Arnold, Betsy & Bill	Betsy is Pat's friend from Summit, N.J.
Ashford, John	Peacham road commissioner
Atkinson, Tom	Married Corinne Blodgett
Baldwin, Phyllis & David	Friends of Pat & George from Dummerston, Vt.
Barlerin, Iness	Annie's friend from UVM
Bartell, Robert	Local musician, married Nancy Wason
Bean, Emma & Bob	Peacham neighbors
Beardsley, Anna Hartness	Daughter of James Hartness, employed George's mother Annie
Bentley, Virginia	Danville author of farm cookbooks
Berwick, Jean & Ben	Ben was one of the farm's best workers
Berwick, Chris	Son of Ben and Jean
Berwick, Janice	Daughter of Ben & Jean, worked at Kempton Farm
Bigelow, Raymond	Married George's aunt Elizabeth Shears
Blanchard, George	Kept a store in South Peacham
Blanchard, Bobby	Son of George Blanchard, worked on Kempton farm
Blodgett, Albert	Annie Shears' first husband

Blodgett, Corinne (Reene)	George's half sister, daughter of George's mother Annie, and Albert Blodgett; married Tom Atkinson
Blodgett, May & Ed	Parents of Albert Blodgett, George's mother Annie's first husband
Blodgett, Shirley	George's half sister, daughter of George's mother Annie, and Albert Blodgett; married Eddie Steadman
Boardman, Barbara	Daughter of Jean & Howard Boardman, married Jack Segal, then Bill Hoffman
Boardman, Becky	Daughter of Jean & Howard Boardman, married Dennis Kauppila
Boardman, Betsy	Daughter of Jean & Howard Boardman, married Julian Smith
Boardman, Jean & Howard	Peacham neighbors & close friends
Bond, Gretchen & Duncan	Peacham neighbors & close friends
Bond, Jessica	Daughter of Duncan and Gretchen Bond
Bond, Rebecca	Daughter of Duncan and Gretchen Bond
Bradley, David	Worked at Kempton Farm
Brown, Beppy & Ed	Peacham neighbors
Brown, Susana	Daughter of Reeve and Richard Brown
Brown, Reeve & Richard	Peacham neighbors

Bussiere, Kathy & Michael	Michael was student at Peacham Alternative School & close friend of Kemptons
Carruth, Phil	Peacham neighbor
Churchill, Joan & Bernard	Peacham farmers and neighbors
Claghorn, Judy	Daughter of Connie & David Claghorn
Claghorn, Michael	Son of Connie & David Claghorn
Claghorn, Connie & David	Dairy farmers in Perkinsville, Vt.; Dave was second father to George, who worked for him in 1950, '52, '55
Clark, Jean & Don	Jean is lifelong friend of Pat's from Summit, N.J.
Clark, Julie	Daughter of Jean & Don Clark, married Sam Kempton
Clark, Marjorie	Daughter of Jean & Don Clark, married Dave Sichel
Clark, Steve	Son of Jean & Don Clark
Clay, Stanley	George worked on the Clay farm in summer 1946
Cochran, Colleen	Daughter of Ron & Anne Cochran
Cochran, Andy	Son of Ron & Anne Cochran, worked at Kempton Farm
Cochran, Jamie	Son of Ron & Anne Cochran, worked at Kempton Farm
Cochran, Anne & Ron	Ron was one of Kempton Farm's best workers
Conner, Sharon	Daughter of Anne Connor Rantoule

Coughlin, Dianne Krupsky	Daughter of Josephine Bigelow Krupsky & Steve Krupsky
Craig, Sandra & Jamie	Had a sugaring operation north of Peacham village
Craig, Clara & Jim	Sold their Village Farm in Peacham to George and Pat
Craig, Ron	Son of Sandra & Jamie Craig
Craven, Jay	Teacher at Peacham Alternative School, founder of Catamount Arts, St. Johnsbury
Crisman, Jo & Ron	Peacham neighbors
Crockett, Shirley & Larry	Friends of Pat & George from Dummerston, Vt.
Danielson, Karin & Ken	Close friends, bought Hooker Farm, Peacham
Dawson, Molly	Daughter of David and Beth Dawson
Dawson, Beth & David	Peacham neighbors and close friends
Dillinger, Elizabeth & David	Peacham neighbors, Dave was one of the notorious Chicago Seven
Dutton, Herb	Son of Helen and George Dutton
Dutton, Helen & George	Dairy farmers in Windham, Vt., George worked for them in 1945
Edgerton, Jake	Friend of George's from Newton School
Edson, Jim	Friend of George's from Newton School; traveled with him cross-country
Esser, Sue	Friend of Kempton kids
Falk, Ester & Clarence	Friends of Pat & George from Dummerston, Vt.

Farnham, George	Farmer in Connecticut; George worked for him while at UConn, 1951
Field, Claude	Peacham farmer
Filby, Birthe & Larry	Birthe lived in Peacham with son Sven Eric, married to Larry Filby
Flanders, Helen Hartness & Ralph	Helen was daughter of James Hartness
Fletcher, Clara & Frank	George's father Leonard Kempton's aunt & uncle
Forrai, Hertha & Zoltan	Operated horse-riding school in Peacham
Fuehrer, Sharon & Bob	Peacham neighbors
Gadapee, Lyra & Brent	Brent played baseball with Matt at Danville High
Gailliardi, Martha	Peacham neighbor
Gill, Dorcas	Daughter of Gill family in Peacham
Glasser, Dottie & Jim	Peacham neighbors
Gorlay, Gordy	Friend of Jen & Sam
Green, Jenny & Frank	Friends of Pat & George from North Danville
Green, Samantha	Jenny's friend, daughter of Jenny & Frank Green
Greenleaf, Susan & Alan	Peacham neighbors
Grey, Nathan	Married Loey Ringquist
Gulick, Debbie	Pat's niece, daughter of Richard & Vivian Gulick
Gulick, Gail	Pat's niece, daughter of Richard & Vivian Gulick
Gulick, Mildred & Ivan	Pat's parents
Gulick, Richard & Vivian	Pat's brother and sister-in-law

Gulick, Robin	Pat's niece, daughter of Richard & Vivian Gulick
Gulick, Sandy	Pat's niece, daughter of Richard & Vivian Gulick; married Wayne Parker
Gulick, Wendy	Pat's niece, daughter of Richard and Vivian Gulick
Guyer, Adrian	Pat & George's grandson, son of Annie and Mike Guyer, b. 9-27-82
Guyer, Leona & Frenchie	Mike Guyer's parents
Guyer, Mike	Married Annie Kempton
Guyer, Nicholas	Pat & George's grandson, son of Annie and Mike Guyer, b. 8-15-84
Hansberry, Barbara	Annie's friend from UVM
Harris, Joy & Graham (Wink)	Steve Harris' parents
Harris, Christopher	Pat & George's grandson, son of Jenny and Steve Harris, b. 2-22-84
Harris, Steve	Married Jenny Kempton
Hartness, James	Entrepreneur and politician in Springfield, Vt.; employed George's mother Annie
Hartswick, Nancy	Peacham neighbor
Herbert, Elizabeth	Daughter of Judy & Peter Herbert
Herbert, Judy Bruno & Peter	Peter boarded and worked on the farm; with wife Judy & daughter Elizabeth became part of family
Holland, Gerald	George worked on his Reading, Vt. farm 1947
Hooker, Paul	Worked at Kempton Farm

Hough-Ross, Richard	Minister at Peacham Church
Hummon, Doris & Serge	Bought Swamp Lot from Kemptons & built a house
Jackson, Midge	Pat's classmate at nursing school
Kalischer, Clemens	Photographed Kempton family & farm for a coffee-table book
Kauppila, Dennis	Moved to the Northeast Kingdom in the 1970s looking for alternative lifestyle; married Becky Boardman
Keeney, Ben	Son of Jim & Randy Keeney
Keeney, Dinah Yessne	Jim Keeney's second wife
Keeney, Dorigen	Daughter of Randy & Jim Keeney
Keeney, Eleanor (Randy)	Jim Keeney's first wife
Keeney, Jim	Student at Newton School and George's lifelong friend
Kempton, Annie	Daughter of Pat & George, b. 9-21-60; married Mike Guyer
Kempton, David	Son of Pat & George, b. 12-4-58; married Cindy Ladue
Kempton, Ethel & George Leonard	George's grandparents
Kempton, Frances	George's aunt, his father's sister; married Andrew Martin
Kempton, Patricia Gulick & George	Authors of this book
Kempton, Jennifer	Daughter of Pat & George, b. 12-14-57; married Steve Harris
Kempton, Leonard	George Kempton's father, son of Ethel and George Leonard Kempton
Kempton, Mata	George's father Leonard's second wife

Kempton, Matthew	Son of Pat & George, b. 8-8-61; married Dawn Richards
Kempton, Melissa	Pat & George's granddaughter, daughter of Cindy and David Kempton, b. 9-17-85
Kempton, Sam	Son of Pat & George, b. 10-1-56; married Julie Clark
Kempton, Tiffany	Pat & George's granddaughter, daughter of Cindy and David Kempton, b.7-30-83
Kenary, Jim	Friend of Kempton kids
Kimball, Lori	Peacham girl
Knapp, Fred	Dairy farmer in Dummerston, Vt.; George worked for him after he and Pat married
Knowlton, Debbie & Jerry	Peacham neighbors
Krupsky, Josephine Bigelow & Steve	Josephine was daughter of Elizabeth Shears Bigelow; married Steve Krupsky
Krupsky, Stephanie	Daughter of Josephine Bigelow & Steve Krupsky
Ladue, Cindy	Married David Kempton
Laird, Lori & John	Teachers at Peacham Alternative School
Langford, Billy Lee	Friend of Randy Keeney, worked at Kempton Farm
Larrabee, Jennifer	Friend of Dawn & Matt
Larrabee, John	Friend of Dawn & Matt
Lederer, Corrine & Bill	Peacham neighbors; Bill was an author of note
Lewis, Kyle	Daughter of Corinne Lederer
Lunt, Marilyn & John	Peacham neighbors

Lyons, Jesse	Minister at Summit Methodist Church; married George and Pat
MacLean, Margaret & Bruce	Peacham neighbors
Magnus, Marilyn & David	Peacham neighbors; David taught at Peacham Alternative School
Marceau, Ruth & Glen	Glen worked for many years at Village Farm
Marceau, Lisa	Daughter of Ruth & Glen Marceau; married Don Moore Jr.
Marcotte, Craig	Worked at Kempton Farm
Marcotte, Cary	Worked at Kempton Farm
Marcotte, Diane & Chris	Chris worked at Kempton Farm
Martin, Andrew	Married George's aunt Frances Kempton
Martland, Agatha & Tom	Peacham neighbors
McLam, Buddy	Competent jack-of-all-trades from Barnet, Vt.
McLam, Dennis	Son of Buddy McLam, also handyman
Mercadante, Barbara & John	Owned a neighboring farm on Green Bay Loop, which Kemptons bought in 1990
Metz, Stephanie & Charles	Peacham neighbors
Miller, Anne	Daughter of Eloise & Richard Miller
Miller, Gladys & Dwight	Friends of Pat & George from Dummerston, Vt.
Miller, Frank	Son of Eloise and Richard Miller & close friend of Kemptons
Miller, Jean	Daughter of Eloise & Richard Miller, married Dominic Dedam

Miller, Lois	Daughter of Eloise & Richard Miller
Miller, Mary	Daughter of Eloise & Richard Miller
Miller, Eloise & Richard	Kemptons bought Millers' farm in Green Bay, Peacham
Miller, Rosemary	Richard Miller's sister
Mills, Anne & Gordon	Bought Sugar House Hill from Kemptons & built a house
Mold, Fred	Curator at Fairbanks Museum
Moore, Francis	Sold maple sugaring supplies in East Peacham
Moore, Deanne & Don	Don is Francis Moore's son, was Kempton's fieldman, is good friend
Moore, Sonia	Peacham neighbor
Morrison, Les	Peacham neighbor, started grain business in Barnet
Murphy, Mickey	Friend of Mike Guyer, became good friend of Kempton's
Newton, Amos	Son of John & Jane Greenwood Newton
Newton, Becky	Daughter of John & Jane Spross Newton
Newton, Gram	Mother of Pappy Newton
Newton, Jim	Son of John & Jane Spross Newton
Newton, Mike	Son of Dave & Margaret Newton
Newton, Mikey	Son of John & Jane Spross Newton
Newton, Peter	Son of John & Jane Spross Newton

Newton, Margaret (Mom) & Dave (Pappy)	Heads of Newton School & second parents to George
Newton, Jane Greenwood	John Newton's second wife
Newton, Jane Spross	Pat's friend in nursing school, John Newton's first wife
Newton, Jill	John Newton's third wife
Newton, John	Son of Dave & Margaret Newton and close friend of Pat and George
Ninninger, Maureen (Moe) & John (Ninny)	John worked with Sam to build Kempton cabin on Mack Mountain Road
O'Boyle, Diane & Peter	Peter was a Peacham lawyer
O'Brien, Cathy	Daughter of Sue & Stuart O'Brien, married Bruce Roy
O'Brien, Shane	Son of Sue & Stuart O'Brien
O'Brien, Susan & Stuart	Peacham neighbors; Sue served with George on Peacham School Board
Packard, Polly & Jerry	Peacham neighbors, George rented their land
Parker, Mac	Friend of Kempton kids from Danville
Parker, Meghan	Daughter of Sandy and Wayne Parker
Parker, Wayne	Married Patty's niece Sandy Gulick
Parker, Zachary	Son of Sandy and Wayne Parker
Parsons, Omri	Peacham neighbor
Perkins, Ken	Friend of George from Newton School, worked on Alaska railroad with him
Petrie, Marilyn	Peacham neighbor

Powden, Carl	Son of Drusilla & Russ Powden
Powden, Mark	Son of Drusilla & Russ Powden
Powden, Drusilla & Russell	Peacham neighbors
Powers, Frenchie	Worked & boarded at Village Farm
Quimby, Gary	Son of Jim and Mary Jo Quimby
Quimby, Mary Jo & Jim	Jim was Peacham carpenter
Randall, Roy	Peacham farmer
Randall, Anne	David Randall's second wife
Randall, David	Peacham farmer
Randall, Erica & Don	Don was son of Frances & Gib
Randall, Frances (Frank) & Gib	Peacham farmers; Gib is son of Roy Randall
Randall, Susan	David Randall's first wife
Rantoule, Anne Connor	Pat's friend from Summit, N.J.
Richards, Dawn	Married Matt Kempton
Ringquist, Loey	Helped with Kempton kids in Dummerston & Peacham, lived on farm several summers, married Nathan Grey
Rough, Joan & Bill	Teachers and friends of George & Pat
Rowe, Alice & Ed	Peacham neighbors
Roy, Bruce	Farmer, married Cathy O'Brien
Ryan, Peggy & Frank	Teachers and St. Johnsbury neighbors
Schoolcraft, Clifton, Sr.	Operated a hen farm in Peacham
Schoolcraft, Gary	Grandson of Clifton Schoolcraft, Sr.
Schwartz, Pat & Bob	Friends from St. Johnsbury
Segal, Bill	Married Barbara Boardman

Shears, Annie	George Kempton's mother, married Albert Blodgett, then Leonard Kempton
Shears, Caroline Eliza Godden	George's maternal grandmother
Shears, Caroline	George's aunt, his mother Annie's sister
Shears, Charlotte	George's aunt, his mother Annie's sister
Shears, Elizabeth (Bess)	George's aunt, his mother Annie's sister, married Raymond Bigelow
Shears, Henry, Sr.	George's maternal grandfather
Shears, Joseph	George's uncle, his mother Annie's brother
Shears, Louisa	George's aunt, his mother Annie's sister
Shears, Henry, Jr.	George's uncle, his mother Annie's brother
Sinclair, Pinky & Kirk	Pinky worked at Kempton Farm
Skoller, Jeff	Friend of Matt from Kirby, Vt.
Skoller, Larry	Friend of Matt from Kirby, Vt.
Skoller, Matt	Friend of Matt K., from Kirby, Vt.
Slaight, Hannah & Hamilton	Peacham neighbors; Hamilton was Sue O'Brien's father
Smith, Julian	Married Betsy Boardman
Snively, Joan & Cub	Joan was Patty's friend from Summit, N.J. They had two sons, Todd and John
Sorrow, Anne & Bob	Bob worked & boarded at Kempton Farm
Steadman, Eddie	Married George's half sister Shirley Blodgett

Steadman, Gary	Son of Shirley Blodgett & Eddie Steadman
Stetson, Doris & John	John was vet in West Barnet
Strayer, Ham	Worked & boarded at Kempton Farm
Strickler, Carol	Friend of Sam's
Swainbank, John	Local attorney
Wallace, Ina & Charles	Peacham neighbors, moved to Norwich, Vt.
Wanzer, Ann & Sidney	Bought land from Kemptons and built a house
Wason, Helen	Mother of Nancy Wason
Wason, Nancy	Friend of Jenny's, married Robert Bartell
Western, Mary Newton & Dave	Mary was daughter of Dave and Margaret Newton
White, Thelma	Peacham neighbor
Wilson, George	Peacham neighbor
Young, Herman	Had a hen farm in Perkinsville, Vt.
Zagaradni, Mike	Worked and boarded at Kempton Farm

ACKNOWLEDGMENTS

I T IS A WONDERFUL TREAT TO BE ABLE TO LOOK
back on your life. This story wouldn't be here if it weren't for
Patty's journal and her love. The importance of the journal is easy
to understand. You have an unusually frank description of a young
family getting started farming and getting used to each other as they
adapt to new situations. The love is less easy to describe, but it's the
glue that makes the farming venture work. In this old man's opinion,
Patty's love continues to make it all work, I can see signs of it in our
children, grandchildren, and great grandchildren.

Dawn, Matt's wife, upgraded the farm computer and gave me
the old one, and she showed me how to use it. Since then, mostly
Jenny but others of the kids also have taught me how to use it, and
after a few months of transcribing Patty's journal, I'm a little faster.

Jenny gets the credit for not letting the journal get lost in a box
full of loose-leaf notebooks. Soon after Patty died, Jenny located
most of the journals, organized them by date, and began transcribing them.

Diane Krupsky Coughlin, my mother's sister's granddaughter,
gave me information about my mother. Cam O'Brien from Danville
worked the computer magic with Ancestry. I will be forever thankful
for her bringing up my mother's amazing past.

As I write this acknowledgement I recall that Nancy Shaw
encouraged Patty to keep writing in her journal and emphasized
its importance. Thank you, Nancy.

There is no question that the person that makes this story read-
able is my editor, Lynne Lawson. I don't know what she does, but
she takes something that I've written and polishes it, and it sounds

good but still sounds like my voice. My kids say to me, with a hint of surprise in their voice, "You write very well, Dad."

My children have been very supportive and when I would get bogged down they would pick me up.

CPSIA information can be obtained
at www.ICGtesting.com
Printed in the USA
LVHW020921030121
675560LV00018B/3017